THEIR SECOND REPUBLIC

To el-Tag Fadalla—
to our sisters Zienab, 'Ayisha, Tayba, Wāsila, 'Abida, Souād and Sāmiya and their children and grandchildren—we are all made rich by your compassion, example and generosity, brother.

Their Second Republic

Islamism in the Sudan from Disintegration to Oblivion

ABDULLAHI A. GALLAB
Arizona State University, USA

Routledge
Taylor & Francis Group
LONDON AND NEW YORK

First published 2014 by Ashgate Publishing

Published 2016 by Routledge
2 Park Square, Milton Park, Abingdon, Oxfordshire OX14 4RN
711 Third Avenue, New York, NY 10017, USA

First issued in paperback 2016

Routledge is an imprint of the Taylor & Francis Group, an informa business

British Library Cataloguing in Publication Data
A catalogue record for this book is available from the British Library.

The Library of Congress has cataloged the printed edition as follows:
Gallab, Abdullahi A.
Their second republic : Islamism in the Sudan from disintegration to oblivion / by Abdullahi A. Gallab.
pages cm
Includes bibliographical references and index.
ISBN 978-1-4094-3572-3 (hardback) 1. Sudan--History--1956- 2. Sudan--Politics and government--1985- 3. Islam and politics--Sudan. 4. Islamic fundamentalism--Sudan. 5. Turabi, Hasan. I. Title.
DT157.673.G35 2014
962.404--dc23

2013049237

ISBN 13: 978-1-138-27157-9 (pbk)
ISBN 13: 978-1-4094-3572-3 (hbk)

Contents

Preface

I wrote this book in close relationship with my 2008 work *The First Islamist Republic: Development and Disintegration of Islamism in the Sudan.* This relationship goes beyond the study of one specific Sudanese phenomenon. In both books, I deal with Islamism, its representation, history, and transformations in the Sudan. In both books, I also deal with the serious problems that led to its demise. But in essence, in both books, I address a manifestation of a sociopolitical experience with local, regional, and global dimensions. The problems I see in contemporary Islamist movements—which are not monolithic—stem from complex developments that came with and relate to the complications of the modern conditions of communities and entities that emerged from the colonial and postcolonial experiences. These conditions are better understood, in my belief, if we can look at them from the following three perspectives. The first is the remnants of the colonial state that reproduces itself by expanding its dominant and coercive institutions. The second is the expansion of the growing of "community of the state" as it developed into a diversified class of military and bureaucratic elite ideologies that concentrated power in its own hands by identifying each one's political, civil or military group with the state. The third is the different forms and attempts of creating fields of liberation within the realm of civil society that have countered the coercive polity and political order, which has been using the state and its violent capacity as a system of control and performance of power over the society.

Here, the Sudanese experience of Islamism stands as a very important one in the history of the Sudan, the region, and in general. This is not because of its success but because of its total failure. It proved that what has been advocated as *al-hal al-Islami* (Islam is the solution) or an Islamist state, made within the Islamists' concept of Islamism, is itself an unachievable idea neither by default nor by design. It was the savage separation between the state and religion that designated the state as the field of coercion with worse excesses of greedy forms of *tamkeen*[1] and the expulsion of religion to the private sphere as part of public

1 *Tamkeen* is a Quranic term associated with "those who, [even] if we firmly establish them on earth remain constant in *salah* (prayer) and render *zakah* (alms levy), enjoin the doing of what is right and forbid the doing of what is wrong; but with God rests the final outcome of all events", al-Jajj 22: 41. For Sudanese Islamists *Tamkeen* represented a takeover moment by using the state to extract as much wealth as possible and to climb up the highest level of political and state power by appropriating the most senior government positions to their members.

relations and self-promotion. I describe this model of separation as savage because the state is tailored to the security imperatives of the regime for which the state operates as a coercive–intensive structure to subdue, appease, discipline, and even kill citizens including the Islamists themselves when a need arises. It is not by any means a secular model of separation; it is a model of total control of the state indispensable to the administration of violence. The Islamists, themselves, now understand that through such a creation, it is as Ḥasan al-Turabi has stated: they "tarnished the image of Islam." Those founders of that state, or the Islamist republic, did not speak of Islam for a long time. This was either because they turned "the idea of Islam" through their experience into a paradox of political life or because it made of them an embarrassment that pales in comparison. That did not mean that the issue of Islamism disappeared from the political discourse. It means, rather, that Islamism has been driven to oblivion through the development of this experience and replaced by violence, wilding, and self-interest, only to satisfy their lust for money, power, and sexual desires (multiple marriages).[2] On the one hand, the General/President is supposed to represent this state of savagery to marshal, even coerce, the public into a counter-revolutionary movement against any form of human liberation, right to life, and freedom or political empowerment. On the other hand, religion as exercised in the private sphere is neither a piety reflected in conduct nor judicious comprehensive guidance followed especially by those in power. The Sudanese satire describe this situation by saying *talau diyna wa 'alagou fi l-hiat* (they squeezed out our religion and they displayed it at the front of state buildings walls).

The premise of this book might be seen by many to be about Ḥasan al-Turabi. That might be true to a certain extent. Ḥasan al-Turabi has remained an albatross around the neck of the Islamist movement; the Islamist movement remained as an albatross around his neck too. However, a future book about Ḥasan al-Turbi might come sooner or later. Ḥasan al-Turabi might be one of the most important political figures in the Sudan and the Muslim world. There might be reasons for some to overlook this fact. Some of these reasons could be attributed to Ḥasan al-Turabi himself. Yet, what makes him such an important personality is not his successful theory of value. What makes him important is his failure to see and accept as a moral, religious, political, and civil value the necessity to pay attention to the process by which people as citizens agree according to their free will without coercion or a military coup and the violence that emerges out of it. It is not only violence, antagonism, and exclusion that sustains Islam; but it

2 Upward mobility for some Islamists in power is a complex matter as in addition to crossing class and social status lines, entrance to metropolitan middle-class community is often sought through multiple marriages to city or Khartoum middle-class women as well. Such marriages, to borrow Dipesh Chakarabarty, provide for some "a site of self-presentation, cultivating a certain style of being in the eyes of others." 'Umar al-Bashir, a polygamist himself, made multiple marriages an unofficial state/Islamist policy by encouraging his ruling Islamists to marry more than one wife.

is solidarity, togetherness, and respect for human dignity and citizens' rights that makes it sensitive and responsive to the habits of the heart.

This raises, perhaps, important questions about the Sudan, the country, its people, and its human experience. Since 1821 and until its recent split in 2011, the Sudan was the largest country in Africa and the Middle East with about one million square miles and a human quilt of Muslim, Christian, and other African religions, and, the Sudanese as a nation or historic people have existed within their imagined borders and real, complex past experiences for a far longer time than that. With or without the creation of different borders, confirmation of archeological evidence and the conceptualization of peoplehood, the whole period from time immemorial to the present could be considered as the origin time of the Sudanese. Within and throughout this origin time, the Sudanese's human experience—before the founding of the Sudan as a geographical and human space—has turned in and transformed into a series of complex developments and different forms of interrelationships. The different modes and systems of these developments and their environments have created the Sudanese as a people. Significant human experiences have molded and shaped the Sudanese mutual encounter with time and place, along with other external factors and internal conflicts and tensions, acting together and separately to internally and externally provoke violence. These changes have allowed for systems of domination over nature, over each other, and over means of production and modes of regulation. Moreover, acts embodying all that continued to stimulate, assemble, construct, and weave together of the social, lived, and imagined histories and the material and immaterial lives of the Sudanese. Hence, there is more to the Sudanese experience in its complexity than meets the eye and what skin color alone can capture. At the same time, the Sudan as a geographical space and a meaning that has been reinforced by the establishment of a territory is one form of this Sudanese experience.

The Sudan was organized in 1821 through human sufferings. Muḥammad 'Alī Pasha's invasion to the country at that time marked a serious point of departure by splitting the world into violent aggressors and helpless victims. Those helpless victims were continuously physically and emotionally abused because they were no match for the colonial and colonizer's modern, heavily armed, and well-trained system of coercion. The invasion and its regime abused all Sudanese people, but some were uniquely marked for additional abuse and maltreatment. Egyptians too were victims of Muḥammad 'Alī's oppressive regime as could be observed when Egypt was subject to a strange type of colonization. That colonial system was under the rubric of the Ottoman field of authority; but in a sense, it leased Egypt to Muḥammad 'Alī and his family to reign over it. The Wali's administration "consisted of a nucleus of men, Wali's family and retainers who formed an inner circle, and a large out circle of Egyptians who were co-opted to work for the government and enjoyed a share of the profits; a share that they stood to lose were the government to be overthrown."[34] In view of this, Cairo's role can only be understood as part of the historic advancement of, and the Egyptian reaction to, this peculiar form of colonial enterprise. Through a process of a coercive system of governance, the regime implemented its twisted objective to control and dominate all of the Sudanese and Egyptian people. Egypt was depicted as a façade of *fellaheen*,[5] who were forcibly drafted in mass, while the Sudan was considered as property acquired by right of conquest. The major form of violence that filtered out of that through the Sudanese collective memories of that experience was that their new country was divided into an open district for hunting slaves where slavery became a function of the state. Hence, the Sudanese, who were depicted as Negros, were "fair game" for servitude. Within that continuum of oppression and domination, the Southern Sudanese were oppressed and abused the most. In the other parts of the country, which was less black, their everyday world was turned into a closed district for heavy taxation. Out of these desperate situations, different impulses, discourses, and forms of resistance emerged and progressed.

In the Sudan, the residue of that abuse and oppression piled up in the collective memory and popular consciousness that shaped an individual and a group worldview. All versions of violence continued to have their distant historical resonance. Yet, the nature and intensity of each form of violence could offer a starting point for the consideration of the historical result of difference and distance that emerged out of that experience. The symbolic and physical consequences, and the forms of violence that originated and sustained out of such an impulse, has since reflected and planted its roots in various types of violence over time that included conquest and its consequences. Eve M. Troutt Powell argued that "the outlook of the colonized colonizer began to shape in the last decade of Muḥammad 'Alī's reign and emerged full-blown by the 1870s."[6] While this is true, it was far more than complex. It was the territorial differentiation that emerged out of that experience, with each region subjected to its own distinctive form of violence, oppression, and control, which planted and maintained something that has reached beyond generalities and generations. Within that situation, Cairo battled between

3 Muḥammad 'Alī Pasha (1769–1849) was the Ottoman wali or Governor General of Egypt (1805–49), and is often recognized as the founder of Muḥammad 'Alī's family dynasty that extended its rule in Egypt till 1952. Muḥammad 'Alī is often cited as the builder of modern Egypt. He conquered and extended his power over the Sudan in 1821. Muḥammad 'Alī conquered the Sudan to seek gold, ivory and other strategic row materials for his treasury, to expand and enlarge his empire, and to acquire slaves for his army. The Turco-Egyptian administration (known as the Turkiyya) ruled the country till 1885.

4 Afaf Lutfi al-Sayyid Marsot, *Egypt in the Rein of Muḥammad 'Alī* (Cambridge: Cambridge University Press, 1984), 196.

5 Singular *fallah* is the Arabic term for peasants. During the reign of Muḥammad 'Alī and after the ruling Turkish aristocracy, people looked down to them.

6 Eve M. Troutt Powell, *A Different Shade of Colonialism: Egypt, Great Britain and the Mastery of the Sudan* (Berkeley, CA: University of California Press, 2003), 65.

its two divided selves. A range of consequences and deeper effects was attributed to each form of oppression in the region.

From the beginning of the creation of the Sudan in 1821, the Mahdiyya, throughout the British colonial era and to some extent ever since, saw their lifeworld colonized, civil experiences constrained, and evolution of their civil society deferred. Such is the failure declaration issued on July 9, 2011, by the Islamists in power who, while seeking to exercise a tighter grip over the Sudanese lifeworld, split the country into two states and turned it into hot or cold battlegrounds between them and other Sudanese groups and individuals. Yet, that leads us to the three issues which are central to the book: (a) a complete withdrawal from Islamism as an ideology as it changed hands from al-Turabi's Islamist *laïcité* to 'Alī 'Uthmān's savage separation of religion and state; (b) forcing the South to walk away from the Islamist regime and its state but not from the Sudan field of action; and (c) walking away from the Sudan and cocoon themselves into 'Abdel Rḥim Ḥamdi's triangle as a focus on where their imagined "core regime supporters" are concentrated to the neglect to the rest of the country.

As I said before, I will say again: after so many years of colonial rule, militaristic governance and totalitarian control, are the Sudanese people ready yet to look back into this long and complex human experience and ask how the Sudanese civil society has been deferred and—the most serious question—have the Sudanese people been liberated yet? Here, as in many areas of inquiry, Sudanese and non-Sudanese scholars might not give up on seeking answers to persisting questions. However, many may be inclined to attest that the Sudanese themselves have not given up. They might have tried several times, but liberation comes in as many different ways. Yet, here and in this particular juncture, it would be likened not only to totalitarian rule only but to two distinctive practices that must be better defined if they are to become germane. That includes the liberation from myriad series of contrivances and mentalities of "totalist" politics, ideologies, and systems and from the devices the state created to give effect to such a rule. As such, the state that the Islamists created is the most violent in comparison to previous states the Sudanese experienced. It might be unique in this sense, but it is none other than how Islamism and the Islamists clarified its and their own desires. If so, it seems that the Sudanese Islamist model stands as an example of profound importance that demonstrates to others that Islamism as a state is something they ought not to embrace. Many would agree that it is the Egyptians who learned the lesson first, whereas the argument of this book that Islamism, similar to other isms, is on its way to oblivion.

Acknowledgments

I am indebted to a number of friends and colleagues who read some or all of the drafts that led to this book and who supported my research in different ways. My work has been enhanced by their encouragement, criticism, comments, and suggestions. I owe deeper appreciation and gratitude to Professor Peter Woodward, John Voll, Asef Bayat, Abdel Majed Ali Bob, Aḥmed Kamal Eldin, Aḥmed Ibrahim Abushouk, and Noah Salmon, who have read parts or all of the manuscript in various phases. The last few years were very rich with discussion with colleagues at ASU's African and African American and Religious Studies departments, their students, and Centers, together with other scholars, especially those who read or reviewed my previous books, and our ongoing conversations on issues and developments in the Sudan and their insightful ideas and critical skills through the years. I would like to acknowledge the many contributions of other scholars in the fields of Islamic studies, sociology of religion and social science whose research, insights and publications into the fields of Sudan studies, Islamism and religion and politics in general have illuminated our way by adding to our knowledge and taught us a great deal. An important outcome of that is I feel indebted to many individuals that I have never met before, and they are more than I can recall in this instance.

Over the years, I have valued the friendship and the ongoing intellectual debates with Moḥamed Aḥmed Maḥmoud, 'Abdullahi 'Ali Ibrahim, El-Sir Sid-Aḥmed, Salman Moḥamed Aḥmed Salmān and other Sudanese friends and members of discussion groups and communities in Diaspora, Sudan Studies and other academic associations, and Alex de Waal and Magnus Taylor and those who contributed reviews or comments to the debate about my books in African Arguments, Making Sense of Sudan, Royal African Society and Social Science Research Council (SSRC) blogs and websites.

Over the last few years, I have benefited from conversations and interviews which I have had on the topic of Islamism in the Sudan with many Islamists, politicians, journalists, and intellectuals whose views helped to either form or shape my ideas about the Sudanese experience of the Islamists in power and their state. I wish to express my gratitude to Dr. 'Alī al-Ḥaj Moḥmed, Dr. Ghazi Salāḥ al-Din al-'Atabāni, the late Yasin 'Umar al-Imam, and professors El-Tag Fad Allah, al-Tayyib Zain al-'Abdin, and Ḥasan Makki for the valuable time they rendered me during long interviews in Khartoum, Bonn, and other places.

I am obliged to Dean Patrick Kenney and the Institute of Social Science Research, Professor Mary Margret Fonow and the School of Social Transformation, Arna Alexander Bontemps and my colleagues at the African and African American

Studies and the Center for the Study of Religion and Conflict at ASU for their continuous support. Special thanks are also due to my gifted and efficient graduate and undergraduate research students who were assigned to me by these departments. I am very grateful to Samiha Topal, Hannah Schimdl, Joseph Thomason and Egbit Abraha whose help has been greatly appreciated.

I am grateful to my publisher Ashgate for being endlessly patient and the anonymous peer reviewers for their helpful comments on the manuscript. I would like to acknowledge my gratitude to them all, especially, Kayleigh Huelin, my editor, for her professionalism and quality of work. I am also grateful to the professional and careful editing from Jerryll Moreno. My thanks go to Professor Christine Szuter director and professor of practice at the Scholarly Publishing Graduate Certificate Program at ASU for suggesting Jerryll for me as a proof editor.

For the last twenty-something years, if not more, my wife Souād T. ‘Ali and our children Aḥmed, ‘Azza, and Shiraz and our families in the Sudan did everything to provide their unrelenting support, forbearance, and encouragement which made research an enjoyable endeavor, writing an inspirational and elevating intellectual exercise, and life better.

While all these colleagues and friends have been helpful in different ways, any remaining deficiencies or inaccuracies are solely my responsibility.

Note on Transliterations and Other Matters

For the transliteration of Arabic and Sudanese names of people, places, and institutions, I followed a simple style based on *The Chicago Manual of Style*, sixteenth edition, and the *International Journal of Middle East Studies*. However, generally accepted English forms of Arabic words and names, such as Islam, Sudan, Khartoum, and so on, are used as they appear in their English forms without diacritical marks. I have italicized any Arabic and Sudanese words followed by a translation of the word or concept. I have tried to be consistent for any given name, especially commonly cited historical names, for which I have tried to follow the most frequently cited spellings. I have, however, left many of the Sudanese and Egyptian spellings that authors have used for their names. Finally, unless specified, all translations from Sudanese and Arabic sources, poetry, proverbs, and other expressive culture are mine.

For this study I used several sources and resources in the field of Sudanese studies written in English, Arabic, and translated into these two languages. It is gratifying to notice how this corpus of knowledge has grown through time. In addition to that, there is a similar corpus of Sudanese expressive culture. Taping, synthesizing, and blending these two gigantic bodies of knowledge is both intellectually edifying and investigatively rewarding. I would like to thank all those who contributed to that body of knowledge.

Chapter 1
Introduction

This book, *Their Second Republic: Islamism in the Sudan from Disintegration to Oblivion,* is a continuation of the study of Islamism in power in the Sudan from 1989 to the present. However, it is not by any means volume two of a book series in the study of Islamism in the Sudan. The previous study,[1] covered the period from 1989 to 1999. This study not only affirms the continuous disintegration of the Islamist movement, but it also takes a critical look at Islamism in the Sudan, the runaway countenance of the entire experience as its institutions, and their ideological and rhetorical stances that foundered into oblivion.

The Islamist regime claimed to turn the Sudan into a state-directed society controlled by an Islamic ideal similar in its purity to the Muslim's during the rule of 'Umar Ibn 'Abdul 'Aziz (682–704 AD)[2] 14 centuries previously. That was to be accomplished, according to its polemicists, by fusing all the aspects and activities of life and living into one. That totalist dream and program did not survive.[3] To quote Hamid Dabashi, "history does indeed, as Marx once frivolously put it, repeat itself (once as tragedy, once as farce)—but the world will not."[4] Such politics of nostalgia, which existed in the early days of the Islamists' rule, soon dissipated as the day-to-day practices of the regime proved to be, at their

---

1 See Abdullahi A. Gallab, *The First Islamist Republic: Development and Disintegration of Islamism in the Sudan* (Burlington, VT: Ashgate, 2008).

2 'Umar Ibn 'Abdul 'Aziz was the eighth Umayyad caliph AD (682–720). Unlike previous Umayyad caliphs, he was not a hereditary successor to the former caliph. He was appointed to that position by the will of his predecessor, the caliph Sulaymān ibn 'Abdulmalik AD (715–717). He was known for being extremely pious, highly respected as caliph, and disdainful of luxuries. During his short rule, AD 717–720, he commenced a policy of internal consolidation based on justice and the rule of law. He dismissed unpopular governors, reformed the taxation system, and abolished the *Jizya* tax for converts to Islam. He also expanded special welfare programs for orphans and the needy and granted the *Mawālī* (non-Arab Muslims) the same fiscal rights as Arab Muslims. He was credited with ordering the first collection of the *Ḥadīth*. Today, he is considered one of the great rulers not only in the Umayyad dynasty but also in Muslim history as a whole. Some Muslims refer to him as the Fifth (and the last) Rightly Guided Caliph.

3 See 'Abdel wahāb el-Affendi, *al-Tawra wa 'l-Islah al-Siyassi fi 'l-Sudan* ([*Revolution and Reform in the Sudan*] London: The Averroes Forum, 1995), 25.

4 Hamid Dabashi, *The Arab Spring: The End of Postcolonialism* (London: Zed Books, 2012), xvi.

best, "attitudes lacking a common intellectual method."[5] In his book, *al-Haraka al-Islamiyya al-Soudaniyya: Dierat al-Daw wa Khiout al-Dhalam* (*The Sudanese Islamic Movement: The Circle Light and the Threads of Darkness*), al-Maḥboob 'Abdelsalaam admitted that from the regime's early days, *al-boas al-fikri* (the poverty of knowledge) of all those who claimed to be specialized in classical Islamic fields of studies and even those who lived within the Islamist experience became clear.[6] If his claim is to be accepted, it is not entirely surprising that the Islamist state—considered central to having an Islamic system enforced—has been constrained from the start by the ignorance of those who were supposed to write down and apply God's constitution. Ultimately, such a model of governance can take any form of "contentious politics." Accordingly, the Sudanese satire is appropriate in describing *al-Kizan*[7] (the Islamists): *dakhaluna al-jami'i wa dakhalu hum al-Souq* ('the Islamists' sent us to the mosque while they scrambled to the market). That Sudanese joke and other similar ones are often circulated and cited by Sudanese community members as evidence of not only their deep-seated disdainful views but also what Islamism has turned into and how it is seen by fellow citizens who suffered a lot from their rule for more than two decades. This book looks at the patterned ways these developments have taken. It offers a portrait of how visible and invisible environments worked together—and sometimes separately—to corrode the internal and external layers of both the first and second Islamist republics. Furthermore, both republics owe much to the debate about the essential nature of Islamism itself; the colonial and postcolonial states and their communities of the state; and the long debate about Islam, politics, and the state.

The three experiences in the last two centuries that continue to have the deepest effects on Sudanese life are the two colonial experiences, the postcolonial states, and the October 1964 Revolution.[8] The first colonial experience (1821–1885) was responsible for the creation of the Sudanese borders that remained until 2011.

---

5 Eric J. Hobsbawn, *The Age of Revolution: 1789–1848* (New York: Vintage Books, 1996), 290.

6 Al-Mahboob, 'Abdelsalaam, *al-Haraka al-Islamiyya al-Soudaniyya: Dierat al-Daw wa Khiout al-Dhalam* ([*The Sudanese Islamic Movement: The Circle Light and the Threads of Darkness*] Cairo: Maktabat Jazīrat al-Ward, 2009), 120.

7 A pejorative term used particularly in the Sudanese daily conversations to ridicule the Islamists. The term refers to an old-fashioned cheap handmade water cup made of a sheet of tin.

8 The October 1964 Revolution was an unarmed civil disobedience and an all-country strike of Sudanese citizens that started in Khartoum and spread throughout the country. It consciously pursued for the first time in Africa and the Middle East a discourse and strategy of organized fields of power relations to a successful end by forcing the dictatorial military regime of Major General 'Abboud (1958–1964) out. Through the October 1964 Revolution, the country witnessed the rise of a new generation of politicians and a younger leadership in most political parties and associations. One of these new politicians was Dr. Ḥasan al-Turabi, who assumed the leadership of the Islamist movement from that point forward.

It created a center and margins with Sudanese peoplehoods and their social, cultural, and economic differentiations that survived proceeding states. The second colonial experience (1898–1956) added to the growth of both the center and the marginalized areas within the same geography. It also added to the existing condition of social differentiation by creating a new community of the state.[9] The first postcolonial experience of the Mahdiyya was successful in liberating the Sudan from foreign rule. However, neither the Mahdist state nor its leader were immune from using draconian measures and violence against their own population, even as some of that population used collective violence against the regime. On the one hand, everyone agrees that the second postcolonial states (1956–present), who have been dominated by military regimes, have not been up to the task of liberating the country and the state from a myriad series of contrivances and mentalities of 'totalist' politics, ideologies, and systems—or from systems the state created to give effect to such a role. On the other hand, the October Revolution stands as a great movement for the Sudanese enthusiasm for liberation from the accumulative and singular role the central state has played in colonizing the Sudanese life since 1821. Like other Sudanese regimes, the Islamist rule has its similar and dissimilar historical and structural causes and preconditions, as well as the primary impediments for its violent, oppressive, and destructive nature. We need a completely different analytical framework to understand what happened in the Sudan in the past quarter century of Islamist rule. Such a framework leads us to look at the Sudanese experience and its complex and complicated developments and the way it has been informing the Sudanese's present experience, its complexity, and the rising Muslim—not Islamist—and global consciousness that provided for technologies of change, meaning, and liberation from tyranny. My approach builds on my previous two books, *The First Islamist Republic* (2008) and *A Civil Society Deferred* (2011, 2013) to provide some necessary background to explain the essence of the Sudanese Islamism and its relationships and forms within which it has been partly or wholly interwoven. Building on my previous colonial and postcolonial research, Chapter 2 provides three points on the Sudanese Islamist fields of action, conditions, and relationships in which the Islamist movement originally emerged and then developed, rose to power, degenerated, and rapidly regressed into oblivion. With a similar approach, Chapter 4 provides a deeper look at the

9 The community of state represents a new form of organization of power that emerged out of the rise of small class of public-educated Sudanese citizens who continued to grow through the expansion of public education since the colonial period. This community of state includes a white-, blue-, and khaki-colored state employee in addition to white *'arrāqi* peasants of new farming projects, such as the al-Gezira scheme. This community of the state continued to find its legitimization within its invention of a progressive self-image and cultural identity as being an important part, if not the only part, of modernity in the country. See Abdullahi Gallab, *A Civil Society Deferred: The Tertiary Grip of Violence in the Sudan* (Gainesville, FL: University Press of Florida, 2011).

October Revolution through the lens of collective revolutionary and counter-revolutionary practices associated with the succession of political developments in the field of al-Turabi's Islamism, in particular, thereafter.

Furthermore, this study—by looking into the essence of Islamism—argues that the prevailing state of consciousness not only provides the beginning for what lies ahead, but it also endows us with the material evidence that the belief behind pursuing Islamism as a rendezvous with an Islamic, Muslim, or even Islamist state and system has proven to be irrelevant. Here lingers the most serious question: does that projection not simply signal the end of the Sudanese model of Islamism or does it also signal the beginning of the end of Islamism itself as an ideology and political project? This study aims to show that through demonstrations in which Islamism itself has been deprived of any meaningful significance, and while all elements of failure open up in the Sudanese project, pronouncements of other models might express the nature and reveal the shape of these ventures of Islamist representations elsewhere. This interpretive claim, as Frederic Volpi says, represents an effort to free this approach "from rigid analytical framework" to what amounts to "making sense of the modern developments in the light of the past but not predetermined by the past."[10]

From Karl Mannheim's *Ideology and Utopia* and Daniel Bell's *The End of Ideology* to Francis Fukuyama's highly controversial book *The End of History,* the literature on the demise of regimes and their ideologies is massive and wide ranging. Narratives and counter-narratives within the realm of the human production of knowledge have been making an "effort to provide a coherent set of answers to the existential predicaments that confront all human beings in the passage of their lives."[11] The end of Islamism and its totality of social and political ideology—what is impatiently foreseen by many as inevitable—is a project and order coming to fulfillment. Many would argue that the Arab Spring has come as a self-fulfilling prophecy and a self-justifying objective that revealed the power of the active forces of the corrosive actions of inner, covert, and overt realities incongruous to the ones shimmering at the top. Such realities manifest themselves behind an alternative reality that continues to interrogate, challenge, and confront the essence of Islamism. Hazem Kandil, reported that he "asked the old, bearded man standing next to me in Tahrir Squire why he joined the protests. 'They promised us that Islam is the solution,' he replied. 'But under Muslim Brotherhood rule we saw neither Islam nor a solution.' The country that invented Islamism may well be on its way to undoing its spell."[12] Many would argue that in addition of the brothers' dismal performance in power, the poor performance of the Sudanese

10 Frederic Volpi, *Political Islam Observed* (New York: Columbia University Press, 2010), 42.

11 Daniel Bell, *The Cultural Contradictions of Capitalism* (New York: Basic Books, 1978), xv.

12 Hazem Kandil, The End of Islamism (London, LRB, July 4, 2013: http://www.lrb.co.uk/blog/2013/07/04/hazem-kandil/the-end-of-islamism/#more-16058).

Islamist was an eye opener for 33 million of Egyptian citizens to march against the Islamist rule.

This study will address all this, largely through a sociological analysis of the Sudanese Islamists' movement, which can be viewed, in part, as a continuing movement of political Islam or Islamism seeking certain kinds of sociopolitical change that would colonize all of the religious, social, and cconomic life of the population by holding the state and using it as a vessel for violent and nonviolent ways to reach that end.

Similar to *The First Islamist Republic*, this study is organized primarily around the following sources: (1) close observation and writing as a journalist and a sociologist on one of the most significant developments of our time—that is, the emergence of different Islamists' movements in the Muslim world in general and in the Sudan in particular; (2) previous and continuing fieldwork and direct interviews with primary sources, including major players in the political field of Islamism in the Sudan, university professors, journalists, intellectuals, and different Sudanese politicians including those who are supportive and sympathetic of and in opposition to the idea of Islamism in the Sudan and elsewhere; (3) a thorough reading of Sudanese, Arab, and international newspapers, magazines, websites, and journals; and (4) synthesizing the primary research, recent books and articles written in Arabic and English or translated to these two languages by Sudanese and non-Sudanese Islamists, academics, journalists, and other writers about certain aspects of the development of the Islamists' state in the Sudan and Islamism in general.

Now one might immediately ask the implicit question: why is a second book about the Islamist experience or the Islamists in the Sudan necessary? The answer to that question is that the study of Islamism and the Islamist experience in the Sudan goes beyond the course of that particular event in time to the very nature of Islamism itself as a reflection of a sociopolitical and, to a certain extent, religious phenomenon. This study involves the structure of power in which the sociopolitical processes and their never-ending conflict with their renewable individual and group ambitions evolve and lead the directions they have been taking. It offers an explanation to an interlude of thought, a record to a human experience, of why the Sudanese Islamism (what I call al-Turabi Islamism) has been called into question by the Sudanese and others and why it faced resistance before and after its decay and descent into oblivion. It is true that many scholars, observers, and even Islamists from outside the Sudan—for reasons we need not get into here—exclude the study of the Sudanese Islamist experience from the study of the other prevailing grand schemes of Islamist developments worldwide. It is also true that Islamism as a phenomenon "had been largely excluded from the mode of inquiry developed by social movement theorists in the West until recently, when a handful of scholars have attempted to bring the Islamic activism into the realm of 'social movement theory.'"[13] Moreover, closing the gates of discourse on religion and Islamism—and its promotion, in particular—as opposed to on the state itself in most Muslim countries, entailed harsh treatment and responses from these ruling regimes that led one way to prison and torture, another to the growth of underground dogma, and a third way to a state-manufactured religious datum. While the title of this book indicates that it addresses a specific Islamist model and experience, it is important to look at how individuals could use Islamism, its codes and ideologies, in a similar way as in other totalitarian experiences. From that, some conclusions might be drawn about the future directions of Islamism in general.

What Is Islamism?

One more time, the question "what is Islamism?" arises. Specifically, the debate about Islam within certain global sectors now undertakes Islamism from start to finish. Hence, one does not need to look far to find an array of terms, definitions, and statements by scholars, politicians, intellectuals, and journalists who then use those definitions to try to create theories about Islamism. Some are not without an element of irony. As Robert Cox argues, theory "is always for someone and for some purpose."[14] In fact, Muslim and non-Muslim scholars, as well as those labeled "Islamists," have debated the terms immensely. The most important element of that debate is that the issue at hand is rather of an *ideology* than of a *theology*. This ideology presents itself, in the words of Karl Marx, as "anxiously conjur[ing] up the spirits of the past to [its] service, borrowing from them names, battle slogans, and costumes in order to present this new scene in world history in time-honored disguise and borrowed language."[15] The terms *Islamist* and *Islamism*—widely used to denote a choice of political ideology unified in well-defined ways and differentiated from other Muslims in specific doctrinal ways (rather than the simple fact of being born Muslim)—are applied here to describe current individuals, groups, and manifestations of Islamist movements, political Islam, and those who are sometimes described as fundamentalists and neo-fundamentalists. That is to say, "if *Islamist* is normatively closed, in effect, *Muslim* is empirically open."[16] Bassam Tibi, who argues that "Islamism

13 Asef Bayat, *Life as Politics: How Ordinary People Change the Middle East* (Stanford, CA: Stanford University Press, 2010), 4.

14 Robert W. Cox, "Social Forces, State and World Orders: Beyond International Relations Theory," *Millennium: Journal of International Studies* 10, no. 2 (1981): 126–55.

15 Karl Marx, *The Eighteenth Brumaire of Louis Bonaparte* (Rockville, MD: Serenity Publishers, 2008), 7.

16 Donald Emerson, "Inclusive Islamism: The Utility of Diversity," in *Islamism: Contested Perspectives on Political Islam*, eds Richard C. Martin and Abbas Barzengar (Stanford, CA: Stanford University Press, 2010), 26.

is a cultural political response to a crisis of failed postcolonial developments in Islamic societies under conditions of globalization," claims that "though Islamism is political, it remains religious."[17] He further raises the question: "how can we understand Islamism as different from Islam without denying the connection between them?" His answer is: "in Europe, the dialects of Enlightenment in a time of great crises led to Communist and fascist rule. Just as these European ideologies contradicted the Enlightenment, Islamism contradicted the humanism of Islam."[18] For some reason Tibi dropped Nazism and colonialism. However, when it comes to Islamism and its relationship to other "isms"—secularism, fascism, Nazism, and communism—things might be more complex than Tibi's conclusion allows. And it would be easy to show that Islamism has relationships to all of those, as I do in this book. Ḥasan al-Turabi's Islamism, which has been blamed by some of the Salfis of Sudan and Saudi Arabia as secular, has its relationship with the French *Laïcitė* as explained in chapters 4 and 5. Moreover, many of those who oppose Islamism in Egypt and the Sudan emphasize what they see as a fascist origin of Islamism. In doing so, they refer to discourses and practices of its founders and focus on its inherent violent impulses and legacy. In the Middle East, as well as in the West, some scholars prefer the term "political Islam" because, as Beinin and Stork argue, those scholars "regard the core concern of these movements as temporal and political."[19] They further explain that these movements use the Qur'an, the Ḥadith, and other canonical religious texts to justify their stances and actions. Further, Beinin and Stork maintain that "today's Islamic thinkers and activists are creatively deploying selected elements of the Islamic tradition, combined with ideas, techniques, institutions, and commodities of the present and recent past, to cope with specifically modern predicaments."[20]

On the other hand, many in the 'East' and in the 'West' reject the term *fundamentalism* because it comes with its own baggage. Often capitalized, the term Fundamentalism originated from an organized American twentieth-century Protestant movement emphasizing the Bible's infallibility. As every word of it is divinely inspired, accordingly, literal interpretation of the text is fundamental to the Christian faith, life, and teachings. Historically, the term originated in the United State when booklets titled *The Fundamentals: A Testimony of the Truth* were published and distributed among churches between 1910 and 1912. The booklets outlined the "fundamental" beliefs that are supposed to be the true tenants of Christianity. Fundamentalism, with its evangelical character and its strict adherence to specific theological doctrines, is usually understood as a reaction against the encroachment of modernism and modernist theology.

---

17 Bassam Tibi, *Islamism and Islam* (New Haven, CT: Yale University Press, 2012), 3.

18 Ibid.

19 Joel Beinin and Joe Stork, eds, *Political Islam Essays from Middle East Report* (Berkeley, CA: University Press of California, 1997), 3.

20 Ibid.

Because of its resolute and dogmatic empathy to a fixed and irreducible pattern of belief, Fundamentalism is sometimes used as a pejorative term, particularly when used to denote its emotive force, religious closed-mindedness, or right-wing conservativeness. Hence, the problem with the category of fundamentalism, as Bobby S. Sayyid explains, is "that it is a category which can only be sustained by avoiding the radical recontextualization. The recontextualization that the advocates of an analytical fundamentalism seek is that of transcending the origins of the term in Protestant Christian circles."[21] Sayyid succinctly continues saying that the term fundamentalism can only "operate as a general category if it situates itself within the discourse of the liberal-secularist enlightenment project and considers this project to be the natural state of affairs. ... To theorize, fundamentalism requires an unproblematic conception of religion and its difference from politics and truth. If one does not accept the hegemony of such a division, then the category of fundamentalism expands to include the political itself."[22] Hence, connecting the term fundamentalism with projects that "assert a Muslim subjectivity ... [is] superficial or secondary and prevent[s] the pursuit of other more fruitful lines of enquiry."[23] Once, not long ago, to many observers' surprise, Ḥasan al-Turabi prided himself as "a typical fundamentalist"[24] when he introduced himself to a mostly Catholic audience in Spain.

In a similar disposition, and to a certain extent in an equally nuanced fashion, some Muslim scholars in particular object to the term *Islamism*. Hassan Hanafi argues that "definitions of invented terms such as *Islamism* are biased, heavily loaded by prejudgments and ideological presuppositions, pro and con and mostly con. Islamism is linked to terrorism, violence, backwardness, fanaticism, oppression, and so forth. These pseudo-definitions are oriented and formulated by security forces and intelligence services."[25] He adds that "sometimes transliteration is used to put forward some names that have negative connotations such as *jihād, jihādists*, and *jihādism* rather than using terms such as decolonization, liberation, resistance, freedom fighter, and so forth."[26] But, indeed, this idea is similar to Shakespeare's idiom: "this is, to give a dog, and in recompense desire my dog again."[27]

21 Bobby S. Sayyid, *A Fundamental Fear: Eurocentrism and the Emergence of Islamism* (London: Zed Books, 1997), 16.

22 Ibid.

23 Ibid.

24 Ḥasan al-Turabi, 'Islamic Fundamentalism in the Suni and Shai Worlds': A lecture by Ḥasan al-Turabi delivered in Madrid on August 2, 1994 to a mainly non-Muslim audience: memorizejuzamma.org

25 Hassan Hanafi, "Islamism: Whose Debate Is It?" in *Islamism: Contested Perspectives on Political Islam*, eds Richard C. Martin and Abbas Barzengar (Stanford, CA: Stanford University Press, 2010), 61.

26 Ibid.

27 William Shakespeare, *Twelfth Night: The Oxford Shakespeare Complete Works* (Oxford: Oxford University Press, 2005), 239.

Across the Muslim World and in other parts of the world many scholars agree with Bobby Sayyid when defines Islamism as "a political discourse, and as such, is akin to other political discourses such as socialism or liberalism."[28] His definition agrees with Olivier Roy's, who adds that the "Islamist sphere of influence spans the entire spectrum of activist groups who, in the second half of the twentieth century, see themselves as an extension of the concepts elaborated by the founder of Muslim Brotherhood in Egypt, Ḥasan al-Banna (1906–1949), and by Abū l-'Alā Mawdūdī[29] (1903–1978), the creator of the *Jamaat-i-Islami* party on the Indian continent."[30] Roy systematically classifies these groups according to each one's instance to power. As a result, there will be at least two categories in which these movements are defined. First, Those Roy describes "neo-fundamentalists"[31] (generally the reformists) are those who aim to see the establishment of an Islamic order in terms of its privatization—"Islamization from the bottom up." In other words, for those reformists, social and political action aims primarily at re-Islamizing the society through different types of political education and mobilization from the lowest level up, "bringing about, *ipso facto*, the advent of an Islamic state."[32] Second, the Islamists seek "Islamization from the top down" (the revolutionary pole, for whom the Islamization of the society occurs through the state power) and they see the establishment of an Islamic order necessitating intervention in public affairs—the capture of the state. The revolutionary pole, however, is differentiated by the way each one's thoughts and actions are territorially bound (local jihādists) or global in scale (global jihādists).[33] Nelly Lahoud vehemently argues that there is an inherent tension between jihādism in its different forms and Islamism, as the former "signals a complete rupture from Islamism with respect to their respective visions of how Islam is to be embraced by individual believers and as an organizing element in the governance of the affairs of the community."[34] Any of these constitutions and formations most likely has nothing, or very little, to do with a theology or a doctrine specific to any form of Islam as a religion. Their common assumption is that the social field and the natural materials that produce useful determinants of politicization of Islam occur

---

28 Bobby S. Sayyid, *A Fundamental Fear: Eurocentrism and the Emergence of Islamism* (London: Zed Books, 1997), 17.

29 There are different spellings of his last name that include but are not limited to: Maudoodi, Mawdudi, and Modudi.

30 Olivier Roy, *The Failure of Political Islam* (Cambridge, MA: Harvard University Press, 1994), 1.

31 Clearly Roy needs to reconsider using the term fundamentalism as the word has a different connotation as explained here before.

32 Ibid.

33 Ibid.

34 Nelly Lahoud, *The Jihādis' Path to Self-Destruction* (New York: Columbia University Press, 2010), 14.

by virtue "of an access of zeal rather than with clearly defined goals."[35] The crucial juncture in this process is that the evils of the Islamists have ruled in the Sudanese experience from 1989 to the present, and the violent impulses of other Islamist groups should not be epitomized or even deliberated on outside this realm. The evils unveiled themselves when the Islamists assumed power in the Sudan and established their republic as the first of its kind in the Muslim world, even as their violent impulse characterized their chosen path of jihādists, "engaged in a war … of both violence and ideas."[36]

Within any categorization of the current Islamist movements, there are five main, important characteristics in the landscape of these groups that need to be identified.

1. As a political project in its different forms and representations, the Islamists within their different strategies and discourses have advocated a political ideology that they claim it is based on Islam. They assert the primacy of Islam using *al-Islam-howa-al-hal* (Islam is the solution) and call for an Islamist order. The Islamists are not different from other postcolonial elites—those whom I call a "community of the state"—who thought they had a compact with modernity and hence despised other forms of Islamic representations, such as the *'ulamā'* and Ṣufi, as backward or relicts of the past. Not only that, but they have always perceived the secular and the non-secular Other—to borrow from Thomas Metcalf—as having no "intrinsic validity."[37] So, in one sense, the Islamists perceive themselves as *fiaa qaliyala* [small group]—"surrounded by an atheist, pornographic, materialistic, secular culture which worships false gods: money, sex, or man himself."[38] In another sense, in its historical development, the resurgence of Islamism could be attributed—in addition to what Tibi illustrated above—"to the failure of the naïve liberalism of the 1930s and Third World socialism in the 1960s and 1970s, and partly because of tremendous influx of rural folk into increasing politicized subproletariats and petit bourgeoisie."[39]
2. The emerging breeds of Islamists are closely associated with the development and the spread of public education. The Islamists, as other members of the community of the state, share a background of public and Western education. Some of them earned their graduate degrees from

35 James Piscatori, *Islam in the Political Process* (Cambridge: Cambridge University Press, 1983), 1.

36 Bassam Tibi, *Islamism and Islam* (New Haven, CT: Yale University Press, 2012), 10.

37 Thomas Metcalf, *Ideologies of the Raj* (New York: Cambridge University Press, 1997), 34.

38 Olivier Roy, *Holy Ignorance: When Religion and Culture Part Ways* (New York: Columbia University Press, 2010), 8.

39 Michael M.J. Fischer, "Islam and the Revolt of the Petit Bourgeoisie," *Daedalus* 111, no. 1 (Winter, 1982): 101–25.

Western schools. While the formal structure of these movements is firmly related to that "tremendous influx of rural folk," the correlation between social origin and academic success reduced their homogenizing operations despite the fact that "they live with the values of the city—consumerism and upward social mobility."[40]

3. As explained in *The First Islamist Republic*,[41] the Islamist groups have developed a self-image and an assurance of their origin's history that position them within their own specific time and place parameters. Although adopting Islam could be perceived as a positive thing within a Muslim society, that by itself does not qualify such Islamist groups to perform the functions of the *'ulamā'* who gained and solidified their legitimacy from institutionalized religious knowledge and their functions as judges, imams, and teachers who issue *fatwa* in matters relating to Islamic knowledge and Muslim life. Accordingly, they "will not be the ones to open up the *'ulamā'*s' corpus." The Islamists "reproach the *'ulamā'*" as they claim to be thinkers and to stand out as self-proclaimed spokespersons of Islam as *deen wa dawla* (religion and state). At the same time, they go further to tell their secular competitors that their compact with modernity could be pronounced in a more authentic fashion. Bassam Tibi observes that Islamists "seem to overlook the distinction between two different traditions of knowledge in Islam: Islamic religious sciences and rational sciences (philosophy and natural sciences)."[42] This discourse, which differentiates their ascribed authenticity, is entangled with competing understandings of both Islam and modernity, as well as with essentialist definitions of both Ṣufi Ṭariqa and the *'ulamā'*. Clearly, this brings in a self-imaging invention of the group that has underlain its actions all through its life. At the same time, such self-imaging and narration of the history of the movement has an enduring impact on the mood and politics of the movement. In a broader perspective, this invention of self-imaging reproduced three important developments in the life of the Islamist movements. First, by promoting such a self-image and the rhetoric associated with it, the movement defends "the essence or experience itself rather than promote[s] the full knowledge of it and its entanglements and dependencies on other knowledges." In this sense, they "will demote the different experiences of others to a lesser status."[43] Second, as Mohammed Ayoob explains, such "decontextualizing Islam allows Islamists in theory to ignore the social, economic, and political milieus

---

40 Olivier Roy, *The Failure of Political Islam,* 23–6.

41 See 'Abdullahi A. Gallab, *The First Islamist Republic.*

42 Bassam Tibi, "The Worldview of Sunni Arab Fundamentalists: Attitudes toward Modern Science and Technology," in *Fundamentalisms and Society: Reclaiming the Sciences, the Family, and Education,* eds Martin E. Marty and R. Scott Appleby (Chicago and London: The University of Chicago, 1993), 73–102.

43 Ibid.

within which Muslim communities exist. It provides Islamists a powerful ideology that they can use to 'purge' Muslim societies of the 'impurities' and 'accretions' that are the inevitable accompaniments of the historical process, but which they see as the reason for the Muslim decline."[44] Finally, the most important aspect of this discourse and its historical narration is that it makes the Sudanese Islamists a self-sufficient political association rather than a religious movement.

4. Fourth, Mark Juergensmeyer points out that the Islamists "are concerned not so much about the political structure of the nation-state as they are about the political ideology undergirding it."[45] That might explain how and why the Sudanese Islamist model turned into that savage separation of religion and state. According to that separation they transformed the state into a coercive force to protect and maintain their political identity and exclude others by distributing power and resources in unequal ways.
5. Finally, the masses that follow these movements are young, educated men and women who live with the values of the modern city. They constitute what Roy labels as "*lumpen intelligentsia*."

The Islamist State: The Sudanese Way

As the first and only one of its kind in the Sunni Muslim world, the Islamists' regime in the Sudan propagated a distinctive ideology with the declared aim of creating a primary model of an Islamist state. The Islamist regime came to power in 1989 through a military coup led by Lieutenant General 'Umar Ḥasan Aḥmad al-Bashir. The coup—inspired and engineered by the National Islamic Front (NIF), a small Islamist political party—ousted an elected civilian government, dissolved all political bodies and institutions, shut down privately owned media, and initiated a reign of terror in order to create their new state and implement their ideology. Dr. Ḥasan al-Turabi, the former Secretary General of the governing National Congress Party (NCP), speaker of the National Assembly, and theoretician and religious reference, was believed by many to be the regime's supreme architect and leader—sometimes in occultation and sometimes in all intents and purposes but always the possessor of the real power. That might be what most Sudanese and observers believed; however, it was not the reality. This study shows the evolution of a new class of Islamists who perpetuated themselves within a new development that emerged even before the 1989 military coup. They have taken the coup and the state that came into existence out of it as a *kasb* (opportunity or gain) with self-serving motives as this new relationship made this new class belong to the

44 Mohammed Ayoob, "Political Islam: Image and Reality," *World Policy Journal* 21, no. 3 (Fall, 2004): 1.

45 Mark Juergensmeyer, *The New Cold War: Religious Nationalism Confronts the Secular State* (Berkeley, CA, and Oxford: University of California Press, 1993), 6.

state and its republics rather than to al-Turabi or his Islamism. Aspiring to higher positions or more *kasb* among domineering and power-hungery members of this group sometimes turn into beastly game. This development is explained in chapters 6 and 7.

A major turning point of the development of the Islamist republic was on the night of December 12, 1999, when President 'Umar al-Bashir appeared on national television and announced that he was dissolving the parliament and imposing emergency measures for three months until elections could be held. As a result of that action, al-Turabi lost his position as speaker of the parliament, from where he had been taking legislative steps to strip the president of some of his powers. That palace coup against Ḥasan al-Turabi radically changed the political environment in the Sudan and to a lesser extent in the wider region. It gave rise to an uneasy feeling among most Sudanese citizens and even political groups, who vigorously debated whether or not the coup was merely another game—similar to the events of June 30, 1989, when al-Turabi was sent to prison as a cover-up—the Islamists were playing. It soon became clear that the conflict was real and that the end of the first republic and the beginning of a new Islamist republic was at hand. However, it took a long time for al-Turabi's remaining followers and Sudanese and non-Sudanese observers to come to the conclusion that al-Turabi had been the ingenuous Don Quixote silently fighting windmills created by his own Islamism. My approach here builds on, and goes beyond, the approach I explained in *The First Islamist Republic* about the transformation of the Islamist political party into a corporation. I move beyond to explore the present political dynamics of al-Turabi's Islamism as it turned into a close-knit group within a relatively small class under the leadership of 'Alī 'Uthmān Moḥamed Ṭaha to control either from within or from without the First and Second Islamist Republics. This current book is based, as was the previous one, on the way power has been organized and contested in the Sudan, as well as in the Islamist movement, especially after the October 1964 Revolution.

Today, after more than 24 years of oppressive and totalitarian rule and more than 14 years for the Second Republic in power, it is clear that Islamism in practice and the Islamists as operative groups and individuals have undergone significant metamorphoses. These processes of metamorphosis have led the idea of Islamism into oblivion. The historic leaders of the movement, especially Ḥasan al-Turabi, turned into a Faustian character licking deep wounds, suffering an ever-progressing feeling of betrayal, and wanting to show the world that the malevolence of some of his disciples are precisely what is behind his demise. President 'Umar Ḥasan al-Bashir is in no better situation and has become the first national sitting leader in the history of the heads of states to be indicted by the International Criminal Court (ICC). Those Islamists—'Alī 'Uthmān and his new class—who came together one day as *verkhushka* to control the First Republic and lead the Second Republic ended up as frenzied "egoliterians" with a high degree of mistrust and even hate toward each other. When Ali 'Uthmān, Nafie Ali Nafie and Awad al-Jaz, "the sacrificial lambs of the NCP's [National Congress ruling Party] reform agenda, effectively purged out of government in company with allies last December"[46] 2013, it was once more affirmed that Islamism has been created to receive its homage and delights in such different arrangements of violence, suffering and human carnage. Moreover, the Islamist experience has subjected the entire country to a series of humanitarian crises. This development has come within a very important period in the history of the country and Islamism as the possibility of the fragmentation of the country into more than two mini-states becomes a looming threat especially after the secession of the South in 2011.

Degenerating Silhouettes of the Islamist Façade

With its diversity, fundamental changes, and regional and global transformations, Islamism has attracted scholars from different parts of the world. By studying each one of these Islamist movements separately or/and contrasting their histories and developments over the last five decades, many scholars have come to different conclusions about the future of Islamism. Some scholars, such as Asef Bayat, argue for a post-Islamist transformation. Others, such as Olivier Roy, claim that Islamism has failed. A third group of scholars, especially those of the European Stability Initiative (ESI, the Berlin-based nonprofit research and policy institute), perceive an emergence of Calvinist Muslims out of the Islamist experience in Turkey. A fourth group, including Raymond William Baker, poses the centrist Islamist question "whether an Islamic project of the center, speaking for an Islam without fear, can address effectively the demands of our global age."[47] This new "Islamist trend," as described by Baker, formulated its manifesto in the 1980s and published it in 1991 in *A Contemporary Islamic Vision* by Kamal Abu al-Magd. The manifesto elicited wide discussion within Egypt intellectual circles; yet, as Sayyid Yassine of al-Ahram argues, there is "nothing 'new' and little that is distinctively 'Islamic' in the manifesto."[48]

Central to the debate about the Sudanese Islamist experience in power are some of the second and third generations of the Sudanese Islamists—'Abdel wahāb El-Affendi, Al-Tayib Zein al-'Abdin, al-Mahboob 'Abdel Salaam, al-Tijani 'Abdel Qadir, Ḥasan Mekki, 'Uthmān Merghni, 'Adil al-Baz, 'Abdel Rahim 'Umar Muhi al-Din, and 'Abdel Ghani Aḥmed Idris—who have written articles and books either bemoaning the providence of the movement or blaming Ḥasan al-Turabi, the coup, and some of the movement's leadership for its tragic fate. Some of those who survived or replaced Ḥasan al-Turabi in power, particularly Ghazi Salah al-Din, argue that "the Islamist did not rule the country" during or through

46 Magdi El-Gizouli, *"New" Sudan: Back to the Future*, Sudan Tribune, (February, 15, 2014) www.Sudantribune.com/spip.php?article49969.

47 Raymond William Baker, *Islam without Fear: Egypt and the New Islamists* (Cambridge, MA: Harvard University Press, 2003), 1.

48 Ibid.

the National Salvation (al-Ingaz) regime. Ghazi, once an aide to president Bashir and head of the ruling party's parliamentary caucus, declared his resignation from the ruling National Congress Party (NCP) on October 26, after publicly scolded and annihilated by being summoned to face a disciplinary party committee headed by Aḥmed Ibrahim al-Tahir the Speaker of the Parliament. He refused to attend nevertheless the committee called for his dismissal and two of his close associates, Ḥasan 'Uthmān Rizig and Fadlalla Aḥmed Abdalla, from the party and the suspension of several others for a year. The cohort of NCP figures, chief among them Ghazi, had issued an open letter to president Bashir at the height of the September riots in Khartoum protesting the brutal security crackdown and calling for the reversal of the government decision to lift fuel subsidies. In their letter, which called for reform, they openly said to al-Bashir "the legitimacy of your rule has never been at stake like it is today."

Although one can admire the courage of the voices who were open with their criticism of the regime, this criticism was never anything more than a reaction to the shortcomings and failures of the regime as each critic saw it. The critics did not see yet the idea and the fundamentals of Islamism, in essence, as a seedbed of totalitarianism, and as the Sudanese example attest, how it provided an example—in spite of itself—of a wide range of ruthless forms of violence demonstrating its providential viciousness and its destructive drive as its principal index.

The combined force of all this soul searching among some of the Islamists and the enquiries among others might help explain, in part, the anxiety and thinking of those working within Islamism's system of reference and of those studying or observing its developments. At the same time, it might also inform about the essential nature of Islamism and its future as one of the "isms" that emerged, extinguished itself, and faded away during the last century. For this research in particular, for some in the academic community, for the Islamists in the Sudan and worldwide, and for other observers reflecting upon the Sudanese experience in power, what has been happening in the country represents a foundational event that has caused a shift in the understanding of the essential nature of Islamism itself. This shift has drained its content and future, which would most likely assign it a fate similar to that of other "isms."

Islamism from Disintegration to Oblivion

My argument partly stems from an attempt to go deeper into issues lingering beneath the surface of many of those reproductions floating up to the surface of a world that my argument seeks to describe. Its contrasting answers are based on the examination of how Islamists in power acted in a specific way to colonize the lifeworld of the Sudanese society and how they used their power and violent capacity of the state as a mode of governance and system for *tamkeen*, extraction or *kasb*. The consequence of both provoked the state to exercise an open-ended violent capacities to promote and maintain what the Sudanese citizens describe as *fasād* or corruption as the fundamental inequalities based on a system of exploitation.

The end result of that experience, the deterioration of the movement from disintegration into oblivion, led to my new argument concerning the "essential nature" of Islamism. The critical point of departure behind Ḥasan al-Turabi's Islamism that initiated the discourse and made the break with other forms of Islamism—the school of the Egyptian Muslim brotherhood—possible and made Ḥasan al-Turabi a leader can be found in the October 1964 Revolution. And it was this break that made routes to both revolution and counter-revolution possible. Hence, the emergence of Ḥasan al-Turabi, his Islamism, and the class of young Islamists from that development is quite crucial when taking a look at the transformations that have followed.

According to this argument, the essential nature of Islamism is the extirpation of the restless and ceaseless motion toward "digging its own grave." This conclusion is informed by the study of the Islamists' first and second republics in the Sudan from 1989 to the present. The logic of this argument has moved through the study of this experience from the imagined and speculative sphere of the October 1964 Revolution—social practice—to that of the facts that turned Islamism into a system of politics that pursues life and politics as an opportunity. The goal of this research project is to situate the Sudanese experience within the local, regional, and global context of Islamism as a sociopolitical phenomenon.

Book Scope and Significance

First, this book is a continuation about how the social world of Islamism, its moral value, and the knowledge at its disposal has completely eroded it as its practitioners wrestled with its ambiguities, with other Sudanese power groups, with the state, and among themselves. In effect, these practitioners have turned Islam into an advertisement hording for their violence. The book provides an entry point into Islam's local regimes and their disintegration as they were associated with the internal degradation of its ideological, practical, and social modes of regulation. The book addresses the profound transformations that stem from the anachronistic qualities of political Islam as it grows and fails. It also focuses on the need to deploy violence to maintain power, which affects the state's dynamics of coercive force in a way that converts the entire experience into a flexible regime of opportunism that seeks survival through these modes of regulation. Addressing this brand of sociopolitical issues of Islamism here we notice different manners of the same personalities. They were inseparable from the effects of these modes of regulations, as they metamorphosed while fighting to secure or dislodge what they perceived as maintained or lost as *tamkeen* and *kasb*. The book addresses the interplay of nonideological elements in the adaptation of conventional (blood relations) and nonconventional (the state as provider of rewards and punishment) factors and means to establish and consolidate privilege, power, and prestige on individual and clique levels.

Second, the book presents a study on the innate problem, ambiguity, and emptiness of the Islamist theory or slogan *al-hal al-Islami* and the relationship of these problems to the practice of the Islamists in power, the model of their state, and the evolutionary and dialectical processes—factors of serious corrosion from within.

External forces further erode the regime by working together and independently to deconstruct the regime and lead Islamism into oblivion. The book argues that a major challenge to the regime has been expressed in terms of religion. As people started to recognize the challenge to their religious commitment and vocation, their feelings of alienation and otherness soon turned into a push-back against the regime's encroachment without becoming an enemy of their faith promise.

Finally, this book's main concerns are different from other works in the field of the study of Islamism in the Sudan and worldwide. It provides a social description and explanation for current phenomenon connected to the Islamists' experience in power; as the broad reality and the social action of this "unique" occurrence not only are and continue to be in the process of decay, they are steadily phasing themselves out. Ultimately, the main focus of the book is to provide a socio-historical analysis of certain developments and transformations of actual historic forms of Islamism and its "runaway" model. By placing them into the context of the essential nature of al-Turabi Islamism, as well as situating it in its local and global contexts, the end of Islamism is readily apparent.

Islamism in Condition and Practice

The genealogy of Islamism as a theory has to be traced back to the concepts of, ideas of, and attempts at mobilization of Islam in the political and social spheres. That, in part, goes back to Ḥasan al-Banna (1906–1949), Abūl-'Alā Mawdūdi (1903–1979), and to a certain degree to Sayyid Qutb (1906–1966). It has also developed in different directions and has been given numerous forms by others, such as Aymen al-Zawahiri, by the *Wasatiyya* group, and by people like Ḥasan al-Turabi in the Sudan, Rachid al-Ghannouchi in Tunisia, and Sayyid Yassine in Morocco, to name a few. For the purpose of this study, Islamism in theory is understood as a system of political *ijtihād* that has used the language of Islam as a self-assertion and a mobilization factor, in the space of the last century, and has started to grow and splinter in different ways into different groups. As Bassam Tibi rightly explains, "the term Islamism reflects a common approach of adding the suffix 'ism' to reflect the conversion of an original idea into an ideology." He goes on to say, "adding an 'ism' to the name Karl Marx reflects an effort to transform the thoughts of his European humanist into an ideology that is not always consonant with Marx's original thought. Marxism was further developed by Leninism to totalitarian communism, which was never Marx's intention." By comparison, and in a similar vein, "the politicization of Islam is a process by which this religion is used for the articulation of political concerns that are not in line with Islamic faith."[49] The Islamists are a product of a variety of factors; chief among them is the growth of a new breed of public-educated individuals and groups or communities of conversation created by the colonial and postcolonial states. Of particular note and as an important development in the history of Islamism, Ḥasan al-Turabi, dutiful child of the Sudanese community of the state, has created his own version of Islamism that departed in most aspects from other schools of Islamism. This book gives great attention to its characteristics, emergence, transformations, and dilemmas that led it to oblivion. Under these conditions, this study gives unprecedented attention to 'Alī 'Uthmān Moḥamed Ṭaha, who has been perceived by many as a shadowy figure behind al-Turabi, and to his fortunes that turned into misfortunes in the entire Islamist experience.

Within the state, Ḥasan al-Turabi's Sudanese Islamist "disciples"—who later turned into "intimate enemies" at one stage and "bitter enemies" at the other—have advanced themselves as a class inside a closed community, perceived by many as a coherent group that tried to rule over the population by assuming power through a military coup and establishing a totalitarian system within the first Islamist republic and an authoritarian one through the second. Those who were bound together one day by the flimsy canopy of an ideological sense of togetherness transformed and at a specific time emerged separated by a desperate state of "egoliterianism" governed by an underlying spirit of wilding that bred selfish individualism and corroded not only their own togetherness but also their ethics, morality, trust, and all aspects of the common good. Hence, the disruption of what could be described as a Sudanese Islamism community of the state reached an unprecedented dreadful moment. Up to then, there has been no another Islamist group worldwide that assumed power in a way comparable with that of the Sudanese's experience.

In January 1987, the Sudanese Islamists, under the leadership of Ḥasan al-Turabi, issued what they described as the Sudan Charter: National Unity and Diversity.[50] In that Charter, the Islamists laid down what they advocated as an alternative regime that based its ideology on the following principles: "intellectual, spiritual, and cultural values springing from our subservience to one God and our belief that He is the sole authority in this world and the world after." These guiding principles, the Charter explains, are "the only guarantee for a righteous society." In this respect, the Charter outlines an Islamic code of moral behavior in Sudanese public life. Jihād against internal and external enemies of the "the state, its religious and Islamic affiliation," is a religious obligation to defend that "righteous society." After about a quarter century of ruling the country, nothing in the Islamists' first republic was either righteous or civil or even guided by that ideology. To turn their

49 Bassam Tibi, *Islamism and Islam* (New Haven, CT: Yale University Press, 2012), 7.

50 For the full text of the Charter, see Abdullahi A. Gallab, *The First Islamist Republic,* 169.

idea of Islamism into action, al-Turabi's disciples and their regime used all forms of state force, private and state violence, and different methods of coercion to transform the Sudan into a model of an Islamist state in the Sunni Muslim world. From the early days of the first republic, both its champions and benefactors saw themselves and their regime as marking a momentous break with the past in the Sudan, the Arab/Muslim world, and the world at large. From 1989 to1999, the Sudanese Islamists, under what was presumed to be the leadership of Ḥasan al-Turabi, reassured themselves and their fellow Islamists worldwide that the road for taking and maintaining power had been paved, and a pilot model of an Islamist state and the reference book for such pursuit had been set. However, and from the early days of the first republic, many major developments—including al-Turabi's prison arrest and home arrest in 1989, the aftermath of the attack on al-Turabi in Attawa in 1992, and the assassination attempts of the Egyptian president Husni Mubārak in Addis Ababa in 1995, to name a few—have shown that neither Ḥasan al-Turabi nor 'Umar al-Bashir was in control. Some of the Islamists, such as 'Abdel wahāb El-Affandi and al-Tijani 'Abdel Qadir, have argued that it was the Super Tanzim, or a hidden government, that was in control. This study tries to trace the development of 'Alī 'Uthmān Moḥamed Ṭaha and his clique that grew within a new class of Islamists as the true power behind the two republics.

Between 1989 and 1999, the institutional voice and the advocated theory of the regime's protagonists and approach to governance was addressed within a single paradigm: *al-ḥal al-Islami* or *al-Musho'u al-Ḥadari* (the civilizational project), in which Islamists systemically and methodically pursued different types of coercive and totalitarian measures to achieve their designs. This paradigm propagated that there exists only one social order, *al ḥal al-Islami,* and one constitution, the Qur'an. Together, their ideology provides the means to the Islamization of society. This ideology and the subsequent state model that the Islamists attempted to establish demonstrates three key features of totalitarianism: the ideology of a single order, the autonomy of the state, and the system of security oppression.

The Sudanese regime grew out of this ideology. The bureaucracy created by the ruling Islamists is an outcome of its direct involvement with the different patterns of authority and power exercised by ruling Islamists throughout the state. It is also the outcome of the interacting dynamics among the competing forces of ongoing sociopolitical developments and the attempts of the ruling Islamists to monopolize the local political, religious, economic, and social markets. Since the first day of the coup, the Islamist leaders have believed that their hold on power was threatened. Fear, along with challenges and conflict with opposing political actors, has shaped the modus operandi of the governance against all types of imminent or anticipated threats to their power. This is why, in order to understand the practices of one of the most horrifying bureaucracies in the history of the Sudan, one must keep in mind the kind of threats the regime had been facing since their first day in power.

The end of the first republic, the beginning of the second republic, and their ultimate outcome do not necessarily mark the end of Islamism in the Sudan or even the end of al-Turabi's political career. It means the end of this particular version of Islamism, which—together with totalitarianism, and regime transition—worked to shape and hone the second republic. In tandem, and equally crucial, the end of the first republic and the beginning of a second one has not been kind to Ḥasan al-Turabi, his intimate enemies turned to real enemies, or their regimes. All three—al-Turabi and his Islamists, their detractors, and their regimes—have been living in a "state of suspended extinction" ever since that day. Each side has been turned by the other into an object to be eliminated through the tools that they both know very well from the days when these tools were used on mutual enemies: the state apparatus of coercion, character assignation, and different forms of violence. Not only that, but also much of the movement has applied to the vision, the plan for the future, and the imagination. After the split, al-Turabi's former disciples discovered that, at least in the eyes of some Sudanese and other Islamists in the Muslim world, they had sacrificed the intelligence they had used to think, plan, and explore new frontiers, only to find themselves and their movement hostage to a new form of control. They traded the potentially soft, though vulgar, power of the *Shaikh* for the intrinsically hard power of a savage, but-do-nothing, general. In effect, they traded Islamism without al-Turabi for a destitute authoritarian military system without Ja'afar Nimeiri.[51] But insofar as that was the case, 15 years elapsed and revealed that the imagined hard power of the general was fading away just as Nimeiri's power did before without materializing anything more than a runaway regime from both Islam and Islamism. At the same time and even more to the point, one of the main questions the study seeks to answer is whether there is a way for that or any other branch of Sudanese Islamism to dislodge itself from the current constraining state of affairs to sprout out of the ashes and embark on a new

51 Ja'afar (or Ga'afar) Moḥamed Nimeiri (or el-Nimeiri; also spelled Ja'afar Muḥammad al-Numayrī; Nimeiri also spelled Nimeiry, Nemery, or Numeyri; 1930–2009) ruled the Sudan from 1969–1985 after leading a military coup in 1969 that overthrew a democratically elected civilian government of the Sudan. He was briefly overthrown by a Communist coup in July 1971. In September 1971, he was elected president in a plebiscite with 98.6 percent of the vote. He was credited with bringing about the Addis Ababa peace negotiations that led to the settlement of a violent conflict with southern Sudan, which according to the agreement was granted autonomy in 1972.

His attempts to apply an Islamic Shari'a law in the Sudan in 1983 alienated many citizens in the country including non-Muslims in the southern region. His abrogation of the 1972 agreement that had granted southern Sudan autonomy added to the factors that helped fuel the resumption of war with southern Sudan. Mahmoud Moḥamed Ṭaha was executed in 1985 at the age of 75, after protesting the imposition Nimeiri Shari'a law.

In April 1985, while he was in the United States, Nimeiri was overthrown by a popular uprising (*intifada*). He sought refuge in Egypt where he spent 14 years in exile. After his return to the Sudan in 1999, he was not actively involved in Sudanese politics. He did run in the presidential elections in 2000, but he failed.

stage in the evolution of Islamism. Chapter 10 addresses the "hollowing out"[52] of the most oppressive system in the history of the Sudan.

Book Organization

This book opens with an introductory chapter on the socio-historical background of the emergence of Islamists in the Sudan, how they assumed power through a military coup, and the resultant retreat of the Islamist project as it took the state as its object. The Islamists in power (as they were not confined to the declared objective of their movement), their regime, and the country went through an interplay and succession of different events, actions, and reactions that have transformed the entire social, political, and cultural developments to create a wide local, regional, and international outrage directed against the Islamists and Islamism itself. Different issues, profound crises, and strong opposition to the regime emerged out of that experience; and different forms of violence and counter-violence, as well as internal conflicts among the Islamists themselves, shaped and characterized the rise and fall of the first republic. This could have much to say about the essential nature of Islamism, the metamorphoses of different power groups of the Islamists in the country, their competition for power, and the use of state power or lack of it to eliminate the other.

Chapter 2 addresses three points on the Sudanese Islamist fields of action: conditions, and relationships in which the Islamist movement originally emerged and then developed, the circumstances in which it rose to power, the process of degeneration, and the rapid regression into oblivion. It investigates the historical development of the Islamists as a group, their political, religious, and worldly construction, and the subsequent disintegration of the movement as it was on the brink of the second republic. In addition, it investigates the group's surrounding local, regional, and global spheres of influence and its place within this context.

Chapter 3 discusses the contributing factors that led to the second republic: (1) Dr./*Shaikh* Ḥasan's rise and fall—the failure of his ambition and his way to establish a Sunni *Wilayat-e-Faqih*; (2) the historical grounds and the underlying currents of the growth of Islamist artisans—'Alī 'Uthmān and his new class (see chapters 7 and 8)—and their continuous transformations as power struggle deemed essential to the foundation of the a savage separation of religion and state that came with their first and second republics; and (3) the genesis of the order of practice, the order of representation of Islamism as a regime, and its fall from disintegration into oblivion.

Chapter 4 gives a detailed analysis of the history and development of Ḥasan al-Turabi and his Islamism, or his Islamist *laïcité* before and within

52 Eva Bellin, "Coercive Institutions and Coercive Leaders," in *Authoritarianism in the Middle East: Regimes and Resistance,* eds Marsha Pripstein Posusney and Michele Penner Angrist (Boulder, CO: Lynne Rienner, 2005), 21–41.

the environment provided by the October 1964 Revolution. In many ways, this revolution is the most prominent, single event in the history of the post-independent Sudan. It unleashed, provoked, and marked the most serious reactions to comparable and incomparable aspects of deliberating the power and authority of an emerging Sudanese civil society. Most of those who contest that now, however, tend not to grasp that a new liberation could have been realized—that an open material world, a state, and a good society could have emerged and led the way toward the possibility of a new Sudan.

Chapter 5 addresses al-Turabi's Islamism as a counter-revolution and how the Islamists and the left paid a high price because of their struggle against each other. Both the left and the Islamists representations were born again via the October 1964 gestation of a new society. The born-again Islamist movement of the post-October 1964 Revolution is not Islamism in itself or by itself; it is something different. The same thing applies to the post-October 1964 Sudanese left. But both groups paid a high price—the hubris of each and the acknowledgment of the emergent developments that ended with the military coups of 1969 and 1989 and their respective regimes—as their rapacious impulses turned into counter-forces, violence, and totalitarian rule. That, however, has engendered new experiences of a world violated by the requisites of the violence and deviation from the liberation agendas and schemes that the spirit of the October 1964 Revolution inspired and aspired for, but that was vulgarized by the two brutal military coups of 1969 and 1989.

Chapter 6 addresses the withering of Sudanese Islamism. It also projects the end of similar forms of Islamism, and it might help us conceive a new investigation of what might come to outmode "passé" Islamism, profoundly transform it, and push it into oblivion. By seriously addressing these issues, this chapter explores the Sudanese Islamist experience within ironies that came out of its webs of significance.

Chapters 7 and 8 discuss three ways related to this particular development that might help us address the significance of this event as a landmark in the augmentation of the withering of Islamism in the Sudan. The first has to do with 'Alī 'Uthmān Moḥamed Ṭaha as a person. The second has to do with what I call "the opportunity of absence" as 'Alī in particular and other of younger al-Turabi Islamists climbed the movement's ladder by taking advantage of the absence of their leaders while they were in prison or exile. The third one deals with the "pathology" produced and the community created out of that development. All this makes the withering of Islamism in the Sudan a unique experience with nothing to compare it to, as no other Islamist group has ever assumed power the way the Sudanese did. In this sense, such developments have made the Sudanese Islamism a "one-item set" in the society in which it occurred; nevertheless, it sheds light on and adds a lot to the study of the essence of Islamism at large. It is most likely from this view one can understand one of the routes to the end of Islamism Chapter 9 focuses on three aspects of a single phenomenon though are not identical, but they constantly intervene with one another to add to the complexity of the idea of the Sudan within its particularities, deep reaffirmation of its moral and human universe and its multilayered realities and differences. What is so new and equally important, however, in the Sudanese consciousness and their understanding of their political, moral and human considerations that this type of rule—the Islamist system—has been more gratified than many pre, colonial and postcolonial regimes in giving insignificant opportunities and reasons not only for its ideology to disintegrate but also for different Sudanese communities to walk away from the regime and its state. This is, was and has been a chief source of the deeply embedded counter-revolutionary attitude of the Sudanese Islamism in which it has been imprisoned for ages. This attitude has been permeated by other "isms" including colonial and postcolonial totalitarian traditions and experiences.

Chapter 10 is the conclusion. It looks at what is called the 8th Islamic Conference, which was convened in November 2012, in Khartoum. The conference represented an open book for the developments and the dramatic oppositional events of the last 24 years of the Islamist regime and the runaway world of al-Turabi Islamism in the Sudan. The fact that development came from within—and is somehow a reflection of the essence of Islamism and a product of the failure of its champions—made the regime more terrified but not did not make it more civil. This chapter looks at what could come next, an uneasy anticipation of the outcome of past developments. This leads to looking at the Islamists' movement toward oblivion and the runaway world within its local and global representations from an indiscriminate perspective. Could the developments in the Sudan indicate the passing of the Islamist order? There is, of course, an example at hand and other clear indications.

Chapter 2

The Making of Islamism in the Sudan

For the Sudanese in general and the Islamists worldwide, the period after the night of December 12, 1999, was starkly different from the period after June 1989. The sharp difference and the harsh dissimilarity is generated and ascertained by the resultant and the most vicious fight that ensued among the ranks of the Sudanese Islamists after December 1999, and continued ever since. The term *conflict* or *division* is obviously a misnomer for what happened that night and followed after among the Sudanese Islamists, which they themselves described as *mufāṣala.*[1] That night, which incidentally was the fourth day of the holy Muslim fasting month of Ramadan, ʻUmar Ḥasan Aḥmed al-Bashir, the same person who led an external military coup against the democratically elected government of al-Ṣadiq al-Mahdi[2] in June 1989, lead an internal or what has been described as a palace coup against Ḥasan al-Turabi, the speaker of the Sudanese parliament, who for many inside and outside the Sudan—has been perceived to have effectively organized and led the Islamists since 1964. Ḥasan al-Turabi not only touts his

1 *Mufāṣala* is the term used by the Islamists to describe the split that occurred among their ranks and contributed to the downfall and demise of Ḥasan al-Turabi.

2 Al-Ṣadiq al-Mahdi (1935–) was the leader of the Umma Party and Imam of the Ansar and the great grandson of Mohammed Aḥmed al-Mahdi (1844–1885) who led a successful religiously inspired revolution from 1881–1885 against the Turco-Egyptian rule in the Sudan. Al-Ṣadiq came into the political limelight in 1964 when he played a significant role in the wide public discussions that led to and accompanied the October 1964 popular uprising. After restoration of democracy in 1964, he became the leader of the Umma Party in 1966. At the age of 31, he became Sudan's youngest elected prime minister (1965–67). Al-Ṣadiq was the prime minister of the democratically elected government (1986–89) which was toppled by a military coup directed by ʻUmar Ḥasan al-Bashir in 1989. In 1995, Ṣadiq's Umma Party joined the National Democratic Alliance (NDA) in Cairo. The NDA was formed of a group of 13 political parties, officers of the Sudanese Armed Forces, trade unions, rebel armed groups (SPLA/M), and independent national personalities who signed the NDA's National Charter of October 1989, to oppose the new Islamist regime of ʻUmar Ḥasan al-Bashir. The NDA was organized in Khartoum under the leadership of Moḥamed ʻUthmān al-Merghani, the political leader of the Democratic Unionist Party (DUP) and the religious leader of the Khatmiyya *ṭariqa*, when the leaders of those parties were arrested and detained in Kober prison the first day of the coup. Later, the NDA moved its leadership to Cairo and Asmara. In 2000, al-Ṣadiq left the NDA and returned to Sudan. He refused to participate in the government or any form of elections and insisted on a constitutional conference for the restoration of democracy in the country. Since that time he declared what he called *al-Jihad al-Madani* (Civil Jihad) against the regime.

legacy as the master mind behind the coup in Sudan in June 1989, but he also bitterly admitted that he was the person who courted al-Bashir to rule the country when he "instructed 'Umar al-Bashir to go to the palace while he went to prison."[3] It may well have been on that very same day of the 1989 coup many characteristics of the Sudanese Islamism, the persons in its leadership and the project that they were planning to pursue by holding the state through a military coup, started to reveal itself in the open. The visible and invisible undercurrents of the power struggle between Ḥasan al-Turabi and his disciples were deeper and earlier than that day's event (chapters 7 and 8). However, nothing could be more characteristic of 'Umar al-Bashir and Ḥasan al-Turabi, or better bring out the contrast between them—when they were legitimated by history not the free will of their people—than the way their movement and its project degenerated from disintegration to oblivion during each one's accent to power. In addition, it is this one aspect, above all others, of the Sudanese experience that affected the Sudanese Islamism through which one can clearly see the character and characteristics of Ḥasan al-Turabi. That is to say, in what this character and characteristics, the persistence and the continuous struggle—throughout his long tenure as a leader of the Islamist movement since 1964 until his tragic ideological and power collapse in 2000—have produced. The paradox is that none of this happened by accident as the growth of his personality cult (see Chapter 3) morphed from Dr. Ḥasan to *Shaikh*[4] Ḥasan, together with the serious transformation of the younger Islamist members of the party into a class for itself, the movement from a party to a corporation, and both into a republic under what appeared to outsiders under his guidance. The turning point of 2000 and the demise of *Shaikh* Ḥasan might be difficult to understand—within the logic of things—because al-Turabi himself was perceived by many as the chief artisan[5] of the movement, the CEO of the corporation, and the

3 Abdullahi Gallab, *The First Islamist Republic*, 4 (see Chapter 1, no. 1).

4 The *Shaikh Ḥasan* was formulated and exclusively used to replace Dr. Ḥasan (Ph.D. from Sorbonne) after the 1989 coup in order to personify his role as the chief ideologue of the Islamist movement. The term *shaikh* meant no more than a title of respect for a senior religious or tribal personality. A closer look, however, shows that the title *shaikh* gained a meaning to describe the role of al-Turabi as the grand jurist and the supreme religious and political reference to the movement and the regime before 1999. Out of that narrative, an innovative and modernized Sunni equivalent of *velayat al-faqih* (guardianship of the Juris consult), tantamount to the divinity of *Shaikh* Ḥasan, emerged to reinvent an infallible personality.

5 There are two important aspects of the Sudanese Islamist movement: the first was its emphasis on and success in the organizational enterprise, which stifled other ideological thought, political discourse, and democratic needs, as well as opening the door for totalitarianism to emerge even before assuming power in 1989. This has, in turn, helped the creation of a strict centralization of all decision-making in the hands of an unchallenged leader. The second significant aspect is that this emphasis on the organizational enterprise turned the movement into an organizer generating institutions. The organizers who survived and dominated the movement were not original political thinkers, but merely political

executive officer of the Islamist bureaucracy and its party (see chapters 3 and 4). Late John Garang described that as an unprecedented event in the time of the kittens that eat their father.[6] For many, it has been striking to see, when any one of them examines events of that period closely, how the long-time disciples of Dr./*Shaikh* Ḥasan, whom he handpicked, groomed, and nurtured and who were nourished by ascending to the highest levels of power within the ranks of party and the state under his dictatorial gaze were happy to replace him with an obscure ready-made dictator: Lieutenant General 'Umar Aḥmed al-Bashir. However, it would be easy to understand why *Shaikh* Ḥasan could not reprove his disciples with a clear conscious for carrying out a coup against him because he himself initiated similar practices before against a different group of Islamists and a democratic government. Hence, he could not lead an effective denunciation to the oppression inflected upon him or lead a trustworthy opposition movement against the regime that annihilated him when he himself initiated or kept silent about oppressive measures against real or anticipated opposition to the regime all the time before his demise. The ranking Sudanese Islamist and al-Turabi's close ally once before, Aḥmed 'Abdel Raḥman said that day that Ḥasan al-Turabi "drank from the same cup that he had given to others." That might be one of the reasons why at that moment of dire need, however, there was no longer spur-of-the-moment mass support from the members of a party he built and led for almost half a century because he had cut himself from them, according to some of the Islamists who turned against him. Many Islamists and Sudanese and non-Sudanese scholars and observers might agree with Dr. Ḥasan Makki,[7] Ghazi Ṣalāḥ al-Din al-'Atabāni,[8]

---

actors with a skill for intrigue, secrecy, and toxic rhetoric. These have become the artisans of the movement. In an interview with Ḥasan Mekki, he argues that the movement lacked a genuine Islamic inspiration and coherent political thought that could be derived from such inspiration from the beginning. For more about the movement see Abdullahi Gallab, *The First Islamist Republic* (Chapter 1, no. 1).

6 It was related to late John Garang that during his first meeting with 'Alī 'Uthmān Moḥamed Ṭaha during the Naivasha negotiations between the SPLM (Sudanese People's Liberation Movement) and ruling National Congress (2003–2005) he said jokingly "we have heard of that revolution that eats its children, the cat that eats its kittens, but we have never heard of the kittens that eats their father."

7 Dr. Ḥasan Mekki, professor of political science at the African University in Khartoum, was the first Islamist scholar to write the history of the movement. In his book *Harakat al-Ikhwan al-Muslimin fi l-Sudan 1946–1969*, which was published in Arabic by Dar al-Fikr in 1980, Mekki presented to a large extent the movement's early history mixed with its imagined myths of origin as narrated through the formal chain of memory concerning details of its early emergence.

8 Ghazi Ṣalāh al-Din al-'Atabāni (1951–), Ph.D. (Surrey), MBBS (Khartoum), is Advisor to the President of Sudan, Leader of the Parliamentary Majority, and one of the closest disciples of Ḥasan al-Turabi before, who turned against him to join the signatories of the memorandum of 10 which paved the way to the ouster of al-Turabi from power. Since 1990, he assumed several ministerial positions and party responsibilities including

and other former disciples of al-Turabi who described the 1989 coup as an introductory phase of al-Turabi's own project to rule the country. According to Ghazi al-Ṣalāḥ al-Din al-'Atabāni,[9] al-Turabi used the Islamist movement as a ladder to climb to the peak of power and then threw that ladder away when he thought that he reached the peak. However, when he realized that he needed it the most, as he had not yet reached the peak, he could not find that ladder.[10] According to appearances or what might look as the reality of the situation, al-Ingaz or its First Republic was al-Turabi's project; but according to the real thing, it was not. Different arrangements and conditions came to rule all state affairs and the movement, and to an unyielding degree, to draw the regime, its state, and its party away from al-Turabi's real control. All things to be considered, however, the rise of Lieutenant General 'Umar al-Bashir that day could be seen as a representation of the eclipse of the stars of *Shaikh* Ḥasan (the First Islamist Republic), the end of his role at the helm of the Islamist movement, and the advent of a new epoch (the Second Islamist Republic). But to strengthen its hold, nonetheless, the new Republic and its regime did not need to wage a new war against all the preceding values, the First Republic's Islamist rhetorical stance, its propaganda system, and its claim to Islam or to put right its savage separation between religion and the state. The paradox is that the night of the palace coup served as a reminder that everything that related to 'Umar al-Bashir and his relationship to the coup and the Islamist Republic happened by accident as the Brigadier 'Umar al-Bashir[11]—a

---

the Minister of State for Foreign Affairs, Minister of Culture and Information, and Adviser to the President for Peace Affairs. He led the peace negotiations and signed the Machakos Protocol with Salva Kiir in 2002. His rivalry and competition with 'Ali 'Uthmān, whom he labeled with Nafie 'Ali Nafie as 'problem people' within the regime, came with very high cost for him. He lost in every single round between him and 'Ali 'Uthmān . He was forced to pass the regime chief negotiator position to 'Ali 'Uthmān to begin the negotiation with John Garang and conclude and sign the Nivasha CPA agreement. Ghazi lost the battle for the position of Secretary General for the Islamist movement against 'Ali 'Uthmān in 2008 and 2012. He heightened his criticism to the policies of the regime especially after the 8th Conference in 2012. He led what was called the 31 Islamist dissidents who sent an open letter to the president, deploring the killings of demonstrators of December 2013 when the regime security forces fatally shot and killed about a thousand young demonstrators. Ghazi and his group, who described themselves as reformers, were suspended by the party. In October 2013, Atabāni, and his group announced that they were resigning from the NCP. They formed a new party which they called *al-Islah al-Aan* [Reform Now].

9 Ghazi Ṣalāh al-Din al-'Atabāni, interview with the author, recording, Khartoum, Sudan, January 4, 2006.

10 Abdullahi Gallab, *The First Islamist Republic*, 78 (see Chapter 1, no. 1).

11 Most Islamists and observers agree on the fact that 'Umar al-Bashir was neither the first nor the second candidate of the Islamists to lead the 1989 coup. The first candidate, Brigadier Kamal Ali Mukhtar died when his plane was shot down by SPLA force in 1988. The second candidate was Brigadier 'Uthmān Aḥmed al-Ḥasan, the leader of the Islamist group in the Sudanese Armed Forces who insisted that the army should have full control

virtually unknown officer not only among the Sudanese population, but among the Islamists themselves—was transformed from obscurity to the longest reigning president in the country's history. Hence, what has happened in the Sudan since the coup of June 30, 1989, goes beyond what could be described as al-Turabi's project, his demise, or an ordinary military regime that contributed to the rise of 'Umar al-Bashir and the end of Islamism and its ideology. It is worth examining carefully that the dawn of Sudanese Islamist Republic and the runaway world of Islamism during a time some might consider as the rise of Islamism in the Middle East as one of the consequences of the Arab spring. That might enable us to elucidate the road that Islamism has taken from its formative years and from its disintegration to oblivion. At the same time, it might be possible to see all these social formations and relationships of "collision and collusion" as they unleash the beast in the Islamist groups and individuals and reveal their kinships, and within all of that we can witness the runaway world of Islamism. As Pierre Bourdieu explained within a different setting, examining such "pathways of transmission of privilege and by recognizing competing, and even antagonistic, claims to preeminence within its own order, the field of the elite schools insulates and placates the various categories of inheritors of power and ensures, better than any other device, the *pax dominorum* indispensable to the sharing of the spoils of hegemony."[12] Hence, and as noted well, "it is not this or that establishment but the field (that is, the space of objective relations) they compose, that contributes *qua field* to the reproduction of evolving matrix of patterned differences of constitutive social order."[13] This chapter addresses three pointers on the Sudanese Islamist fields of action, conditions, and relationships in which the Islamist movement originally emerged, developed, rose to power, degenerated, and then rapidly regressed into oblivion. In doing so, we might be able to bring out and trace the essence of Sudanese Islamism as an important example that has become so significant in featuring the rise—which was neither out of vacuum nor divine—and the fall—which is not due to a curse nor a conspiracy—of Islamism. But rather, it is like other "isms" that produced conditions that forced the disintegration of their regimes, dismantled their claims, and turned their actors to serve as a travesty of their own ideology. But with compositions, environments, geographies and situations that "varied significantly enough to make the classifications a 'useful analytical tool.'"[14]

---

over political power after the coup. The Islamists replaced him with 'Umar al-Bashir a few days before the coup.

12 Pierre Bourdieu, *The State of Nobility, Elite Schools in the Field of Power* (Stanford, CA: Stanford University Press, 1996), xii.

13 Ibid.

14 Rogers M. Smith, *Stories of Peoplehood: The Politics and Morals of Political Membership* (Cambridge: Cambridge University Press, 2003), 77.

Pointer One: The Rise of the Community of the State

For a while, some Western and Muslim intellectual narrative especially that subscribes to Max Weber's[15] sociology of religion presented Islam as an old-fashioned, reactionary, and 'anti-modern' movement. As such assessment continued to sediment through time to become almost a taken-for-granted part of the discourse for some in the West and in the Muslim world, a reductionist impulse continued to grow as well, and Islamism became both the internal and the external negative Other. Others in the West and Muslim world continue to contribute to a line of debate that attributes the origin of the Islamist movement—especially during its infancy—to British Intelligence, the Freemasonry lodges, or/and in certain aspects in its history, made common cause with the Nazis first and the CIA later. So rigid some of these assessments might be, many would agree with Bobby Sayyid's denunciation of all attempts that explain the rise and the cause of Islamism as "either an external force acting upon some notion of a significant Islamic presence," or see Islamism "to be a superstructural response to structural crisis."[16] Sayyid also criticizes "attempts to explain the rise of Islamism [that] begin with a general process which acts as fuse to a powder-keg. ... the powder-keg being some form of Muslim society, the resulting explosion being Islamism."[17] He argues that "it is one thing to accept and enumerate a series of structural problems within Muslim societies but it requires that another step be taken to explain why these problems meet their response in the form of Islamism."[18] To find a new way for considering the nature and essence of Islamism, one might have to look at the state—colonial and postcolonial—and its capacity to conceive of a cosmos and produce categories of individuals and groups of citizens entrenched in a web of complex relations "independent of their consciousness and will," as Karl Marx once asserted. One of these groups could be the community of the state, which was produced by the public education that was steeped in and introduced by the colonial state and continued in expansion ever after. As a product of the introduction of public education and its system of bestowal of degrees, and conferring according to their credentials of a prestigious governmental and social status, an elite and

15 For more information about Max Weber's ideas on Islam see, Bryan Turner, *Weber and Islam* (London: Routledge and Kegan Paul, 1974). In his summary to that Turner argues that, "when Weber came to analyse Islam, he focused on the political, military, and economic nature of Islamic society as patrimonial form of domination. He treated the role of values as secondary and dependent on Islamic social conditions. ... his analysis was not far removed from Marx and Engels who claimed that the Asiatic mode of production, characteristic of India, China and Turkey, produced an enduring social order which was incompatible with capitalism."

16 Bobby S. Sayyid, *A Fundamental Fear: Eurocentrism and the Emergence of Islamism* (London: Zed Books, 1997), 23.

17 Ibid.

18 Ibid.

new structure of social and cultural stance emerged with a self-image and collective faith in the legitimacy of their role as a community. Later, that status and those individuals and groups became, within the new order of things, the essential element of a different economic and social capital "that not only guarantees preferential and speedy access to positions of command"[19] but also to "its high degree of autonomy and internal differentiation according to the same anatomy between money and culture that organizes the field of power at large [and] enables it also to internecine conflicts by recognizing rewarding diverse claims to scholastic, and thence social, excellence."[20] All that became the base for a new sociopolitical differentiation in the Sudan, as well as other colonized countries. I call those individuals and their groups the community of the state. Who, within their acquired specialized knowledge and system of education were connected to a progressively economically rewarded practice and ascent to higher positions in both the state and the society. That is to say, the state and the higher social recognition within the community of the state endowed those emerging groups, their new system of practice, and the privileges they gained with an open-ended gradational status. In addition, these new particular educational institutions and their graduates continued to dictate the rules of the space of possible virtues or vices attributed to state endowment of power and prestige together with the social rewards, and lack thereof. No other form or system of indigenous, religious, or traditional education played such a major role in the structure of merit, social space, and distribution of cultural capital, power, and prestige.

As the public education continued to grow and become increasingly operational in producing and adding to the professional, cultural, and religious groups of the community of state, the human capacity that developed within that community, the ideological models, the world views, and the self-images they established as a modern community were carefully crafted with the intention of establishing these groups as a class of their own created to adhere to the rules that served that state, to create secular hierarchies incompatible with the traditional order, and to present them as 'intimate enemies' of that colonial state. Those rules were harmonious with the colonial ideals to "meet the approval and support of the British public and of the English-speaking race," to civilize the Sudanese.[21] The population of the country was enticed to see the future of their children transformed into positions of power and prestige through public education and to trust the fact that they would be better informed through the new media. The same new system of communication and knowledge dissemination and instruction, however, was firmly fitted in constituting a system of domination as an extension of the state power and hegemony. The new educational system has

19 Pierre Bourdieu, *The State of Nobility*, xi.

20 Ibid.

21 Janice Boddy, *Civilizing Women: British Crusades in Colonial Sudan* (Princeton, NJ: Princeton University Press, 2007), 45.

set the boundaries and fault lines between the elite and different groups of the local and other populations. The colonial state was not only able to define routes to status, power, and prestige through colonial radicalization and historically structured social realities, but it was also able to exercise "the power to define the nature of the past and establish priorities in the creation of a monumental record of a civilization, and to propound canons of taste, [which] are among the most significant instrumentalities of rulership."[22] Within these developments, the growing Sudanese cultural, economic, and political communities of conversation developed their own courses of action and ways of thinking about themselves, their colonizers, and the world. Considered together, the colonialists were able to exercise their material and hegemonic power to construct a form of institutional state structure and to determine its directions and deeper effects in the Sudanese life.

The Sudanese society began to experience a new form of organization of power and resistance to colonial role out of the rise of the small class of publicly educated milieu (the community of the state) that continued to grow through the expansion of the public education. A new form of internal resistance gradually replaced the old forms of external resistance—taking arms—against the colonial system. These new arrangements of resistance grew to find their elementary forms as a civilizing mission in reverse. But the community of the state continued to find its legitimization within its invention of a progressive, growing self-image and cultural identity as an important part, if not the only part, of modernity in the country, as noted before. This, however, is an identity "from whom one is already somewhat abstracted and alienated. Such splitting of one's self, to protect one's sanity and to insure survival, makes the subject an object to himself and differentiated the violence and the humiliation he suffers from the 'essential constituent"[23] of his self. That is to say, "it is an attempt to survive by inducing in oneself a psychosomatic state which would render one's immediate context partly dreamlike or unreal. Because, 'in order to live and stay human, the survivor must be in the world but not of it.'"[24] These inward-looking groups and their exclusivist self-image developed a worldview and political ideologies of self-affirmation that were reflected in the practice and the discourse of the elite of political parties in their multiple centers and in the civilian groups of the military regimes. The reproduction of this class within its self-image, as they continued to enter the political sphere, introduced a new form of stratification that devalued their local majority Other—within their different forms of religious, social, and regional representations—as backward. This situation made this social groups, not only an intimate enemy of the state,

22 Bernard S. Cohen, *Colonialism and Its Forms of Knowledge: The British in India* (Princeton, NJ: Princeton University Press, 1996), 10.

23 Ashis Nandy, *The Intimate Enemy: Loss and Recovery of Self under Colonialism* (Delhi: Oxford University Press, 1998), 109.

24 Ibid.

but also an intimate enemy of their own society as well. In this connection, Partha Chatterjee describes similar situations as "imitative in that it accepts the value of the standards set by alien culture. But it also involves a rejection: 'in fact, two rejections, both of them ambivalent: rejection of the alien intruder and dominator who is nevertheless to be imitated and surpassed by his own standard, and rejection of ancestral ways which are seen obstacle to progress and yet cherished as marks of identity."[25] This cognitive representation through which these groups assembled made them representative of themselves. In this sense, this self-representation animates and embodies hegemonic impulse perceived through a status and power deferential, endowed by the state. Such a situation Bourdieu describes in a different as the state "is first and foremost the 'central bank of symbolic credit' which endorses all acts of nomination whereby social divisions and dignities are assigned and proclaimed, that is promulgated as universally valid within the preview of a given territory and population."[26] Moreover, "the academic title is the paradigmatic manifestation of this 'state magic' whereby social identities are manufactured undercover of being recorded, social and technical competency fused, and exorbitant privileges transmuted into rightful duties."[27] Within the community of the state, the Sudanese population are always described as plagued by *al-jahl, wa al-jū' wa al-marad* (ignorance, hunger, and pestilence) out of their own choice. At the same time, these members of the community of the state are described as a vanguard destined or who "started to look to life and Sudanese society through the modern spectacles and evaluate them within the modern standards, which were a mixture of authentic religious culture and the irresistible European culture."[28]

There were additional implications that directly resulted from the seemingly improved and modernized sphere of public boarding school education and the degradation of the indigenous systems of both education and forms of work. The introduction of public education represented a radical break with previous or traditional systems of learning. What was unprecedented, without a doubt, was the state "acting as agent as the central bank of symbolic credit, … [where] the academic title is a public and official warranty, awarded by a collective recognized authority, of a competence whose technical and social boundaries and proportions can never be disentangled or measured, but which is always independent of subjective, partial evaluations (those of the bearer himself or his close relations, for example)."[29] As a result, the behavior and attention in public

25 Partha Chatterjee, *The Partha Chatterjee Omnibus: Comprising Nationalist Thought and Colonial World, The Nation and its Fragments, A Possible India* (Oxford: Oxford University Press, 1999), 2.

26 Pierre Bourdieu, *The State of Nobility*, xvii.

27 Ibid.

28 Aḥmed Khair, *Kifah Jil: Tarikh Harakat al-Khirijin wa Tatawurha fil-Sudan,* 2nd ed. (Khartoum, al-Dar al-Sudaniyya, 1980), 18.

29 Pierre Bourdieu, *The State of Nobility,* 376.

education as a tool for upward mobility not only prejudiced the livelihood and image of indigenous education including all mosques and other religious and other non-British based systems education such as al-Azhar,[30] but also governed the way to the admission to the closed society of the community of the state. Accordingly, this steady lowering of the standards and status of all types of indigenous schooling and those who lacked public education together with the professions related to it meant that those growing numbers of individuals who continued to do such works remained poor and were considered illiterate. One result of this structural poverty, or the modernization of poverty,[31] was the disinterest in and marginalization of the old system of education, work, and their resulting products. The colonial state, as Binan Chandra rightly cauterizes its function, "follows, in the long run, anti-industrialization and anti-development policies. And it does so precisely because it is guided by 'the national situation' not of the colony but of the metropolis."[32] As more people plunged into poverty, the majority of the population plummeted into an uninterrupted slide toward an all-encompassing development of illiteracy and poverty or to add to and impair the position of existing marginalized population and their spheres. More people were transported away from their homes to be turned into workers in the emerging colonial government capitalist project in the creation of the infrastructure, such as railways, river-way transportation, and ports. In addition, dams and other construction projects, as well as a Gezira scheme and other colonial extractive economy activities, to name a few, allowed wealth and poverty to take on a different shape. Within this new development, public education and government jobs were made a criterion of modernity. A new form of stratification of upward and downward mobility and aggregates of mass produced poor population emerged concurrently as a new social phenomenon and as a result of this development. The colonial state formed its homogenous system and salient characteristic, as most groups became dependent on its opportunities and "good will" as the job provider for both the educated and the uneducated. At the same time, other groups were subjected to structural underdevelopment as an overt consequence of a style of extraction, a system of control and incentives and disincentives of rewards and punishment. That is/was what made "colonialism as shared culture which may not always begin with the establishment of alien rule in a society and end with the departure of the alien ruler from the colony."[33]

30 Many Sudanese consider Egyptian university education and former Soviet Union and Eastern European university education is inferior to the University of Khartoum and British university system.

31 See Galan Amin, *Modernization of Poverty: A Study in the Political Economy of Growth in Nine Arab Countries 1945–1970* (Leiden: Brill, 1980).

32 Binan Chandra, Karl Marx, His Theories of Asian Societies and Colonial Rule, in UNESCO ed. *Sociological Theories: Race and Colonialism* (Paris: UNESCO, 1980), 437.

33 Ibid.

On the other hand, all sectors of the population, rich and poor, educated and uneducated, became increasingly dependent on what the government provided in the field of employment, transport, education, medical, and other services. Machines powered by steam, coal, and electricity, which were a monopoly of the state, and the growth of their material production, in addition to new efficient communication and transportation systems, had a profound effect on the power, capacity of material production, and security of the state. The connection between poverty production and the government's mode of operation points to the distance between the colonial system and its institutions on one side, and various groups of the population on the other.

Another factor of this new system in the Sudanese life was that the majority of people were left behind within the realm of traditional types of work or production, including rain fed agriculture, rural economy, and simple jobs, which meant they remained poor and turned into an underclass. Thus, when viewed from the bottom, it might be even clearer to see the progress of structural poverty and the human sacrifices offered at the altar of the colonial state. Most profoundly affected were the rural poor in the entire country who were rapidly driven into the bottom of the new marginalized social stratum in the country. In a short time, the colonial state was not only the original core of the capitalist development, which dominated and transformed the social structure, but it was by far the most important agent in the importation of the most pressing needs—from the train to the pencil—and the sole exportation body for all raw material, from cotton to gum arabic, and other products. Within the Sudanese community of the state, Islamists emerged as what Rogers M. Smith describes as a "political people" and "a potential adversary of other forms human associations, *because* its proponents are generally understood to assert that its obligations legitimately trump many of the demands made on its members in the name of other associations." The Sudanese Islamists emerged as a 'political people' according to their historians in 1946[34] out of a seven members of a group who met secretly one night at the western sport field at Khartoum University College, discussed the idea of an Islamist organization that might "confront the communist onslaught and resist British colonialism with the intention of establishing a righteous society based on Islamic ideals."[35] Within its transformations which were conflict riddled, the movement turned under Ḥasan al-Turabi into a "strong and wide" political people who depict their group "as a distinct society entitled to ultimately to override the claims of not many but *all* other groups, and entitled to do so not just not in regard to a few issues but *all* issues."[36] Ḥasan al-Turabi's Islamism, as chapters 3 and 4

34 For more information about the early history of the Sudanese Islamists movement see, Abdullahi Gallab, *The First Islamist Republic*, 36–44 (see Chapter 1, no. 1).

35 Rogers M. Smith, *Stories of Peoplehood*, 20. Moḥamed Khair 'Abdel Gadir, *Nashaat al-Ḥarkah al-Islamiyya fi l-Sudan 1946–1956* (Khartoum, al-Dar L-Sudaniyya lil Kitab, 1999), 66.

36 Rogers M. Smith, *Stories of Peoplehood*, 22.

depict, emerged and circulated outside all systems of Sudanese political culture to create its political people. Other factors, as chapters 6 and 7 show, played a key part in its transformation today. In both cases, the Islamists held the state, denying it other non-Islamist citizens and turning it into a coercive-intensive to dominate "antagonistic groups, which it tends to 'liquidate,' or to subjugate perhaps even by armed force."[37] At the same time, they used the state to distribute in an uneven manner rewards to some and injustice to other. It is the contingent nature of such exercise of violence, the state-assisted different but violent forms of exploitation and organization of violence within the accumulative behavior and overarching authorities of the Islamists that makes other people feel and see their relationship with those in power and their state in a different light is what I describe as a novel order of separation of religion and the state.

Pointer Two: Islamism as a Subliminal Condition

The official accounts and the Islamists' self-made and academic historians did not consider within their discourse the factors behind the birth of Islamism in the Sudan. Most of them describe it as a self-made, unique development that came from nowhere. In January 2006, I interviewed the late Yasin 'Umar al-Imām,[38] the movement's commissar general par excellence, member of its leadership bodies since the 1950s, a parliamentarian, and editor of its newspaper *al-Mithaq al-Islāmi* 1965–1968 among other leading positions. For some of the Islamists, Yasin represents one of the institutional memories of the Islamist movement. In that interview with him, Yasin reiterated in clear terms the uniqueness of the movement. He noted that "in 1949 a group of young students including Babikr Karrar, Moḥamed Yousif Moḥamed, Yousif Ḥasan Sa'id, and Moḥamed Aḥmed Moḥamed 'Alī came to Khartoum from the rural parts of the country. They formed *Ḥarakat al-Taḥrir al-Islāmi* (Islamic Liberation Movement) at Khartoum University College." Al-Imām adds that the Harakat "advocated high moral standing and it was anti-Marxist." The nascent left movement at the Gordon Memorial College was called the Sudanese Movement for National Liberation.[39] Al-Imām distinguishes between two important aspects of the nascent Islamist movement. While he claims that "it had no relationship to *Ḥarakat al-Ikhwan al-Muslimeen* (the Muslim Brotherhood movement) … it was the Communists who continued to call its members Ikhwan." Other Islamist scholars, such as Ḥasan Mekki, 'Abdelwhab El-Affendi, and some of the Islamist politicians including

37 Antonio Gramsci, *Selections from the Prison Notebooks I* (New York: International Publishers, 1971), 57.

38 Yasin died at his home in Omdurman, June 22, 2013.

39 For more about the early history of the Sudanese left, see Moḥamed Nuri el-Amin: *The Emergence and Development of the Leftist Movement in the Sudan During the 1930s and 1940s* (Khartoum: Khartoum University Press, 1984).

Ḥasan al-Turabi reiterated similar narrations. Moḥamed al-Khier ‘Abdel Gadir, a founding member of *Ḥarakat al-Tahrir al-Islami*, explains in his book, *Nashaat al-Harkah al-Islamia fi l-Sudan 1946–1956*, that the seven members of the group met secretly one night at the western sports court at the Khartoum University College, discussed the idea of an Islamist organization that might “confront the communist attack and resist the British colonialism pursuant to the establishment of a righteous society based on Islamic ideals.”[40] He added that this was the way those who were present understood their mission, “though they had no clear vision of how that idea could work, or from where it should start or what to do next. They just relied on God, sincerity of their orientation, and the resolve of the youth.”[41] ‘Abdel Kadir confirms Yasin’s claim that the groups had no direct relationship to the Muslim Brotherhood organization in Egypt. He adds that some of them had not even heard of that organization. In this case, it seems that “the notion thus possesses a critical normative dimension, and even a political dimension in so far as it designates the way individuals or communities become subjects, outside the establishment and its powers and norms—even if new forms of knowledge and power come into being in this process.”[42] In other words, it is important to see the different paths and courses that movement has taken from one development within the Sudanese social movements, society, and its development through time. For most of its detractors, Islamism has been described as a disease outbreak that infected the Sudanese body politic as early as the 1940s of the condominium rule in the country. Indeed, since the birth of the movement, these three currents with their conflicting accounts or silence have been persistently underlying a cold culture war between the Islamists and their secular and other political opponents and may be mistrusted by other academic or elite individuals or groups. This complicated phenomenon seems to be deeply rooted in an intellectual quest that sees Islamism in essence as a less composed configuration of a religious rather than a political movement. Or one that perceives it as a religious movement void of religiosity. Hence, a cautious inquiry of the movement and its emergence could therefore serve four important endeavors: (1) prevent simplistic appending of the movement to nowhere; (2) dispute such arguments and claims that the movement is a unique and novel phenomenon; (3) challenge the notion that it was an outbreak from history’s quarantine house; and (4) confirm that the elementary form of the movement is like other developments within the Sudanese community of the state’s sociopolitical life with multiple sources and sets of reproduction that could be subject to or associated with certain self-affirmations of factors that might be rooted in that particular existential experience of Sudanese colonial encounter.

This encounter, and with the introduction of mass public education, inculcated in generations of Sudanese “a culture of the self,” the new forms of division

---

40 Moḥmed Khair ‘Abdel Gadir, *Nashaat al-Ḥarah al-Islamiyya fi al-Sudan 1946–1956* (Khartoum, al-Dar L-Sudaniyya lil Kitab, 1999), 66.

41 Ibid.

42 Rogers M. Smith, *Stories of Peoplehood*, 20.

of labor. These new forms of labor, with their close relationship to the state, produced the state's organic and nonorganic intellectuals as well as a new sense of citizenship and characteristics of other, different, political formations and demands. These developments combined and divided five different communities of conversations, discourses, and ambitions to hold the state together. The first includes regular and civil service personnel (white-collar workers). The second group includes members of trade union organizations (blue-collar workers). The third group (khaki-collar workers) includes the military, in the first place, and, in the second place, regular forces. The fourth group refers to the private khaki-collar workers, who include the Christian guerrilla forces and insurgency organizers and leadership in the south. In addition, the colonial distribution of labor brought a new peasant community (of white *'arrāqi* workers).

Simultaneously, the structural change that came with public education brought with it political organizations that included Islamists, Communists, other types of Leftists, and Pan-Arabists in the northern part of the country, while church education produced most of the southern political elite. Each one of these political groups and organizations committed itself to certain exclusivist ideologies that followed or propositioned doctrinaire order for the state, modernity, and society. Further, each group entertained self-assurances that only their group represented a self-contained model of political representation. By virtue of their upbringing, these different political schools and their representations among the community of the state developed a self-image which claimed that, although they might be a minority in terms of numbers, they were a majority in terms of status. Hence, they either openly rejected or discreetly undermined the rules and the results of the democratic game as long as the democratic game gives the Umma party or their other "sectarian" rivals, the Unionist party, to have and maintain an advantageous position.

Primary opposition between the different ideological schools and their varied political affiliations reflects a self-image and underlies, to a certain degree, a life-style and selective affinities that grounded each one of those ideological schools and the political affiliations they each produced. This primary opposition reflected its secondary opposition within the political discourse as well as rivalry and antagonism that reflects a degree of status inconsistency. At the same time, within the minority political representational discourses, neither the Islamists nor the Leftists saw themselves in that way. These representational discourses embodied, from one side, a reductionist impulse as they describe the majority parties and their selective affinities as *taqlidi* (traditional), *tāifi* (sectarian), *rajii* (reactionary), and/or *muhāfis* (conservative). They all share the view that these parties and the social groups that support them were part of an old, static order, which was inimical to social and political progress, and which had to go. At the same time, the attitude of these minority groups toward each other was less benign than one might imagine. The modes of reductionism in which these parties were interlocked have paved way for a remorseless and never-ending war of attrition between the Islamists (with all of their different feathers), the Communists, and the regional leftists. The main political parties and their religious and social associations in their totalizing discourses perceived these minority parties as *tanzimat aqāidiyya* (ideological organizations) either born out of alien *musturada* (exported ideologies) or as a product of the rejection of the mainstream associations. In retrospect, we have seen, within the last five decades, both sides living in a "state of suspended extinction." That is, each side has been turned, by the other, into an object that should be eliminated through the state apparatus of coercion and/or private violence. Both state and private violence grew stronger over time, especially during military rule, when the ruling elite and their rivals continually resorted to different sorts of armed violence. Moreover, these modes of reductionism and the mutual hostilities have generated the most enduring and consequential political and cultural wars, with aims of not only humiliating the "other," but also of eliminating them completely, whenever possible. Within such an environment, public debate becomes unconducive to reason and civility. All too often, a military coup, which progresses into a dictatorial rule, has silenced all kinds of public debate and, with it, has stifled any possibility for reason and/or civility. It is not surprising, therefore, that this state of affairs continued to enlist military aid to resolve political conflicts. This process of coercing opponents through military rule forced most, if not all, political organizations to take turns in acting as clandestine organizations, receiving harsh treatments from different regimes. And through the mode of the coup or violence, each group transforms its 'Othering' impulses and past negative feelings or hostilities into an organized form of subjugation of the "dreaded Other." Behind every military coup in the Sudan—successful or abortive—has been a civilian political party or a group of conspirators. All the while, groups of civilian, as well as military collaborators, took part in every military regime. Hence, the self-fulfilling prophecy about the Islamists as *jihaz fashisti*, "a fascist apparatus," as their communist enemies used to describe them, has become both the living example and the enduring legacy of their rule during their republic, especially in the period between 1989 and the present. Chapters 4–5 and 7–8 cover these developments, which led the movement from disintegration to oblivion as headed by Ḥasan al-Turabi and 'Alī 'Uthmān Moḥamed Ṭaha.

Pointer Three: The Visible Hand of the System from Modernity to Colonization of Religion to Savage Separation of Religion and the State

There was another way the colonial state influenced the Sudanese way of life. It was through the "visible hand" of the system which had the upper hand in transforming the state into a structure of enterprises and through market control and elimination of competition to imports which were advertised "as a magic medium 'through which England's power and influence could be enforced and enlarged in the colonial world.' Commodities are not simply the vanguard of imperial rule;

they create the empire all by themselves."[43] J.S. Furnivall argues that "it is indeed, generally true that colonization has arisen out of commerce, and not commerce out of colonization: the doctrine that trade follows the flag is quite modern, and in history the flag has followed trade."[44] At the same time, "neither imperialism nor colonialism is a simple accumulation and acquisition. Both are supported and perhaps even impelled by impressive ideological formations that include notions that certain territories and people *require* and beseech domination: the vocabulary of classical nineteenth-century imperial culture is plentiful with words and concepts like 'inferior' or 'subject races,' 'subordinate peoples,' 'dependency,' 'expansion,' and 'authority.'"[45] The structural grasp of all these colonial fields of action, power, extraction and domination relates directly and indirectly to long- and short-term systems of creation of imagined and real periphery, modes of differentiation, production of both homo- and auto-referential racism, and the construction of peoplehood through different forms and exercise of cultural hegemony and direct forms of violence. *Al-Suq al-Afrinji*[46] was not only an epitome of the leadership of trade over the state, it is an open-air advertisement and main supplier for "a host of commercially produced 'things' to sustain a civilized life."[47] Consumption groups of the community of the state—Scotch drinkers, double-breasted suits wearers, cigarette smokers, Derby shoe wearers—grew assuming and opening new perspectives appealing to such mass-marketed merchandise and connecting such patterns of consumption to a culture concomitant to modernity. Ḥasan al-Turabi expressed a similar false consciousness of modernity when he claimed that "Islam is the only modernity, because if the modern sector in our society represents modernity, then the modern sector is dominated by Islamic currents, students and university graduates everywhere represent modernity as they are the only current which exercises any measure of *ijtihād*."[48] He adds, "the modern elite, mostly Western educated and probably younger. Even their dress sometimes is different."[49] Even the remaining disciples of al-Turabi after the 1999 split among the ranks of Islamists and the removal of *Shaikh* Ḥasan from power claim that he taught them

---

43 Janice Boddy, *Civilizing Women: British Crusades in Colonial Sudan* (Princeton, NJ: Princeton University Press, 2007), 38.

44 J.S. Furnivall, *Colonial Policy and Practice: A Comparative Study of Burma and Netherlands India* (New York: New York University Press, 1956), 4.

45 Edward W. Said, *Culture and Imperialism* (New York: Vintage Books, 1993), 9.

46 Literally the European market. It was a shopping center designed and zoned as fashionable modern shopping area dominated by foreign and mainly European businessmen and stocked by European goods and merchandises. *Alsuq Al-Afranji* stood in contrast to *al-suq al-Arabi* [the Arabic or the local Market] and physically separated al-Suq al-Arabi from the official sector of the colonial capital Khartoum. For more information about that see, Abdullahi Gallab, *A Civil Society Deferred: The Tertiary Grip of Violence in the Sudan.*

47 Janice Boddy, *Civilizing Women*, 35.

48 Arthur L. Lowrie, ed., *Islam, Democracy, the State and the West: A Round Table With Dr. Ḥasan Turabi* (Tampa, FL: The World and Islam Studies Enterprise, 1993), 20.

49 Ibid.

libs al-shal wa Istimal al-jawal, that is to say that he changed their appearance to look fashionable wearing the neck scarf and using the cellphone. Such excursions that dramatize modernity by connecting it to such a particular group's appearances "which may be experienced as unhappy consciousness, sometimes disguised as arrogance, is also a source of their pretention, a permanent disposition towards the bluff or usurpation of social identity which consists in participating 'being' by 'seeming', appropriating the appearances so as to have the reality, the nominal so as to have the real, in trying to modify the positions in the objective classification by modifying the representation of the ranks in the classification or the principle of classification."[50]

The 1899 British invasion of the Sudan is often regarded by Aḥmed wad Sa'd (1926d.), the greatest of the Sudanese Mahdiyya ([Mahdist State] 1885–1899) bards (muddaḥ) as the *kuba*, greatest disaster, where and when "our Islam has grown murky and our religion been cursed."[51] In the opinion of wad Sa'd and other Sudanese of the time, the British invasion of the Sudan, the brutal obliteration of the Mahdist state, and the installment of the colonial system was a *kuba*. More than any other, the colonial experience in the Sudan with regard to religion at large and Islam in particular needs deeper investigation and more clarification that should go beyond the *kuba* syndrome, as there are certain aspects of continuity and discontinuity between that historical experience of the colonial state in colonizing religion and the present regime that matters. It matters because it is still inside and outside the fields of power relations and the way the state has been used not only as a colonizing vessel to religion but also violence supreme in relation to human life (see Chapter 9).

That leads us to another major issue of colonizing religion and another similarity between the colonialist and the Islamists experiences. This major aspect of colonizing religion in general, and Islam in particular, during the colonial period was that the state created in and of itself a new religious entity via its monopoly and control over the Sudanese open religious space with its different colors. The state could deploy its authority strategically to regulate, impose certain roles, and deny access to particular religious markets. The enforced social, political, and religious fragmentation turned different religious representations into appendages of the state. The colonial state, from its first day, embarked on strategies that monopolized and organized the course of action through which the regime could pursue its policy to impose control over the entire population. Yet, though the language and the rulers are different the scheme and arrangements of colonizing religion followed by the Islamists are so little different from Wingate's state. However, the Islamists project was capable of overcoming the colonization aspect

---

50 Pierre Bourdieu, *A Social Critique of the Judgment of Taste* (Cambridge, MA: Harvard University Press, 1984), 253.

51 See Qurashi Moḥamed Ḥasan, *Qasaid min Shiaraa al-Mahadiyya* [Poems from Mahadiyya Poets] (Khartoum: al-Majlis al-Qoumi li Ri 'āyat al-Adāb wa al-Finoon, 1974), 176

to the savage separation of religion and state by turning the coercive-intensive state to coercive-only state.

For the colonialist state, one aspect of their strategies arose out of a policy of inclusion, while the second was derived of arrangements of exclusion. The guidelines of this policy were carefully drafted in Kitchener's famous memorandum[52] to the new military provincial governors (*Mudirs*)[53] of the different districts of the Sudan. Kitchener made a clear distinction between "good," which would be accommodated, and "bad" Islam that should not tolerated. The state of affairs for the Islamists, however, has been totally and entirely exclusive as all other religious representations are considered. For them, all other religious representations in addition to those they describe as secularists, who may be different from each other, have been placed within the parameter of bad Islam that should not be tolerated. Hence, both the colonialists and Islamists did not hesitate to employ all forms of particularistic violence, whether described as a civilization mission or orientation, against whoever considered an enemy of the "totalist" state. So, the state has been designated specific function which is the ungodly use of force and the ungodly *tamkeen*, which is a form of extraction through the use of the state as a monopoly of the Islamists.

The other shared aspect of colonization of religion between Governor General Wingate (1899–1916) and the Islamists is the one that Wingate and his right-hand man, Inspector General Rudolf Slatin Pasha employed as one of the predominant determinants of the state policy. Slatin was not only the second high-ranking person in the colonial state, but also the de facto "*Grand Mufti*"[54] par excellence.

52 Kitchener issued as early as March 17, 1899 his famous Memorandum to Mudirs that set his principles of government. The memorandum included the three main principles that to be followed by the colonial government in the coming years. These principles include: (1) the toleration of domestic slavery; (2) low taxation; and (3) the encouragement of what he described as orthodox Islam as opposed to Ṣūfi Islam or what labeled as heretical sects.

53 Mudir was the Egyptian title of the provincial governor.

54 Rudolf Karl, baron von Slatin, was born in 1857, at Ober St Veit near Vienna, Austria, and died in 1932. An Austrian soldier in the service of Charles Gordon governorship before the Madist Revolution in the Sudan, Gordon appointed Slatin Mudir of Dara-South western Darfur in 1878. In 1881 he was promoted to Governor General of Darfur. Slatin was forced to surrender to the Mahdists and held prisoner in the Sudan during the Mahdists rule 1883–1899. He converted to Islam, and renamed himself Abdelgadir in order to improve the morale among his Sudanese troops. He escaped after eleven years and served Lord Kitchener in the re-conquest of Sudan against the Mahdists. His nearly forty years in the Sudan and his knowledge of the country, its people, its languages and religious groups proved to be invaluable for the establishment of the colonial rule and its state in the Sudan especial during Wingate's tenure. He wrote *Fire and Sword in the Sudan* (tr. 1897), which was instrumental in the propaganda war in Britain and Europe against the Mahdist state. In 1900 he was appointed Inspector General of the Sudan, in which capacity his mastery of Arabic and his profound knowledge of the land and peoples proved invaluable in the work of reconstruction undertaken by the Wingate regime to lay

The Islamists similar to Wingate and his *Grand Mufti* Slatin sought to eradicate not only "centers of unorthodox fanaticism," but also to conquer those whom they waged jihad against in the South, Nuba mountains and also those they described as secular groups and orientations. For Wingate and Slatin, and similarly for the Islamists, who both claim to be seeking to regain or support "good Islam". other Muslims and the Sudanese who are not Muslims represent the external Other. But as the colonialists had their grand mufti, the Islamists had their "Mahdi with a Ph.D. from the Sorbonne." If we combine the distance of each one of these two experiences from the culture and their attempts to forcibly impose religion as an ideology void of faith and theological knowledge or "deculturation effect which is not followed by acculturation," we might reach two important conclusions. First, by developing such an ideology both experiences were transformed into a "fundamentalist-type" of governance. Second, as both experiences lacked what al-Turabi describes as *figh al-Hukm* (theology of rulership), both experiences have taken religion to adapt to their own needs and self-interests. These attempts by these regimes to colonize religion has been rejected by Muslim and non-Muslim citizens. Hence, both extreme regimes relied on coercive power to impose submission or to chastise disobedient subject populations. And perhaps equally important, Islamist legitimization does not come from past experience or heritage similar to other religious representations in the country, especially the Ṣūfi *turq* (singular *ṭariqa* or order) that they despise, or the *'ulamā'*, whom they deride and ridicule. Nevertheless, they do not qualify to perform the functions of the *'ulamā'* who gained and solidified their legitimacy from institutionalized religious knowledge and their functions as judges, Imāms, and teachers. However, both the colonial and the Islamist states' form of state interventionism and control of the Muslim life was conducted as a function of the state through reordering the high-ranking *'ulamā'* as state employees.

The most important aspect in the separation of religion and state within the Islamist experience in the Sudan drives from the fact that a situation was created from first day of the coup in 1989. Since that day, the regime positioned itself as a cultural and political minority by a name they chose by themselves and with a religious marker which was political in essence and ignorant of the main tenants of Islam as its leaders admitted and as explained here before. They were tempted by worldly pleasures; and although they advocate that Islam is *din wa dawla* (a religion and a state), it became evident later that their relationships are based on kinship. In addition to that, and maybe out of that, they developed individualistic traits as they were nurtured to consider politics as an opportunity: *kasb*. In an interview conducted with Ḥasan al-Turabi by the Islamist oriented London magazine *Impact International* in March 1993, however, he explained briefly

the foundation of colonizing religion in general and Islam in particular. I describe him as the *Grand Mufti* because he played the role of being the main person whose advices and *fatwas* were sought in matters that laid the foundation of that system of control. In 1907 he was made an honorary Major General in the British army.

his major task in the Sudan which was "to Islamise public life—civil, business, police, military, economy and culture in all their dimensions." He added, "our power lies in our Iman, and we need a lot of *shawkah* (material power) in order to face the challenges that confront us."[55] Some of these challenges he referred to could include the "gap between military and civilian, and this explains perhaps some of the political instability and military takeover; after a while the civilians become very jealous, and the people followed them although most of the uprising was not necessarily popular. It was elites, trade unions, government, professional unions, that's how it all started, most of the time. We want to overcome this."[56] For that reason, al-Turabi perceives the solution in the militarization of the entire society. He argues, "I think the idea is to dissolve the army, just dissolve the army in society, so to speak. The idea of popular defense force goes some way to do that. But people should organize for their own defense. If the army needs to broaden its base, then it can call upon these forces. Otherwise, these forces are people who are engaged in their daily occupations and go only when they are needed."[57]

The militarization of society came out of a grand scheme of what the Islamist called during their heyday *al-Musho'u al-Ḥadari*. Within that grand scheme comes *al-da'wa al-Shamila* as the operational plan. The Islamists' approach to *al-da'wa* targeted first all other Muslims whose understanding, observance, and practice of Islam were viewed by the Islamists as faulty or incomplete. An approach that puts in practice the Islamists' deeply rooted mode of reductionism and disrespect to all other religious expressions and representations. Second, the Islamists "introduced new content into the message of *al-da'wa*. Rejecting the confinement of religion to matters of private faith and ritual, they emphasized that Islam was both *din wa-dawla*. In addition to enlarge the domain of Islamic regulation, the Islamists propagated a new, activist, interpretation of proper Muslim conduct."[58] Consistent with other developments within the Islamist movement in the Sudan for the last two decades and especially during the lifetime of the first republic, an ideology-driven *da'wa* has emerged, and according to professor el-Tag Fadalla's characterization, it turned the *da'wa* into one of the tools of the political pursuit. So, *al-Da'wa al-Shamila* turned out to be the Islamist's burden that could replace the White man's burden. Each one of these projects had its violent dark side. Out of such *al dawa al-shamila* emerged such ideas of jihad against citizens in the south and north, and militarization of society. In the south, the war took a jihādi overtone as the state described its violence against the insurgency there as jihād. In the north, the ghost houses, the Islamists' dwellings of horrors where Islamist torturers "committed the cruelest

55 An interview with Dr. Ḥasan al-Turabi, "Challenging Times, but Madinah is our Model," *Impact International* (London: February 12–March 11), 7–9.

56 Arthur L. Lowrie, *Islam, Democracy, the State and the West*, 29

57 Ibid.

58 Carrie Rosefsky Wickham, *Mobilizing Islam: Religion, Activism, and Political Change in Egypt* (New York: Columbia University Press, 2003), 126

acts of mental and physical torture including beatings, mock executions and sleep and food deprivation." The militarization of society according 'Umar al-Bashir means that the militarized "civilian population [and] has led to the creation of a large Popular Defense Force (PDF)." All of that quickly grew "to fit different situations. In the Nuba Mountains, for example, it has been integrally associated with jihad, while in much of Northern Sudan, it is a component of Islamic social planning." Later, it developed into the *Janjaweed* in Darfur. Many attribute the idea of *al-Musho'u al-Ḥadari* to 'Alī 'Uthmān Moḥmed Ṭaha who established one of the largest ministries in the history of the country under the rubric of the Ministry of Social Planning and who developed the concepts of *al-Da'wa al-Shamila* and *al-Enqlab al-Islami*, the Islamic total transformation, which is a term that might have been borrowed from the Iranians and owe its currency to the Revolutionary Guard *Sepah-e Pasdaran-e Enghelab-e Islami.* The separation of religion and state model of the Islamist regime became manifest when the security, intelligence, and the police state expanded and incorporated all those units. Then the vesting of power and no separation except that between the state and religion was defined. As it turns out, the Islamists were successful in creating a coercion-intensive state separate and standing on an independent base. In addition to that the state became an overseer and protector of a rampant corruption as another form of violence which expanded through *al-tamkeen.*

The other aspect of separation was the action the regime took against the legal community. One of the fundamental issues that the Sudanese achieved through the October Revolution was the separation of powers and within that independence of the judiciary was recognized. At the same time, even before that "after independence, bar association members were uniquely positioned to command the public's trust and lead efforts to mobilize citizens. Many older Sudanese lawyers still speak with pride about the guidance legal professionals provided to nonviolent people's movements to topple both 'Abboud's military regime in 1964 and the Nimeiri regime in 1985."[59] The Islamists quickly took very serious measures in the aftermath of the coup "to set up a parallel system of justice to deal with threats to its security."[60] This system which started by detaining members of the legal profession along with politicians without charge and purging the legal profession continued within the Islamists strategy to immediately put "the sweeping power of the legal profession under executive control."[61] In addition, the regime "captured and imprisoned key leaders of the bar association's main office in Khartoum and quickly reopened it for business with loyalists in command."[62] The regime took

59 Mark Fathi Massoud, *Law's Fragile State: Colonial, Authoritarian, and Humanitarian Legacies in Sudan* (Cambridge: Cambridge University Press, 2013), 123.

60 Carolyn Fleuer-Lobban, *Shari'a and Islamism in Sudan: Conflict, Law and Social Transformation* (London: I.B.Tauris, 2012), 88.

61 Ibid.

62 Mark Fathi Massoud, *Law's Fragile State: Colonial, Authoritarian, and Humanitarian Legacies in Sudan* (Cambridge: Cambridge University Press, 2013), 127.

leading members of the bar either to "Sudan's notorious prisons at Kober and Port Sudan or to 'ghost houses' or other unofficial prisons to be tortured. Ironically, one of these unofficial house prisons was set up in the 'confiscated offices of the … Sudan Bar Association.'"[63]

Another innovation of major importance that the Islamists introduced in shaping their violent state confirms what 'Abdullahi An-Na'm describes "whatever the state enforces in the name of shari'a will necessarily be secular and the product of coercive political power and not superior Islamic authority."[64] To turn the state into a coercion-intensive system the Islamist that their new penal code "cemented the notion that disagreements with government's rule would be akin to disrespect to Islam [crime of *ridda* or apostasy], a crime punishable by death." One of the paradoxes of Islamism in power that Ḥasan al-Turabi who supervised that code one day was threatened later "with trail for apostasy like [Mahmoud Moḥamed] Ṭaha in 1985. A special pamphlet directed against al-Turabi and declaring him an apostate was published by the official *Majal'at Mujama' al-Figh al-Islami* in 2006 under the title *Risalat al Qul al Fasl fi al-Rid ala min 'an al-Asl* wherein al-Turabi's statements which are contradicted by the Qur'an are repudiated."[65] In addition "the Public Order Courts (al-Nizam al-Am) that deal with petty infractions of Islamic law (e.g., dress and alcohol), fail to meet the minimum standards of a fair trial."[66] Moreover, application of these laws "upon non-Muslims and discrimination against women by using Islamic devices such as honor, reputation, and morality are used by Public Order Police (*al-Shurta al-'Ama*) and Popular Committees (neighborhood associations) to protect the 'moral health' of the society."[67] By transforming the state into a coercive vessel, the courts and "corporal punishments, echoing the words of the legal historian Douglas Hays, is routinely used as a 'splendid occasion for lessons of justice and power.'"[68] Many Sudanese courthouses are designed like Western-style motels, with two floors of courtrooms opening onto exterior corridors. Floggings (many, if not most, for alcohol-related offenses) are administered in these open walkways or terraces alongside courthouse buildings, visible and audible to those on the premises and passerby in the street. Many upsetting videos that circulated worldwide show the moment Sudanese women were flogged in the street by the police and how they cried in pain while a judge was in attendance watching. Within all of these practices, laws, and innovation of the system of torture and violence, the Islamists

63 Ibid.

64 'Abdullahi Aḥmed An-Na'im, *Islam and the Secular State: Negotiating the Future of Shari'a* (Cambridge, MA: Harvard University Press, 2008), 7.

65 Carolyn Fleuer-Lobban, *Shari'a and Islamism in Sudan*, 92.

66 Ibid.

67 Ibid.

68 Mark Fathi Massoud, *Law's Fragile State: Colonial, Authoritarian, and Humanitarian Legacies in Sudan* (Cambridge: Cambridge University Press, 2013), 127.

transformed the state into a comprehensive system whose functional designation was to maintain the regime through a coercive mode of operation.

At the same time, the Islamists as a desperate population transformed into identity groups defined by their tribal affiliations, celebrated religion at their homes as *tilawa* (group reading of the Quran), fasted for two days a week, and met with select few confidants for sun-set breaking of the fast and group prayer. Other than that religion, for the wealthy Islamism has become a drive for plural marriages that 'Umar al-Bashir himself encouraged by setting the example for other Islamist officials. I call this separation savage because it has been enforced through coercive means.

In so far, collecting together all these pointers, we can arrive at the essence of Islamism itself and the developments that existed in some of its complex, but savage, forms of governance, that attempts to maintain their monopoly over power, control the population and extract resources through a system that operate through direct and indirect internal and external violence.

Chapter 3

Ḥasan al-Turabi: The Making and Unmaking of al-Turabi's Islamism (1)

The second Islamist republic was born out of the 1999 *mufāṣala*—as described by the Islamists themselves—that is, a change of direction, which some Islamists and observers portray as a palace coup. It was executed by a hidden government or elements of the security and military in alliance with some of the Islamist "artisans," who the executives believed to have been molded by, and who meekly served, their Secretary General[1] for decades. He kept them from following any other ideological leadership except that of their mentor, Ḥasan al-Turabi, who positioned himself as the Sudan's sole Islamist theoretician. In a sense, some of the Islamist members of his party turned their adherence to him into a "political spirituality." Aḥmed 'Abdel Rahman, one of the leading Islamists before the coup, blamed al-Turabi for turning "the Islamist movement into a Ṣūfi *ṭariqa* [brotherhood] and [becoming] its *Shaikh*."[2] Nothing could be more characteristic of the disposition of the mentor who turned the movement into a "regime of practice" and his party members into "artisans" locked up in his iron cage; nor could anything better bring out the sharp contrast between al-Turabi the leader and his rebellious disciples than this turn of events when the hegemonic canopy that shaded the Islamist disciplinary society was shattered.

It is true that the entire internal struggle against al-Turabi had not yet come out in the open, though more importantly, the event, as stated before, gave rise to an uneasy feeling among most Sudanese citizens at home and abroad, as well as in groups of journalists and even among local and regional political groups. Almost all of those groups and individuals vigorously debated whether or not that change of events was a true rebellious moment or merely another game similar to the ploy used in the coup of June 30, 1989, when al-Turabi sent himself to Kober[3] prison as a cover-up while he sent al-Bashir to the palace, a move he admitted to later. But whether that appalling and peculiar incident was due to the Islamists justification—as they evoked the Hadith that *al-ḥarb khid'aa* (war is trickery or

---

1 Ḥasan al-Turabi assumed the position of al-Amin al-'Ām (the Secretary General of the Islamist movement) in 1965 and has been in that or similar positions ever since.

2 'Abdel Raḥim 'Umar Muḥi al-Din, *al-Turabi wa al-Inqadh; Ṣirā'a al-Haw wa al-Hawiya Fitnat al-Islamien fi al-Sulta min Muzkirt al-'Asharaa ila Muzkirat al-tafahum m'aa John Garang* (Khartoum: Marawi Bookshop, 2006), 180.

3 This the Sudanization of the name Cooper. The prison was named after Mr. R.M. Cooper, the first director of the prison.

deceit)—or to al-Turabi's fear of being implicated had the coup failed, it tells about al-Turabi's character, the Islamists' moral competency, and the lust to capture the state regardless of each one's hidden agenda. Moḥamed Ṭaha Moḥamed Aḥmed, an editor in the Islamists' hatchet journalism, opinioned once that the coup could have cost al-Bashir his life, but not al-Turabi had it failed.[4] However that may be, that the coup as single event has continued to present itself as the mode of operation whereby the regime acquired its self-image within the Sudanese mind. Henceforth, that memorable credibility gap has opened up into an abyss, especially because that particular event has never been renounced as a great mistake by any of the Islamist groups regardless of their fighting.

Yet, the more they obscured this complicated and difficult truth, the more its private and public costs grew and charted the course of Sudanese Islamism's route from disintegration to oblivion. Sudanese Islamism, henceforth, was abrogated as an illusion "incongruent with reality" according to its own and others' judgments, as truthfulness was never counted as one of its virtues. That exemplifies an illustration to the essence of Islamism and its Sudanese model, as explained in the previous chapter, especially as "the more things change, the more they stay the same"[5] in terms of its regime of practice.

The second republic came out of three contributing factors: (1) Dr./*Shaikh* Ḥasan's rise and fall—the failure of his ambition to establish a Sunni *Wilayat-e-Faqih*;[6] (2) the historical grounds and underlying currents of the growth of Islamist artisans—'Alī 'Uthmān and his new class (see chapters 7 and 8)—and their continuous transformations as a power struggle deemed essential to the foundation of the hidden government that came with their first and second republics; and (3) the genesis of the order of practice, the order of representation of Islamism as a regime, and its decline from disintegration into oblivion.

Through these developments, the Sudanese Islamist imagination faded, and the regime as a whole lost its claim to any certainty, political representativeness, and long-time-challenged religious legitimacy. Instead, the significance, meaning, and consequences of the Sudanese Islamist experience have clearly extended well beyond the Sudan, the Islamists and their two republics, and the state they used and abused. It has demonstrated the most important example of the limitation and the essence of Islamism, as much of the experience was inverted since its early days into one of the most frightening and fast-moving turnaround forms of violence, wilding culture, and practice, and an unrestrained lust for wealth, power,

---

4 Quoted in 'Abdelgani Aḥmed Idris, *al-Islamiyoun: Azmat al-Roya wa al-Qiyada* (London: Sinnar Publishing House, 2012), 91.

5 The song says "the more things, the more they stay the same."

6 It might not look clear to many how such an idea would apply here, especially the guardianship of the *faqih* in the *shii* model is particularly in the absence of the imam, and thus fits into a larger eschatological schema, which of course al-Turabi doesn't share. Of course al-Turabi was not following a *shii* model, he was reinventing the tradition within a new Sunni model by virtue of being a jurist scholar.

and women. Here and the following chapters, I illustrate some details about Ḥasan al-Turabi and his version of Islamism, his disciples and their state, the specific characteristics of each, and the common patterns and trajectories that relate to the case for or interconnected with the demise of Islamism in the Sudan.

Dr./*Shaikh* Ḥasan and the Way to a Sunni *Wilayat-e-Faqih*

Ḥasan 'Abdalla al-Turabi was as much an enigma who shrouded himself with mystery to those who loved, respected, or feared him as he was to those who disparaged, competed with, or hated him. Throughout his political career, he has been accused—especially by former colleagues and disciples—of numerous shortcomings that include condescension, callousness, opportunism, and even incredulity and *kufr*. No matter how provocative, controversial, and even notorious some find him, he has emerged as a key player—in the Sudan, the region, and the world—as one capable of commanding the attention and support, if not the strict allegiance, of thousands of Sudanese who have streamed to listen to him for more than 50 years. He knew how to attract local and foreign media attention better than the presidents whom he served or opposed.

His strange style, a mixture of sarcasm, mockery, and provocative language, as well as verses quoted from the Qur'an and some concepts reproduced from modern Arabic terms, touched a raw nerve for inexperienced foreign media and ingenuous Sudanese audience. Andrew Natsios, who spent years as the Special Humanitarian Coordinator for Sudan and on President George W. Bush's Special Envoy to Sudan, wrote, "when Western scholars and writers interview him, they tend to accept him for what he appears to be—urbane, charming, witty, and brilliant. Turabi knows how to speak to Western audiences, using language calibrated to be inoffensive but also misleading."[7] Natsios adds, "two Hassan al-Turabi exist in parallel universes: the moderate and thoughtful Islamic scholar who can be found when he is out of power or when he speaks to Western audiences in English or French, and the religious zealot who emerges when he is in power or speaking in Arabic."[8] The Sudanese citizens, who knew al-Turabi better than anybody else, abridged that in their satire by declaring "there are two Ḥasan al-Turabi: one for export and the other for local consumption."

He has an enduring effect on some of his disciples, who emulate his iconic rhetorical and writing style, erratic moves and movement, and the animation of his hand gestures and facial expressions when he speaks. According to Aḥmed Kamal al-Din—an attorney, a former disciple who maintains good relations with al-Turabi, and a self-described independent Islamist—that gives al-Turabi an added

7 Andrew S. Natsios, *Sudan, Southern Sudan, and Darfur: What Everyone Needs to Know* (New York: Oxford University Press, 2012), 86.

8 Ibid.

value of "unclaimed sacredness."[9] Whether unclaimed or not, this sacredness most likely speaks of "a pure charisma [that] depends on devotion to the person, ... [rather than a] successful charisma based on devotion to his work."[10] But the expectation that all members of the party would work harmoniously with the devout followers to achieve the charismatic leader's goals proved to be a different matter. It was within this context that Ḥasan al-Turabi's tragedy occurred, but it did not get the attention that it deserved among those who have been studying his legacy. Al-Turabi's story and his pursuit for power deserves more consideration, as it surpasses all bounds of what he repeatedly describes as the tragic parts of *ibtila'*[11] that are attributed to the brand of Islamism he created, its demise, and the essence of Islamism at large.

The Authoritative Position of Ḥasan al-Turabi

Ḥasan al-Turabi was born in the eastern Sudanese city of Kassala on February 1, 1932. He was born into a famous religious family who had settled in the village of Wad al-Turabi, 52 miles southeast of Khartoum, where his great grandfather was buried. His father, 'Abdalla al-Turabi (1891–1990), joined the Sudanese judiciary as a *Qāḍī shari'i* (shari'a judge) in 1924. 'Abdullahi 'Alī Ibrāhim argues that young Ḥasan al-Turabi, as a son of *Qāḍī shari'i*, was "born on the wrong side of the colonial track, ... [he] witnessed a close emasculation of his father, home and tradition. At a young age he saw firsthand the Manichean worlds of colonialism in which a dispossessed native space such as the qadi's court had been pitted against a merciless modern space such as the civil court."[12]

However, the relationship between the colonial state in the Sudan and Islam, in particular, and religion in general, is more complex. The colonial state created in and of itself a new religious entity via its monopoly over and canonization of the Sudanese open religious space. The state could strategically deploy its authority to regulate and impose certain rules and roles and to deny access to particular religious fields and markets. The enforced social, political, and religious fragmentation turned different religious representations into appendages of the state after making a distinction between "good" Islam, which would be accommodated, and "bad" Islam, which could not be tolerated. As Nandy argues, "colonization colonizes the

---

9 Aḥmed Kamal al-Din in an Internet interview with the author, March 2012.

10 Bryan Turner, *Weber and Islam: A Critical Study* (London: Routledge and Kegan Paul, 1974), 25.

11 An awe-inspiring test by God when the faith of a true believer is being examined.

12 'Abdullahi 'Alī Ibrāhim, *Manichaean Delirium: Decolonizing the Judiciary and Islamic renewal in the Sudan, 1898–1985* (Leiden: Brill, 2008), 330.

minds in addition to the bodies and it releases forces within the colonized societies to alter their cultural priorities once and for all."[13]

At a young age, al-Turabi was exposed to a variety of systems and movements, stories, and experiences that ultimately shaped his ideology. Young Ḥasan al-Turabi lived under the influences of a hegemonic culture and its structures' forces, which supported and maintained the colonial system, as well as under the influences of the national movements, which resisted colonialism in the Sudan. But he also lived through the infancy of the Islamist movement at the University College of Khartoum and the emergence of Bābikir Karār and *Harakat al-Taḥrir al-Islami* (ILM), which arose as an anti-Communist movement. Young al-Turabi lived during the time of the early emergence of Moḥamed Moḥamed Ṭaha, another Sudanese Islamist who was "admired by young Islamists for his combative style, while arousing the hostility of Ṣūfi leaders by touching the same raw nerve the Mahdi touched a century earlier in claiming direct divine mandate to reshape Ṣūfism (and the totality of Islam)."[14]

He also experienced the oral stories about and the legacy of his grandfather Ḥamad al-Naḥlan Ibn Moḥamed al-Bidairi, who was known as Wad al-Turabi (1639–1704). In addition to the everyday stories, Ḥamad's biography was chronicled in the work of Muḥammad al-Nur b. Ḍayf 'Allah, who lived in *al-Ṣultana al-Zurqa* (Funj Sultanate, 1504–1821): *Kitab al-Ṭabaqat fi khusus al-awliya'wa 'l-salihin wa 'l-'ulamā'wa 'l-shu'ara'fi 'l-Sudan.*[15] According to Wad Defalla, al-Naḥlān invented a new way to see religion in the Sudan at that time. He was known as the first person in the Sudan to declare himself as *al-Mahdi al-Muntazar* (the expected Mahdi). Some Mecca *'ulamā'* thought that his ideas were heretical when he tried to advocate being a Mahdi in there during the haj period, and he was badly beaten. According to Trimingham, he "was a *Malāmati*[16] and his claim to be the Mahdi was regarded as one of his excesses."[17] In his article about al-Turabi's theology, 'Abdullahi 'Alī Ibrāhim argues that al-Turabi's chroniclers invariably assume or suggest "that his Islamic revival is by and large a continuation of his family's clerical, Ṣūfi, and Mahdist traditions, which go back

13 Ashis Nandy, *The Intimate Enemy: Loss and Recovery of Self under Colonialism* (Delhi: Oxford University Press, 1998), vii.

14 'Abdel wahāb El-Affendi, *Turabi's Revolution: Islam and Power in Sudan* (London: Grey Seal Books, 1991), 44.

15 One of the most extensive Sudanese compilations of biographies of holy men, scholars, and poets of the Funj Sultanate period. Edited by Dr. Yusuf Faḍl Ḥasan, Khartoum, Khartoum University Press, 1985.

16 *Malāmatiyya* (singular *Malāmati*), according to Wad Defalla, "are a class of Ṣūfis who do blameworthy things in contravention of shari'a in order to incur the people's disapproval. Some seek to destroy their critics, whilst others seek such disapproval for the good of their souls and from fear of the dangers of popularity." Translated in J. Spencer Trimingham, *Islam in the Sudan* (London: Oxford University Press, 1949), 135.

17 J. Spencer Trimingham, *Islam in the Sudan*,150.

to the seventeenth century."[18] Ibrahim adds that al-Turabi's "biographers rightly point out that his family, from Wad al-Turabi's village on the Blue Nile south of Khartoum, has a long tradition of teaching Islamic sciences and practicing Ṣūfism. But the religious compulsions these writers associate with his family diminish al-Turabi to a mere bearer of a tradition."[19]

He is not a mere bearer of tradition, it is true. However, that tradition influences al-Turabi's background more than 'Abdullahi 'Alī Ibrāhim enumerated in his aforementioned article. First, Ibrahim maintains that "al-Turabi does not view his village or lineage as 'traditional' in the sense that others use it in claiming the influence of cultural traditions in his life." Second, al-Turabi, according to Ibrahim, "described his people as adept at forging tradition rather than submitting to its alleged imperative. He described them as 'free' and open to change." Wad al-Turabi villagers, according to Ibrahim, started as Qadiriyya followers one day and later switched to Khatmiyya. Third, during the Mahdiyya revolution (1881–1898), some of the villagers fought with the Mahdists—although later, at the end of the Mahdist state and the advent of the colonial rule in 1898, some "found it convenient to switch back to Khatmiyya, since colonialism showered them with political favors for opposing Mahdism."[20] But neither that openness to change nor convenience of going back and forth from Khatmiyya to Mahdism gave the Islamist Ḥasan al-Turabi or his party a convenient place among those villagers. They did not support his election to the Sudanese national parliament and, during the 1968 election, "he lost his bid to win a seat in his home constituency."[21] Nevertheless, all of these elements worked in the background to promote a personality cult different from any other formations. Most importantly, the realization that the aim of remembering such historical heritage was not to inform an overpowering philosophy or sway his Islamism and Islamist followers negatively left him free to add to his self-image to the Sudanese mind.

On one hand, acceptance of such unmitigated renowned origins, one would suggest, has left no ground for controversy. On the other hand, al-Turabi's origins have not satisfied everybody, especially those who hold that there is more to one's character than a memory of a late grandfather and his tomb. In this sense, there are many aspects of primary self-efficacy actions and their consequences that grew out of al-Turabi's active self and the products that make a claim to his charismatic experience. That becomes even clearer where and when he makes a claim to what his personality bequeaths as it continues to stimulate, subliminally or premeditatedly impressing and affecting in different ways his Sudanese public. However, all of that succeeds only insofar as it adds to his personality cult and convinces some of his followers by adding unique experiences, such as his great

---

18 'Abdullahi 'Ali Ibrāhim, "A Theology of Modernity: Ḥasan Al-Turabi and Islamic Renewal in Sudan," *Africa Today* 46, no. 3 (1999): 195–222.

19 Ibid.

20 Ibid

21 'Abdel wahāb El-Affendi, *Turabi's Revolution*, 84.

grandfather's claim to be al-Mahdi al-Muntazar, fittingly or deleteriously, and his active self as a latter-day Mahdi with a Ph.D. from the Sorbonne.

Later, some of his remaining loyalists boasted that he taught his renegade disciples "*libs al-shal wa istimal al-jawal.*"[22] In this sense, one can see more to in this commotion than that insinuation, especially when other developments such as style, taste, and modernity were not freed but added to the weight of Mahdism in its new and old images. Moḥamed E. Ḥamdi, who claims to be the true chronicler of al-Turabi's "intellectual and political views and positions,"[23] argues that al-Turabi's marriage into the Sudan's first family to Wiṣal al-Mahdi, Sadiq al-Mahdi's sister and the great granddaughter of Moḥamed Aḥmed al-Mahdi (1844–1885), "was a consummation of an undeclared alliance between the Muslim Brotherhood and Ṣādiq al-Mahdi wing of Ansar."[24] Thus, regardless of the threads of history through the great grandfathers, al-Naḥlān and al-Mahdi conceal the posterity of the messianic inspiration that has profoundly shaped the course of al-Turabi's pursuit to power, his awareness of expectations, and the way his personality cult was built. But what has been experienced in this field aroused different and diverse responses from both his followers and detractors. The legend and arrangements that emerged out of that development in its complexity has deeply influenced and typified al-Turabi's ambition, his personality cult, and his cult following by producing a multiplicity of ramifications.

In the first phase of his leadership to the party and as early as the 1960s, the denunciation of al-Turabi as Secretary General by some of the members of the party's executive committee was manifested in four principle forms. The first form, from the early time of his leadership, included some nagging members of this party's executive committee who accused al-Turabi of turning the party into a *trila* (trailer cart) subordinate to the Umma party.[25] However, during that time al-Turabi emerged as a distinguished new leader in the Sudan—especially among students from higher education institution—to give the small and marginal Islamist party a new image. Due to his role during and after the October 1964 Revolution, and especially at the Round Table Conference in 1965 and after, he won a significant majority of the seats of *dawair al-khrijeen* (Graduates Electoral College)[26] in 1965.

---

22 Al-Turabi's remaining disciples after the *al-mufāṣala* of 2000 used that term to show how al-Turabi influenced the lives of the Islamists and made them look fashionable and modern in their attire and use of modern systems of communication.

23 Moḥamed E. Ḥamdi, *The Making of An Islamic Political Leader: Conversations with Ḥasan al-Turabi* (Boulder, CO: Westview Press, 1998), ix.

24 Ibid.

25 'Iesa Makki 'Uthmān Azraq, *Min Tariekh al-Ikhwan al-Muslimin fi al-Sudan, 1953–1980* (Khartoum: Dar al-Balad Publishing, n.d.), 95–121. The word *trila* (trailer cart) was a part of the profound conflict between al-Turabi and Ja'afar Shaikh Idris, which continues up to this day, where Ja'afar continues to accuse al-Turabi of blasphemy.

26 An electoral college closed to university and college graduates.

The second phase was the initiation of al Turabi's strategic vision of *wahdaniyya,* or oneness. Later al-Turabi explained and continued to promote this idea as his deep-seated grand theory of what he calls "unitarianism," which he has assumed, developed, and followed as his operational and high-status stipulation. According to that, unitarianism here represents the "fundamental principle that explains almost every aspect of doctrinal or practical Islam."[27] Hence, through time, the idea of unitarianism, which started as a representation characteristic of "leadership as one," has extended to embrace a total order of "not just that God is one, absolutely one, but also existence is one, life is one; all life is just a program of worship, whether it's economics, politics, sex, private, public or whatever."[28] Hence, leadership as one was initiated and confirmed by "his new grip on the movement [that] was dramatically demonstrated in the decision to issue a communiqué on November 2 in the name of Ḥasan al-Turabi as Secretary General of Ikhwan."[29] This move was "even more significant, given that no such a post as Ikhwan Secretary General' existed then. In fact such a designation contradicted the resolutions of the fifth congress of the party [which was held in 1962] that insisted on collective leadership as a safeguard against what was seen then as the abuse by [the previous leader al-Rashid] al-Ṭahir of his position."[30] What is not surprising was the eagerness the younger college-educated groups, most of whom supported Dr. Ḥasan and his new leadership. They claimed to have drawn inspiration from the October 1964 Revolution and to apply it to the new image and prestige of the University of Khartoum and its environment. That has been a program that al-Turabi and his party continually reproduced, communicated, and accentuated particularly in decisive roles of mobilization and promotion of their own self-image. Al-Turabi repeatedly—especially when called upon to describe his group, mostly to Western audiences of journalists and scholars—claimed that Islamism "is the only modernity." It is in this form that al-Turabi's compact with modernity as he perceives it draws a "marked sense of self-awareness"[31] and a clear line between his and other forms of "traditional" Islamism—the Ikwan in particular—that adopted the term *al-Amin al-'Āām* for *al-Murshid al-'Āām* (the General Guide). Within such an order and the body of politics that emerged out of it comes a very serious foundational aspect of al-Turabi's theory of practice the perception of people as one. According to that, neither dissent nor disagreement could be tolerated, and in this sense, the "Other" has been regarded not only as the enemy but as a threat and a heresy from which society, held together with and sustained by the power-as-one, should be protected. This concept constituted the foundation of the Islamist totalitarian pursuit and the violence that ensued out of it.

---

27 Arthur L. Lowrie, ed., *Islam, Democracy, the State and the West: A Round Table with Dr. Ḥasan Turabi* (Tampa, FL: The World & Islam Studies Enterprise, 1993), 13.

28 Ibid.

29 'Abdel wahāb El-Affendi, *Turabi's Revolution*, 75.

30 Ibid.

31 Moḥamed E. Ḥamdi, *The Making of an Islamic Political Leader*, 14.

The third phase of his transformation transpired out of his evolving leadership condition. He transformed from Dr. Ḥasan, the university professor, into the high leader Dr. Ḥasan, head of the political Islamist party, and then into *Shaikh* Ḥasan, the uncontested leader—at least in appearance—who finally solidified into the totalitarian leader who took steps toward an unfulfilled *Wilayat-e-Faqih.*

Fourth, Dr./*Shaikh* Ḥasan ended up propounded and remunerated for every virtue by some and deprecated for every evildoing by others. All this owes a great deal to al-Turabi's personality cult, his behavior, and his form of Islamism.

Al-Turabi's Personality Cult

Al-Turabi's personality cult did not emerge overnight. To trace the genesis of this development, we need to go back to the emergence of Islamism as a movement whose presence publicly budded outside university and high school campuses after the October 1964 Revolution. Here, step-by-step, Ḥasan al-Turabi methodically and successfully consolidated his power with a strict centralization of all the Islamist party's authority in his hand. Simultaneously, al-Turabi's personality cult grew as a work of al-Turabi himself. He, the brilliant student, the acknowledged university professor, and the "fox-like"[32] politician, had always been celebrated as the heart of his disciples' cult, and he continued to be perceived by them as a representation and expression of an Islamist modern *ṭariqa* whose exceptionalism they liked to believe in and promote as their image to the Sudanese public. Professor al-Tag Fadalla, former president of the Sudanese International University, noted that "al-Turabi's status as a university professor and dean of faculty of law [at an unusually normal promotion, experience, and early age] in addition to his family background endowed him with a cultural and social capital that facilitated his path to the fields of power within his Islamist group and Sudanese society at large."[33] Dr. 'Alī al-Ḥaj Moḥamed[34] attributes al-Turabi's prominence to his outstanding ability of getting ahead and staying ahead. He argues that al-Turabi "is not only a brilliant person but also a dynamic thinker and by staying for so long at the helm of the organization he shaped his leadership position and it shaped him."[35]

To better understand that in relation to the formation of his personality cult, we need to look at the history of the person and his role as part of the definition of the social phenomenon within the growth of the Sudanese community of the state.[36] In one sense, al-Turabi does not strike those who study his legacy as simply a

32 Many of his political enemies describe him as such.

33 'Abdullahi A. Gallab, *The First Islamist Republic,* 5. (see Chapter 1 n. 1)

34 Dr. 'Ali al-Ḥaj Moḥamed is the deputy Secretary General of the Sudanese Islamist Popular Congress Party. He lives in exile in Germany.

35 Ibid.

36 The community of the state includes sets of elite and dissenters produced by public education that later inherited the colonial state and became its surrogate mother. See

successful member of the Sudanese community of the state or as an accomplished scholar. One needs to look deeper, into al-Turabi's personality cult, which was blended with an environment conducive to the Sudanese community of the state's general feeling that their "rendezvous with destiny"[37] had been fulfilled, as they emerged heirs of the colonial community of the state and products of the public school that imposed an unchallenged authority who controlled the postcolonial state. Al-Turabi had the privilege to be one of the few and first Sudanese to be admitted to the University College of Khartoum a year after it was elevated to that position from Gordon Memorial College. After his graduation from the School of Law in 1955, he studied abroad and completed a master's degree in 1957 at the University of London. In 1964, he was one of the first Sudanese awarded a Ph.D. from the Sorbonne in Paris. He wrote his doctoral dissertation on the place of emerging powers within a liberal democracy. In 1961, he visited and toured the United States. According to some writings about his legacy, he was disturbed by the racial prejudice he encountered. "After finishing his dissertation in 1964, al-Turabi traveled extensively in Europe."[38] On his return to the Sudan, Dr. al-Turabi was quickly appointed Dean of the Law Faculty at the University of Khartoum. He left the prestigious university position within a few months to become a member of the post-October Revolution Sudanese Parliament and the Secretary General of the Islamist organization that adopted the name Islamic Charter Front (ICF) instead of that of the Muslim Brotherhood.

The ICF was a small organization of no more than a couple thousand members, who mostly were students from universities, higher education institutions, and secondary schools. It advocated an "Islamic constitution" and an "Islamic state." All of these factors added to al-Turabi's personality cult, "grouping around him some of the younger and more militant members, but at the same time alienating some of the old guard who clashed with him repeatedly."[39] 'Alī al-Ḥaj Moḥamed claims that "those old guard members were not sidelined by al-Turabi but would have inevitably found themselves sidelined regardless."[40] In his book, *Min Tarikh al-Ikhwan al-Muslimin fi al-Sudan* (*From the History of Muslim Brothers in the Sudan*), 'Iesa Mekki 'Uthmān Azraq, one of the elders of the Sudanese Muslim Brotherhood, briefly describes some of these clashes and how some of the movement's leaders complained about the harsh language of their new Secretary General, Dr. Ḥasan al-Turabi. Azraq particularly referred to an incident when some members of the executive committee of the movement demanded an apology from

Abdullahi A. Gallab, *A Civil Society Deferred: The Tertiary Grip of Violence in the Sudan* (Gainesville, FL: University Press of Florida, 2011).

37 Aḥmed Khair, *Kifah Jil*, 18 (see Chapter 2, no. 27).

38 Stephen E. Atkins, *Encyclopedia of Modern Worldwide Extremists and Extremist Groups* (Westport: Greenwood Press, 2004), 323.

39 'Abdel wahāb El-Affendi, *Turabi's Revolution*, 75.

40 'Alī al-Ḥaj Moḥamed, interview by author, audio recording, Bonn, Germany, July 24, 2012.

al-Turabi for publically insulting Dr. Zain al-'Abdin al-Rikābi, another professor, a member of the executive committee, and the editor of the movement paper, *al-Mithaq*. Al-Turabi refused to apologize and said, according to Azraq's story, that he "has never been used to apologizing in public."[41] Such an account holds significance because this behavior continued to be al-Turabi's pattern, even when he was asked to apologize to the Sudanese people for his role in the 1989 military coup and the atrocities committed as a result of it.

Again, he said he would not apologize and stated that he apologizes only to Allah. Hence, he has always placed himself above individuals and colleagues, organizations, the nation, and the state. Accordingly, we are here in front of a personality that floats above history. In his interview with the Egyptian TV host Muna al-Shazali, he explained that by saying that he does not like to padlock himself to any political, partisan, or religious formation. "I would like to talk to the human beings in the world and in existence," he echoed to his interviewer.

It might be important to ponder 'Abdullahi 'Alī Ibrāhim's reflection on the legacy of 'Abdalla al-Turabi, Ḥasan's father, and his "experience as a cleric in a colonial Judiciary that relegated shari'a law to a humiliatingly inferior position in relation to modern, civil law." This experience, according to Ibrahim, deeply influenced al-Turabi's assessment of the broader patterns of change in two significant ways. First, "it makes his point that colonial clericalism, as family jurisdiction divorced from the business of the state, was only one example of the long-standing tradition in Islamic clericalism of separating shari'a from state politics in order to safeguard personal piety." Of course, the view that clericalism was incapable of reconciling Islam with modernity was not unique to al-Turabi, but it was shared by the Islamists at large. By its very nature and relationship to the inherited colonial and the would-be generations of the community of the state, the Islamists have considered that all forms of clericalism, *'ulamā'*, and their institutions amounted to an old-fashioned group "whose education is based on books written hundreds of years ago and who believe nothing better could be produced." Second, "he uses his father's experiences to question the ability of the secular effendis to implement a modernity in which Muslims would feel at home."[42] However, modernity in which Muslims would feel at home has further complexities. These complexities became more serious through time, particularly when al-Turabi assumed power after the 1989 coup. He and his followers saw themselves as having a trust over the religious, moral, and political high ground and a monopoly over its ideals, as they arrogantly claim it. In so doing, they assumed they owned the language, example, and arbitration of ethics, values, and beliefs over and above the ideology. Later, al-Turabi admitted that one of

41 'Iesa Makki 'Uthmān Azraq, *Min Tarikh al-Ikhwan al-Muslimin fi al-Sudan 1953–1980* (Khartoum: Dar al-Balad Publishing, n.d.), 105.

42 'Abdullahi 'Ali Ibrāhim, "A Theology of Modernity," 195–222.

the main problems that their experience in power suffered was a deficiency in the fiqh of rulership.[43]

The implications of this matter for al-Turabi and the Islamists might be clear, especially when he continued to state that the *'ulamā'* represent the relics of the past. He believed in himself as the ideal that emerged from the ideological experience of his own understanding of modernity. According to him, especially when he was in power, these *'ulamā'* needed to undergo an Islamist "Four Cleanups Movement" to become "more enlightened and look at religion in its wider meaning as a force against falsehood and injustice in all areas of life." Hence, the enlightenment of his father's experience as an effendi gave him his education through ordinary public schools in the Sudan and abroad. This experience was an opportunity for him to enter the club of the community of the state as one of the "intimate enemies" of that state. At one time, he asserted that the state should "atone," though he did not explain how and for what reason. The values of the community of that state club suited al-Turabi's personality cult very well because it provided for "separate pathways to transmission of privilege, and by recognizing competing, even antagonistic, claims to prominence within its own order, the field of elite schools insulates and placates the various categories of inheritors of power and ensures, better than any other device, the *pax dominorum* indispensable to the sharing of the spoils of hegemony."[44]

Al-Turabi joined Bābikir Karār's ILM in 1951. It might be difficult to assert such intellectual influence; however, many would argue that Bābikir Karār's intellectual influence on al-Turabi is more than meets the eye. In many respects, Karār's ideas of the Sudanization of the Islamic movement and other unorthodox views regarding women and social justice had a deeper influence on al-Turabi's thoughts. From a very early period, Karār acted as if he was the representation of the conclusion arrived at by such ideological thought and the solution for such questions. Al-Turabi followed Karār's style diligently. Hence, such a position in Islamism endowed him with the knowledge of how to act, how to live, and what schemes of Islamism to consider relevant to the personality cult of "the leader" in a totalitarian setting and to a certain extent in establishing the Islamist republic after 1989.

The Making of an Islamist Political Leader[45]

An important stage in the history of al-Turabi and the Islamist movement in the Sudan started in 1964 when he returned from France with a Ph.D. in

43 In his TV interview with Muna al-Shazali, which can be viewed at http://www.youtube.com/watch?v=ksTo7V0JeIs.

44 Pierre Bourdieu, *The State Nobility*, xxi (see Chapter 2, no. 12).

45 Moḥamed E. Ḥamdi turned his interviews with Ḥasan al-Turabi into a book titled *The Making of an Islamic Leader: Conversations with Ḥasan al-Turabi.*

constitutional law. He started to gain attention as an articulate spokesperson of the Islamists at the University of Khartoum when he gave the greatest statement of his life at a panel organized by the Social Studies Society at the university in October 1964. Members of General 'Abboud's ruling council attended the panel. Chief among them was Major General al-Magboul al-Amin al-Ḥaj. Dr. Ḥasan al-Turabi said that a peaceful resolution to the problem in Southern Sudan lay in extending democracy to the whole country. Recently, he recalled, "I said that decentralization was the solution for the southern problem, which means more freedoms should be given; that means the regime needs to go!"[46] However, most of those who attended that night would agree that he said something closer to what 'Abdeleahab El-Affendi later wrote: "the problem of the south was first and foremost a constitutional problem, reflecting assault on people's liberties both in north and south, although certain additional factors caused the situation in the south to degenerate into armed rebellion. There could thus be only one solution for this problem and the problem of the country as a whole: the ending of the military rule."[47] This single event brought him major nationwide recognition, and after the downfall of 'Abboud's military regime, al-Turabi continued his move up the ranks of the small Islamist movement.

The climax of his popular political history was that he won the highest number of votes in *dawair al-khrijeen* Graduates Electoral College for the parliament in 1965 in the first elections after the downfall of the 'Abboud's regime. That win became the epitome of pride for Dr. Ḥasan al-Turabi, the Islamist "leader" now "unbowed by authority and orthodoxy."[48] These two events helped the propagandists and the conventional storytellers among al-Turabi's followers reshape history to provide him a more significant role in the October 1964 Revolution. al-Turabi and the Islamists continued to claim that he initiated the October 1964 Revolution, which is a claim that has been bitterly disputed by other political parties and historians.

The most dangerous flash point in Ḥasan al-Turabi's history and legacy is that his personality cult positioned his life in the subjective experience of himself. The growth of al-Turabi's personality cult and the progression of his monopoly over a total sense of veracity took an irreversible course. Now, it would be difficult to understand Ḥasan al-Turabi outside of his version of Islamism. Dr. Ḥasan Mekki, in a recorded interview with the author, asserted that "the entire Islamists' project in the Sudan is more or less al-Turabi's project rather than the Islamists."[49] Whether it seems that way to some more than others, Ḥasan al-Turabi's disciples and enthusiasts have no more in common with him than his opponents and adversaries.

46 Quoted in Ismā'il Kushkush, "In New Protests, Echoes of an Uprising that Shook Sudan," *New York Times*, February 23, 2012, A6.

47 'Abdel wahāb El-Affendi, *Turabi's Revolution*, 71.

48 Austin Dacey, *The Secular Conscience: Why Belief Belongs in Public Life* (Amherst: Prometheus Books, 2008), 25.

49 Ḥasan Mekki, interview by author, audio recording, Khartoum, Sudan, December 28, 2006.

Among Islamist intellectuals, Ḥasan al-Turabi, by all means, is an outsider. He is neither a Muslim Brother, nor a typical orthodox mainstream Islamist. To some, he may be a self-made Islamist, but others may seriously doubt whether he is an Islamist at all.

In a special interview with the Egyptian TV host Muna al-Shazali in July 2011, al-Turabi repeatedly affirmed that he is neither a Muslim Brother, a Sunni, nor a Shia and that he would prefer not to lock himself within the confines of any political or Islamist representation.[50] However, he definitely adds a different shade to Islamism's many existing shades. From a critical perspective, by contrast, most of his avowed Salafi enemies label him as a secular person propagating "dangerous ideas."[51] At the same time, other opponents from the left label him as *rajee* (backward looking or reactionary). A former disciple of Ḥasan al-Turabi, Dr. Ghazi salah al-Din al-'Atabāni, questions his integrity. According to Salah al-Din, "Ḥasan al-Turabi used the Islamist movement as a ladder to climb up the peak of power and then throw that ladder away when he thought that he reached the peak. However, he did not find that ladder when he realized that he needed it the most as he did not reach that peak yet."[52]

'Atabāni was not alone; others describe him as an opportunist because of his political performance. William Langewiesche, who interviewed al-Turabi several times, claims that he has heard that "al-Turabi is called the Madison Avenue ayatollah."[53] Others would argue that he has always been an opportunist who uses religion as a useful tool "just to sell you [his] cause," as he conceded in 1989 to Scott Peterson, a *Christian Science Monitor* writer.[54] All this shows how many divergent views of al-Turabi there are that try to define his place in the political and religious fields. Yet, to take all that seriously, it might be helpful to briefly reflect on some of these allegations and how they relate to his Islamism. In the 1980s, the Salafi leader Aḥmed Malik, president of the Muslim Union, wrote under the pseudonym Ibn Malik a book titled *al-Ṣarim al-Maslūl fi al-rad 'Ala al-Turabi Shātim al-Rasūl* (*The Unsheathed Sword, in Reply to al-Turabi, Denigrator of the Messenger* [*of God*]) in which he severely attacked Ḥasan al-Turabi and later

50 Interview with Egyptian TV host Muna al-Shazali, http://www.youtube.com/watch?v=ksTo7V0JeIs&feature=relmfu.

51 Salafi and conservative-leaning Islamists in the Sudan and some of the *'ulamā'* in Saudi Arabia, including the late *Shaikh* 'Abdul-'Aziz Bin Bāz, campaigned locally and abroad against al-Turabi by accusing him of being a secularist.

52 Ghazi Ṣalāḥ al-Din, interview by author, audio recording, Khartoum, Sudan, December 30, 2005. The idea that al-Turabi manipulated the Islamist movement for his own gain was repeated again and again in all the interviews I conducted with Ḥasan Mekki, al-Tayib Zain al-'Abdeen, and Ghazi Salah al-Din.

53 William Langewiesche, "Turabi's Law," *Atlantic Monthly* (1994), 26–33. Vol. 274, No. 2

54 Scott Peterson, "Sudan's struggling government offers to go '100 percent Islamic,'" *Christian Science Monitor*, August 7, 2012, http://www.csmonitor.com/World/Africa/2012/0807/Sudan-s-struggling-government-offers-to-go-100-percent-Islamic.

branded him as an apostate. Later, in the year 2000—when al-Turabi no longer in power—Aḥmed Malik continued to raise these issues about al-Turabi. Al-Amin al-Ḥaj Moḥamed Aḥmed, the teacher of Shari'a studies at the Arabic Language Institute at Um al-Qura University in Mecca also wrote a book that attacks al-Turabi. This kind of criticism of al-Turabi is evidently in line with the Saudi Salafi *'ulamā's'* and activists' official and private views and attacks on him and his ideas. Such criticism of al-Turabi has united the Saudi, Sudanese, and other Salafi and other conservative individuals of the Muslim Brotherhood from other parts of the Muslim world. Through their criticisms and attacks, they have been determined to show how far away al-Turabi and his brand of Islamism stand from what they consider true Islam. But al-Turabi himself has never hesitated to tell the world that there is something about these groups that is not to be trusted. He himself has explained how distant his Islamism is from the Egyptian Muslim Brotherhood. He even refused to give *bay'ah* (oath of allegiance), like Ṣādiq 'Abdullah 'Abdel Māgid, to the Egyptian Brotherhood *Murshid.* He maintains that "the Islamic movement in the Sudan is very aware of its own history. It might in early days have assumed the form of Egyptian experience, which in turn had emulated an earlier model of Islamic life, mainly characterized by education and reform."[55] He claims that there is a distinct difference between the two Islamist representations and describes the Egyptian one as a "traditional form of organization."[56] He describes his Islamism as the one that "developed a marked sense of self-awareness, positioning itself accurately within its own specific time and place parameters."[57]

Indeed, it is not surprising to notice that as one examines when and how al-Turabi muscled his way to "position" his Islamism and leadership and how he shaped the movement "accurately within its own specific time and place parameters" during the sixties of last century. The "traditional form of organization"—the die-hard loyalists to the Egyptian Ikhwan, such as Ṣadiq 'Abdullah 'Abdel Māgid, Maḥmoud Burat, the Ikhwan group led by Moḥamed Ṣaliḥ 'Umer, and al-Turabi's main rival (later became Salafi) Ja'afar *Shaikh* Idris—"made a formidable team that eventually gathered around it the bulk of the Ikhwan old guard."[58] Antagonism against al-Turabi and his "heretical" ideas continued to grow, as did hostility from those individuals and groups together with regional Salafi circles.

It is true that another and different part of the internal struggle against al-Turabi had not come out into the open. More importantly, it is also true that al-Turabi's strategies, maneuvers, and ways in dealing with his old in-house contenders took peculiar ways and means. By replacing his adversaries and competitors one or more at a time, he disarmed most of them. However, al-Turabi's revolving-door syndrome tactics of bringing younger members of the organization in and

---

55 Moḥamed E. Ḥamdi, *The Making of an Islamic Political Leader*, 14.

56 Ibid.

57 Ibid.

58 'Abdel wahāb El-Affendi, *Turabi's Revolution*, 87.

hurling others out ultimately backfired—he was thrown out by the very ones he handpicked to replace some of his antagonists.

Although al-Turabi "complained that he had been the target of a politically motivated campaign of vilification by figures from the Egyptian Muslim Brotherhood, which was behind most of these allegations,"[59] it may well have been that the issue was deeper than that. It is about neither "heresy" nor "dangerous ideas" but primarily about where these forms of Islamism and Salafism collide on the question of ideology and orientation and about where his character had been trying to present itself as different. That, in a sense, reflects on the character of al-Turabi and speaks about the essence of Islamism. Ḥasan al-Turabi is not a Muslim Brother and has never been and never needed to be one. On August 2, 1994, Dr. Ḥasan al-Turabi delivered in Madrid a confusing speech to a mainly non-Muslim audience. He described himself as a typical fundamentalist. What made that speech confusing was by that time there was no person, group, party, or movement in the Muslim world that described itself as fundamentalist as explained earlier. Moreover, by that time, most scholars of Islam had successfully freed Islam and Islamist movements from the labels "fundamentalist" or "fundamentalism," as the term cannot be "transferred from its original context."[60] In that lecture, Ḥasan al-Turabi never mentioned a relationship to the local, Egyptian or international Society of the Muslim Brotherhood. Neither that day nor any day before had al-Turabi ever mentioned, written, or discerned any influence on or relationship of that organization with him or his Sudanese Islamist organization. On the contrary, he described the Egyptian body of Islamism "as traditional,"[61] and he branded its foundation as based on a traditional form of leadership. He asserted that "the earliest Muslim Brotherhood was led by Ḥasan al-Banna in the typical manner of a *Shaikh* with followers; there is little that was democratic about it. And there was a view that the *shura* or consultation is not binding; it's informative, it's persuasive, but it's not binding on the *amir,* the leader."[62] As a result of this major difference between al-Turabi and the Egyptian Brotherhood and its local representations, he proudly boasted of his encounter with the Sudanese Brotherhood as the "biggest shake-up the [Sudanese Islamist] movement had ever experienced to that time."[63] When carefully reading al-Turabi's Madrid lecture, one could see him attempting to come to grips with his own and different ideology. He was adamant about interpreting his ideology as a Muslim phenomenon opting for a historical

---

59 'Abdel wahāb El-Affendi, "Ḥasan Turabi and the Limits of Modern Islamic Reformism," in *The Blackwell Companion to Contemporary Islamic Thought*, ed. Ibrahim M. Abu-Rabi' (Malden: Blackwell Publishing, 2008), 144–60.

60 Bobby S. Sayyid, *A Fundamental Fear: Eurocentrism and the Emergence of Islamism* (London: ZED Books, 1997), 16.

61 Moḥamed E. Ḥamdi, *The Making of an Islamic Political Leader*, 14, 17.

62 Arthur L. Lowrie, ed., *Islam, Democracy, the State and the West: A Round Table with Dr. Ḥasan Turabi* (Tampa, FL: The World & Islam Studies Enterprise, 1993), 18.

63 Moḥamed E. Ḥamdī, *The Making of an Islamic Political Leade*, 14, 17.

movement of change.[64] For this new perspective and that historical movement of change, al-Turabi was the salesperson of his own brand of his Islamism, especially before the 1989 coup. Even after the coup, his Sudanese Islamists tried with and without him to introduce the first major experimentation of political Islam in the Sunni world by the end of the second millennium. In this instance, al-Turabi, the Sudanese Islamists, and their benefactors inside and outside the country had expected the emergence of a model that could reinstate a certain version of political Islam as an alternative ideology and an example after the collapse of the Soviet Union and the demise of East European socialism. For al-Turabi, the demise of that brand of communism coincided with what he believed to be the promise of an emerging Islamist order that would liberate the entire human race "from the clutches of all kinds of material, political, occult, or psychological control."[65] Al-Turabi, himself, advocated that the Sudanese Islamist state model would act as a launching point for "pan-Islamic rapprochement ... proceeding from below." He explains, "if the physical export of the model is subject to Islamic limitations in deference to international law, the reminiscence of the classical Khilāfah and the deeply entrenched Islamic traditions of free migration (*hijra*) and fraternal solidarity would make such a state a focus of pan-Islamic attention and affection."[66]

For Ḥasan al-Turabi, the "present growth of Islamic revivalism means a sharper sense of inclusive-exclusive identity, a deeper experience of the same culture and stronger urge for united action, nationally and internationally." He further elaborates that "once a single fully fledged Islamic state is established, the model would radiate throughout the Muslim world,"[67] which is a concept borrowed from Sayyid Qutb and articulated first by 'Abdalla 'Azzam as *qaidat al-Jihād al-Ṣulbah* (the strong Jihād base or foundation) and later by other Islamists such as al-Qaeda (the Base).

But al-Turabi here doesn't recognize Qutb or 'Azzam. It seems we can read al-Turabi's moment as he saw it emerging within its time and space. He reargued a debated issue in a different manner against the Qutbian perspective. Al-Turabi held the state as a central issue different to and colliding with the Society of the Muslim Brotherhood's dispositions of tarbiya, Sayyid Qutb's vanguard creed, and the Salafi isolationist world view. From such a perspective and a dissimilar structuring of the discourse emerged al-Turabi's calculation. According to al-Turabi's definition of modernity, which he articulated in his meeting with the American scholars, he might have thought of himself as a more educated person with cultural capital superior to that of all the locals, such as Maḥmoud Moḥamed Ṭaha, Bābikir Karār, and regional and local founders of Islamism including Ḥasan al-Banna, Abu A'la' al-Mawdudi, and Sayyid Qutb. His life experience and

64 See *Islamic Fundamentalism in the Sunni and Shia Worlds*, in http://www.islamfortoday.com/turabi02.htm.

65 Ibid.

66 Ibid.

67 Ibid.

relationship with the main discourse about modernity within three metropolitan centers—Khartoum, London, and Paris— represent an added value to that cultural capital as part and parcel wholesalers of his *laïcité*, breaking away from culture, religion, and modernity. Hence, the differentiation processes and functions of his discourse for how and where to assemble and construct his space as an individual and a group with God, according to some prevailing worldviews, has become subject to controversy. In this field, al-Turabi's Islamism represents an unthought-of form of *laïcité*—not secularization—that presents religion as an enterprise and a product that functions through a system of production that could manufacture and distribute its product through a new breed of wholesale and retail vendors. Only in this sense is Ḥasan al-Turabi is similar to Sayyid Qutb. Each one is a wholesale vendor but within his own terms. Nevertheless, for Ḥasan al-Turabi the Sudanese Islamist and Sudanese Islamism and the Islamist each seek a different interpretation.

Ḥasan al-Turabi, who prides himself as *Ibn al-Thagafa al-Francia* (a son of French culture) created his own *laïcité*, not promoted but typified by the Islamist movement. It is more than a personal project. As early as 1962, al-Turabi, as a graduate student in London, submitted a memorandum to the Fifth Congress of the Sudanese Ikhwan that proposed "the movement be transformed into an intellectual pressure group on the lines of the Fabian Society, and not to work as an independent party. Instead it should act through all the political parties and on all of them."[68] At the same time he attested that he started studying the French language while he was in England.[69] On the one hand, Ḥasan al-Turabi's *laïcité* represents a breakaway from culture, religion, and modernity. It depicted culture as primitive by despising the Sudanese Ṣūfi Islam in particular and Sufism in general. It broke away from religion by reproaching the *'ulamā'* and censured modernity by denouncing secularism. Typically, his brand of Islamism differentiates its field of action by designating religion and religiosity in different spheres that advance "politics over religiosity and political action over theological reflections."[70] Within this, however, al-Turabi's Islamism placed itself within a limited and limiting field of the secularism debate. However, al-Turabi attacks secularism and secularists all the time. Here, al-Turabi's Islamism built its own instruments and devices that then functioned outside what could be described as the religious thought-of rationalization. As stated earlier, al-Turabi himself described the field of his Islamism as dominated by "students and university graduates everywhere [who] represent modernity and they are the only current which exercises any measure of *ijtihād*, any review of history."[71]

68 'Abdel wahāb El-Affendi, *Turabi's Revolution*, 64.

69 See, for example, Dr. 'Azzam Tamimi, *Murajaat maa al –Mufakir al-Islami Dr. Ḥasan al-Turabi: Session 1* (London: al-Hiwar TV, November 2009).

70 Frederic Volpi, *Political Islam Observed*, 6 (see Chapter 1, no.7).

71 Arthur L. Lowrie, ed., *Islam, Democracy, the State and the West: A Round Table with Dr. Ḥasan Turabi* (Tampa, FL: The World & Islam Studies Enterprise, 1993), 20.

How his Islamists differ from other groups that relate to modernity, according to that, is based on an assumption and a generalization. He assumes that "liberal politicians and intellectuals are not interested in Islamic history, they are interested in European history; they want to transplant European institutions. They don't know how to grow them in soil. They look so much to the West that they are not actually renewing, they are not deciding any *ijtihād.* If there are any *mujtahidin,* they are the Islamists now."[72] The Sudanese *mujtahdin*, according to him, are "young people who are equal; there was no one who could proclaim to be senior in age to become an absolute *Shaikh.*"[73] These groups, or *lumpen intelligentsia* as described by Guilain Denoeux and Olivier Roy before him, are "not usually clerics but young, university educated intellectuals who claim for themselves the right to interpret the true meaning of religion (their actual knowledge of Islam is typically sketchy)."[74] At the same time, their reference presents the political discourse of al-Turabi and those who blindly follow him in denouncing secularism as a "political discourse in religious garb."[75] In this sense Islamism is inside and outside secularism at the same time. In its "two-sided relation to modernity and the West at the very heart of Islamist ideology, lies a powerful, comprehensive critique of the West and what Islamists see as the corrupting political and cultural influence of the West on Middle East societies."[76] On the other hand, "the Islamists' reliance on concepts drawn from the Islamic tradition also indicates a desire to break away from Western terminology. Hence, Islamism is a decidedly modern phenomenon in at least two critical respects: the profile of its leaders and its reliance on Western technology."[77] Ḥasan al-Turabi added another aspect to his Islamism by being inside and outside Salafism at the same time. While he agrees with the Ṣalafis in denigrating Ṣūfi Islam, he takes a step further within his *laïcité* by bragging that he is a child of French culture and disapproving of the *'ulamā'* and their institutions. Hence, al-Turabi's Islamism has floated free of modernity and its secular underpinnings, free of Islam and its scholarship or *'ulamā'*, and free of culture and its Ṣūfi representations. That such provocation riddled with ideological exceptionalism, one would argue, has set him free to practice his unchecked *ijtihād* and to critically challenge everybody else since only a few people—his disciples—could be conformists. Aḥmed Kamal el-Din argues that al-Turabi "gave himself unlimited freedom" but, I would say, that freedom has gone wild by giving no attention to the conventions and the rules of engagement within the local, Islamist, and Islamic discourse. It developed *laissez-faire* forms of verbal and later physical violence that evolved

72 Ibid.

73 Ibid.

74 Guilain Denoeux, "The Forgotten Swamp: Navigating Political Islam," *Middle East Policy*, 9 no. 2 (2002): 56–81; 62.

75 Ibid.

76 Ibid.

77 Ibid.

around a system of conflict and became a group-binding function for a full differentiation of the group and its individual members from the outside world.

This is one of the most serious problems of the Islamists at large and Ḥasan al-Turabi's brand of Islamism in particular. From that, what can be said is that what characterizes the Islamists is an image and practice of verbal and physical violence; weirdness or fraudulence is a product and an arsenal of its political behavior. For years, Sudanese bystanders directed pejorative designations of profane culture and labels at them, such as *Kizan* (tin cups), *tujar al-Din* (religion vendors), and fascists. At the heart of this stream of epithets that some Sudanese citizens fling at them is something perceived as a representation of a disingenuous, reprehensible faith. At the same time, it is clear that the Islamists have been living a culture of distance, as most of them feel they have been under a state of social siege. Or as Paul Ritter puts it, they are in a different setting, exercising "an instrument of censure"[78]—especially as they have been finding themselves bombarded by such torrents of jokes, satirical remarks, and caricatures portraying them as weird. All of that makes Islamism function as a political and social magnet that attracts some individuals and groups to the movement for reasons other than personal piety and makes climbing up the ladder of the organization to leadership positions a vocational matter that requires conformity among other mundane qualities and requirements rather than adherence to faith.

No wonder we find that some leading members of the organization take pride in describing themselves as *ṣalouk al-jabha* or *ṣalouk al-Ikhwan* (the gangster or the bully of the Brotherhood). That makes faith and piety the least needed factor in the organization's communal life. Hence, within the evolution of the Islamist organization under the leadership of Ḥasan al-Turabi, the *usra*,[79] or the basic unit that unites the brotherhood society has been modified and transformed into a unit similar to a faction within the Communist Party. It is for this reason that the foundation of the organization at its best represents a community that developed personal and communal imagined areas of conflict that leave no room for the kind of beliefs that ponder the absolute for the transitory.

Such a worldview and conduct made this impulse of insensitivity toward their surroundings a recurring phenomenon. In addition, the uncompromising stand of al-Turabi and his Islamists against all shades of non-Islamists—from

78 See Paul Reitter, *On Origins of Jewish Self-hatred* (Princeton, NJ: Princeton University Press, 2012).

79 The term literally means family. However, Ḥasan al-Bana created the system for his society of Muslim Brotherhood in Egypt as the smallest unit. The unit consisted of about 10 members each in a system of study circles (*usra maftuoha* [open unit] and *usra mughlaga* [closed unit]) to serve and achieve knowledge through a two-tiered approach. This structure divides active members of the organization into *usarat al-takween* (the preparation stage unit), open *usra* whose function is to achieve *tarbiah* (education), and *usarat al-'amal* (action unit), a closed *usra* whose function is to achieve the line of political and jihādi activities.

communists to other secular individuals and groups—makes no room for the Other, who is perceived by al-Turabi and other Islamists to constitute a main threat within a Muslim society. Hence, it has become a primary goal of the Islamists to keep secularists at a distance, expelled if possible, or eliminated without feeling remorse. These two modes of impulses have opened the way for a callous and never-ending war of attrition between both the Islamists and their insignificant Other as the presence of each side is perceived as ephemeral. In retrospect, we have seen within the last five decades that both sides have been living in a "state of suspended extinction" as each side has been turned by the other into an object that should be eliminated through the state apparatus of coercion or private violence. Both state and private violence grew stronger over time, especially during the Cold War when the governing elite and their rivals continued to accord and fortify their power pursuit to be exploited and played out within the rivalries and competition between the superpowers.

Nevertheless, al-Turabi made desperate attempts to go to the Sudanese political market, turning to everything from the university campus and wallpapers, to the party newspapers and magazines to sell himself and his version of Islamism to different young generations of Sudanese with poor elementary religious learning. In this respect, al-Turabi's Islamism and Islamists emerged as an autonomous and a self-satisfied entity antagonistic to almost every representation within the local and regional surroundings. It has always been self-denying democracy advocating for a vague notion of *shura*. It has never been a professed commitment to human rights, a policy of choice, or tolerance of the Other, a situation that earned them the reputation of being fascists.

Within this, there are four bare schemes for understanding al-Turabi's subjective experience within his struggle for state power and developing a mode of thought and action for struggle-based violence. The interaction between these two is central to an understanding and better appreciation of the person and his legacy. It is also important for understanding the essence of Islamism as a phenomenon with a totalitarian mindset, its development, and its disintegration and plummet into oblivion under his leadership. Under Ḥasan al-Turabi, the Islamists gradually became a mainstay of political activism and agitation, instigating different forms of violent campaigns—verbal and physical—against what they described as secularists and secularism in general and the Communist Party in particular; this occurred both on and off the campuses of universities and other institutions of higher education. The new generation of Islamists who grew up under the leadership of Ḥasan al-Turabi inherited from the Ikhwan their idea of *wa a'ido* (and prepare against them)[80] and added to it their behavioral glorification of individual and wholesale violence.

---

80 The emblem of al-Ikwan al-Muslimun (Muslim Brotherhood) since the days of Ḥasan al-Banna is a picture of two swords, a part of *ayah* (verse) number 60 from *Surah* 8 (chapter) al-Anfāl, which says: "and prepare against them whatever you are able of power and of steeds of war by which you may terrify the enemy of Allah and your enemy and

But beyond the common features of the Islamists' violence that has been directed toward almost every single group of the Sudanese population, Ḥasan al-Turabi in person became a subject and target of this violence. And he received it with abundance.

others besides them whom you do not know [but] Allah knows." This verse has been taken out of context and internalized to be the battle cry and the rule or prescription for every conceivable situation that one might encounter in routine social interactions, with an open-ended behavioral display of aggression toward the Other or whoever is perceived as an enemy by the Islamists.

Chapter 4

Ḥasan al-Turabi: The Making and Unmaking of al-Turabi's Islamism (2)

In many ways, the October 1964 Revolution is the most prominent single event in the history of post-independence Sudan. It unleashed, provoked, and marked the most serious reactions to the comparable and incomparable aspects of deliberating the power and authority of an emerging Sudanese civil society. Most of those who contest that now, however, tend not to grasp the controversy that a new age where liberation could have been at hand and an open material world, a state, and a good society could have emerged leading the way toward a new Sudan to be a possibility. That could be better understood if we examine the matters of consciousness that could stimulate and inspire citizens to forge their own way to their true political roles and cause them to be cognizant of their actual identities, their social conditions, and how they could order their lives together. Yet, as substantial, tangible, and complex as these issues could be, liberation, might come in many different ways and forms. Perhaps even more telling in the Sudanese situation, the citizens were qualified to liberate themselves not only from the dictatorial military rule but from at least three other distinctive systems and practices that must be well-defined if they are to become germane. These systems and practices include the nature, function, and ideology of the state within the Sudanese historical time and, in particular, within the Islamist experience. There are long-term, deep liberation issues here that need to be seriously scrutinized. This leads us, as this chapter develops, to the quintessential and foundational moment for al-Turabi Islamism in the Sudan in which Islamism transformed into a "counter-revolutionary" movement delivered in that form to the movement's members and later to the Sudanese people at large—before and after the 1989 coup. This development came along with the figure of Ḥasan al-Turabi, for whom there was no distinction between himself and the October 1964 Revolution as he and his disciples believed and advocated that Dr. Ḥasan al-Turabi was not only the leader of October 1964 Revolution but also the soul and incarnation of that revolution. Al-Turabi and his followers might receive most of the blame, not unwittingly so, for describing their leader as a revolutionary and then continuing to claim as much from October 1964, up to this moment. But, since al-Turabi's early days of leadership of the Islamist movement to this moment, al-Turabi's political character has troubled and been troubled by other revolutionary figures, his disciples, the movement, different regimes, and the Sudanese scene. Although the advent of Islamism in the Sudan began in the 1940s, it is al-Turabi's disposition that illustrates the essence of Islamism in the Sudan and allows us to understand how and where the revolutionary and counter-revolutionary movements were related and how they gave rise to the political practices of the first and second Islamist republics.

The Ecology of October 1964 Revolution

The culture of the October 1964 Revolution that overwhelmed the nation and its surrounding societies in African and Middle Eastern fields called for liberation from the oppressive regime and the inherited violent state. October stays as an event in time and as a culture of the most serious conversations and a significant sociopolitical vehemence mitigated by a great awaking of the complex diversity of the Sudanese society. The legacy of the awakening is the obligation for an all-encompassing national agenda for change in the nature, function, and ideology of the state and performance of governmental systems. This towering experience is an embodiment of the earnest national supplication for liberation from a myriad series of contrivances and mentalities of "totalist" politics, ideologies, and systems inherited from the colonial and postcolonial state and from the devices the state cultivated throughout these colonial and postcolonial periods. All of these affected the dictatorial rule of General Ibrahim 'Abboud (1958–1964) and other similar regimes that followed in the identical way that the state acted. The extended release of such reactions transcends time and place, and the deeper meanings of that towering experience. The winning vision of the extended reactions highlighted the fundamental feature that produced the main constitutions of consciousness and "reality-defining" means of comprehension of such a complex Sudanese condition. The fundamental features of that condition include but not limited to:

1. The October 1964 Revolution successfully launched a general civil disobedience movement, sought a different state based on the rights of citizens in social justice, freedom, dignity, and accountability to its citizens. The real significance of the October experience lies in its high degree of innovation and efficiency as a movement, led by unarmed civilians, which spread throughout the country. Civilians consciously pursued for the first time in Africa and the Middle East a discourse and a strategy of organized fields of power relations to an effectual and triumphant end by forcing a violent dictatorial military regime out of power. This was true in three important ways. The first was that Ibrahim 'Abboud's regime was chased out of power by the collective action of individuals, organizations and groups (professionals, workers, students, farmers, and political parties). The second was that 'Abboud's regime contributed to the means of their growth by expanding the public services, such as education; but at the same time, his regime violently infringed upon the public liberties of these individuals, organizations and groups through modes of violence in an attempt to dominate and control the affairs of the country and its citizens.

The third was that war the state waged in the southern part of the country, which was not meant to be described as a civil war, represented an apex of this infringement on public liberties and citizen's rights. The southern Sudanese demanded an act and a program of an imaginative political initiative; however, along the way in which liberation from dispossession could not only put an end to but lead the out of to the construction of marginalization and "development of underdevelopment" in the country at large. The way the state read the southern grievances as an act of rebellion that challenged its authority, ambition, and its ruling elite (the community of the state) was inaccurate; and it was the most dangerous reading in the history of the colonial and postcolonial Sudanese condition. It was also inaccurate and dangerous that the 'Abboud regime and the state perceived the demands of Sudanese citizens to organize political parties, trade unions, and other associations of their choice as an unlawful undertaking that would require anyone participating in or calling for, to be punished: imprisonment, torture and exile.

2. The civil disobedience movement, which was initiated by almost all sectors of the Sudanese citizens in October as a collective social and political action, and the successful execution of this revolutionary process added to the value manifested in the role, the power, and the political capital of the Sudanese civil sphere, which was emphatically secular in its character and composition. The October 1964 Revolution released the latent characteristics of all the aforementioned different social groups together with the marginalized underclass, rural, and urban middle class as they all acted as social units and "predicators of movement and organizational success."[1] So too, all that success gave rise to an alternative social contract based on a new form of belonging. This contract could have helped the state make a serious transformation from a system established as the foundation of the colonial rule to the state of a new Sudan.
3. As in any time and place, there were those who were less fascinated by such narrations and the potential sociopolitical outcome of a new Sudan, its contents, and discontents. Such attitudes go together with the type of predictions that could confuse and gravitate what some would like to keep personal or group treasured or valued resources to themselves. Hence, although transformation is not a stance of a historical determinism, there are continuous forms and forces of collective, another of social differences, and a third of "quiet noncollective encroachment"[2] that worked to counter to such transformation. While roots of all these forces were not necessarily embedded in or inspired by the Sudanese civil imagination, the failure or

1 Mayer N. Zald, and John D. McCarthy, eds, *The Dynamics of Social Movements: Resource Mobilization, Social Control, and Tactics* (Cambridge: Withrop Publishers, 1979), 4.

2 Asef Bayat, *Life as Politics*, 45 (see Chapter 1, n. 12).

success of any one of them could be reinforced by the failure or success of each or both of the other above-mentioned two. For all of these reasons, it might be true, as Robert Bellah elucidates in a different situation that "history of modern nations shows that segmentary rational politics is not enough. No one has changed a great nation without appealing to its soul, without stimulating a national idealism, as even who call themselves materialists have discovered."[3] That is why if the October experience stands for a contemporary political memory, inspiration, or the enduring dream of generations of Sudanese, it is that urge of belonging and aspiration for a new social contract that refuses to accept any reversible condition to the desired Sudanese social life to come and the imagining of that deferred civil society to materialize.

4. The complexity of the construction of the political discourse of liberation, the victory of the October 1964 Revolution as a civil movement, the counter-power that disputed and even sometimes nullified the institutional power of the "old Sudan" and its military state represented and defined one of the most profound developments in the Sudanese political experience in itself and in its search for a new covenant. The eyes of the whole world, together with the Sudanese, were watching that October day to see "how the great experiment in newness is faring;"[4] today there are more lessons that could be gained from this experience. Chief among these lessons is what confirms the general Sudanese belief that the military can take power by force, but there is no way for them to remain in power indefinitely. That is because the military coup and the regime that comes out of it are in essence a manifestation of a counter-revolution as it stands as an impediment outside of the Sudanese mode of political belonging of being active actors in shaping their future. Thus, we can easily see that general Sudanese belief has been confirmed by the successful execution of the April 1985 Uprising against the Ja'far Nimeiri dictatorship (May 1969 through April 1985) and the continuous patterns of encroachments, social movements, and nonmovements[5] in opposition to the current Islamist regime. Remarkable here is that belief is nowhere more apparent than in the understanding that has grown into a form of dual political imagination, which has been persistent in the Sudanese collective mind and its political culture. What could be described as a Sudanese civil religion or a religion of modernity, has emerged out of this dual political imagination. It is

3 Robert N. Bellah, *The Broken Covenant: American Civil Religion in Time of Trial* (Chicago, IL: University of Chicago Press, 1992), 162.

4 Ibid.

5 Nonmovements are what Asef Bayat referred to as "the collective actions of noncollective actors; [which] embody shared practices of large numbers of ordinary people whose fragmented but similar activities trigger much social change, even though these practices are rarely guided by an ideology or recognizable leaderships and organizations." See, Bayat, *Life as Politics*, 14 (see Chapter 1, n. 12).

described here as the great experiment of newness. Related to this were the ideals of freedom, equality, progress, and public welfare. This civil religion has rituals that have commemorated the October 1964 Revolution ever since. Later, it seemed that the April 1985 Uprising that brought down Ja'far Nimeiri's 16-year-long dictatorship was a natural evolution and confirmation of that belief and its authority. The April 1985, *intifada* as the Sudanese describe it, gave considerable momentum to the nation's commitment to the October experience of newness and to its ideals. The paths that led to the ideals of the October 1964 Revolution and the nostalgic commitment to these ideals has reconstructed a civic and sympathetic association with this Sudanese civil religion and its shrines, which includes the University of Khartoum, the birthplace of the October Revolution. It endowed respect to the revolution's poets, entertainers, and artists who contributed to the national discourse and to the articulation of the values of that existential experience. The works of those intellectuals and knowledge workers has stayed alive as an open book recited time and again and sung whenever relevant circumstances arise. Examples of such artists, entertainers, and poets include Moḥamed al-Makki Ibrahim, Fadl 'Allah Moḥamed, Hashim Sidiq, Mahjub Sharif, Mohammed Wardi, 'Abd al-Karim al-Kabli, and Mohammed al-Amin to name a few. The dual nature of the newly awakened Sudanese political imagination is reflected in the considerable nationwide appeal, dialectic of conversation, and motivating power of collective action. It is also mirrored in the enormous fear that military regimes on the other side would feel an expected uprising against their regime as an outcome of their breach of social, political, and constitutional contracts.

This unique Sudanese political experience, however, has given many groups within the political and intellectual sectors more confidence in their power, and it has raised distinctive forms of practices and conversations in different directions. Contrary to what one might imagine, some of these conversations do not keep a balance or harmony between the discourse, ambition, and practice of some groups and the liberating ethos of the October experience and its obligations. Emotional enthusiasm to the revolutionary spirit, which has swept some people away, has revealed itself to them in a deterministic presumption that an uprising to overthrow the Islamists' regime is expected and inevitable as long as the forces that ousted the military could be mobilized the same way before. In an interview with al-Sadiq al-Mahdi, the leader of the Umma Party and the Imam of the Ansar sect, explained that he and his party promote what he called *al-jihād al-madani* (civil jihād) in which the public sphere will be instrumental to unseat the Islamist regime through such forms of civil disobedience. In a sense, this orientation might open up inroads to the province of the "value of pluralism." Especially as other attitudes and ideas about civil disobedience have been published in most of the Sudanese political literature or delivered by groups opposing the Islamists regime for the last 24 years. Moreover, and in every single demonstration against the Islamist regime, the street cry has always been; *'āid 'āid ya* October (coming back again October). Hence, all the lessons learned from fighting this current regime seem to indicate that the Islamists have acted consistently before and after establishing their ruling regime as a counter-revolutionary force to stifle attempts toward a system that the Sudanese would respect and devote their lives to, rather than one that they are forced to obey but puts their lives at risk.

This has been increasingly true in two ways. The first concerns the Islamists' dedicated efforts to betray the progress toward a national covenant for a liberated Sudan. The second is that since the first day of their state in 1989, the Islamists proved to be not only aware that their regime adamantly opposed all aspects of a liberated Sudan, and they took measures to avoid any form of civil uprising against their hold on power. Such pursuit does not arrive from a non-historical field of action. It is part and parcel of a counter-revolution orientation and practice the Islamists persistently pursued.

In the years that followed the October Revolution, there was a seditious reality—sometimes latent but uncontested—in the foreground of the Sudanese political scene, and at the background of everybody's mind, of what remained from the October achievements and what might come out of that. As a result of the October 1964 Revolution, the country witnessed the rise of a new generation of politicians and a new and younger leadership in most of the political parties and associations. These new leaders participated enormously not only in compromising but they also sometimes vigorously and violently acted against the ethos of a possible new social contract for a liberated Sudan. The mutual hostility and conflict within this new leadership was implacable since day one. Whether by default or by design, that was no less true for those who took over from the older generation. The next generation of leaders also devastated the Sudanese political and social landscape during this time and on critical occasions. Each saw in himself and his program a political party or an ideology that was a divinely prearranged "errand into the wilderness." Hence, most of those new players were decidedly narrow-minded and provincial in their partisanships, both in nature and agenda. Individually, they were condescending to each other as well. In other words, because each side functions and maneuvers from an essentially different conception of authority, weight, power, and measure of moral and political sentimentality, neither side will ever be able to persuade the other of the futility of its own claims. Yet, while conversation could be open sometimes, the etiquette, value, or ideal of courteousness and civility is absent. Similar attitudes were clear, also, behind each other's talk to the media, as well as during face-to-face conversations and within their contribution to the public discourse. Of course, it did not take long to discover that the totality of liberation had never reached a reasonable degree of favor in its local constituencies or political parties' programs or expressions. Consequently, the counter-revolution manifested not so much as a break from the liberation ideal but acted as its reversal—a reversal that centered on the role of the state. Hence, the verbal ferociousness, toxic language, and antagonism, in addition to violence, continued to be conjoined and sometimes to have had a mutual tone and temper of absolute disdain. Hence, the identification of irrelevant conflicts easily shifted to other impulses and the ability to differentiate between a number of groups in which the role of liberation was banished or replaced by anti-liberation discourse.

This new generation of post-October leadership included the following figures to name a few:[6]

- Dr. Ḥasan al-Turabi, Moḥmed Ṣalih 'Umer, Moḥamed Yousif and Souad al-Fatih of the Islamist movement;
- 'Abd al-Khaliq Maḥjub, Aḥmed Suliaman, Moḥamed Ibrāhim Nugud, Joseph Garang, Al-Ṭaḥir 'Abdel Bāṣit and Farouq 'Abu 'Iesa of the Sudanese Communist Party;
- al-Ṣadiq al-Mahdi, Moḥamed Ibrahim Khalil, and Imām al-Hadi al-Mahdi of the Umma Party;
- Moḥamed 'Uthmān al-Mirghani, al-Sharif Ḥussein al-Hindi, Musa al-Mubark, Ṣalih Maḥmoud Ismā' il, and Moḥamed Tawfiq of the Democratic Unionist Party;
- William Deng, Samuel Arow, Tobi Madut, and Joseph Udoho of the Sudan African National Union;
- Abel Alier, Bona Malwal, Hilary Lugali, Peter Jat Kouth of the Southern Front;
- Father Philip 'Abbas Ghaboush of the Sudanese National Party: Nuba mountains;
- Aḥmad Ibrāhim Diraij, and 'Alī al-Ḥaj of Darfur Front: later the Umma Party and Muslim Brotherhood respectively;
- Sirour Ramli from Rural Khartoum
- Ḥashim Bamkar from the Bija Congress;
- Sir al-Khatim al-Khalifa, Ja'afar Karār, Mahjoub Moḥamed Ṣalih, and Aḥmed 'Abdel Ḥalim from the left;
- al-ShafiAḥmed al-Shaikh, al-Ḥaj Abdel Rahman of Sudan Workers Trade Union Federation (SWTUF);
- Fatima Aḥmed Ibrāhim of the Women's Union;
- Shaikh al-Amin, and Yousif Aḥmed al-Mustafa of the Farmers Union;
- Ja'afar Nimeiri the army officer;
- 'Abdel Majid Imam and Babikir 'Awad Allah of the judiciary;
- Abdin Ismail, Amin al-Shibli, and Makawi Khoujali, Bar Association;
- Moḥamed 'Umer Bashir, al-Nazier Dafalla (Academics: University of Khartoum);
- Moḥmed Abdel Ḥai. Moḥmed al-Mahdi Majzoub, 'Abdullahi 'Alī Ibrāhim, Moḥmed al-Makki Ibrāhim, al-Nur 'Uthmān Abakar, Ṣalah Moḥmed Ibrāhim, Fadalla Moḥmed, 'Abdallah Ḥāmid al-Amin (Poets and writers);
- Bashir Moḥamed S'aid, Mahjoub 'Uthmān, Moḥamed Mirghani, S'ad el-Shaikh, 'Abdel Rahman Moukhtār (Journalists).

6 This list is not by any means comprehensive.

In addition to those, Moḥamed Moḥamed Ṭaha emerged as a thinker and a political leader of a different Islamist movement called the Republican Party later the Republican Brothers. An auxiliary group of advisors to the dictators, such as Mansour Khalid, Ja'afar Moḥamed 'Ali Bakhiet, Aḥmed 'Abdel Halim, Bader el Din Suliamān, and others continued to fuel the fires of these diametrically opposed legions and their leaders. This new generation of politicians and leaders entered the Sudanese political scene with competing visions or no visions at all. They had conflicting interests and tendencies to resolve political conflicts through different forms of violence that they exercised on each other and on different sectors of the Sudanese population. Most of them tried to get a hold of the state directly or by proxy to turn it into an instrument of oppression in their own hands and forge its coercive power against their rivals. Needless to say, the continuation of these hostilities generated warfare that affected the political, religious, and social fabric of Sudanese life. Hence, along with this power struggle, the continued war of attrition between rival political entities and self-contained models of political representations was affirmed through the language and power of state antipathy or perceived personality. Perhaps the most vociferous expression of that development was creation of a culture of violence deployed from an external field of power that was based around the military coup as a mode of change. In all instances of military takeover, the regimes that emerge subsequent to the coup turn into a system of an uneven distribution of rewards, oppression, and inequalities that in one way or another reinforce the violent face of the state and enhance its instruments as a vessel of coercive force.

A significant corollary of the coup-related violence is the development that resulted from the prism through which most state actors, especially the military, viewed the plight of Sudanese citizens who found themselves marginalized. Depressingly, it is not hard to see the clash between most of those marginalized citizens and the state in its violent and nonviolent actions even after October 1964, and the Round Table Conference, 1965. They showed how the counter-revolution turned all contingencies of marginalization into an extended release of violence. Only through this can one see the rise of resentment and different forms of expression of grievances in the periphery, which the centralized state and its community has never fully understood and which continued to be perceived by different regimes as a rebellion that needed to be firmly dealt with. This, however, turned violence of both sides—the state and the rebels—into one of the main topics of conversation between both entities. Attempts to enforce compulsion—as a way of adding sufficient devotion to the higher national ideals of unity and conformity, as well as the presentation of the state as a grand form of disciplinary actions—ensured the state's continued existence and demonstrated its overarching power. Operations of counter-violent expressions by those who felt excluded or marginalized have become the preferred modus operandi to ensure recognition. The collective attributes of that form of state power and the counter-power over that state has drained human and material resources, and they became an added value to progressive forms of the development of underdevelopment. But this phenomenon involved a causal relationship between the state's reactions to the violent and nonviolent dissension and the demands of the emerging geographies of marginalization and the poverty-enhanced ruralization of urban centers. Rural dislocated poor, who fled marginalization and its discontents of war, famine, and poverty left behind a disrupted way of life and tried to find protection in urban areas in which resources were continuously exhausted and incredibly scarce. In addition to the same processes that created ruralization of the urban centers, other factors caused a swell in migration from these urban centers to outside the country as oppressive regimes drove away workers, professionals, and artisans by the thousands, forcing them, instead, to seek employment in oil-rich Arab countries, in particular, and other countries in general. That phenomenon made the Sudan a country with one of the highest internal and external displacement populations in the world.

It is all a losing battle against what the Sudanese could see through their experience of what liberation is all about. It is not surprising then that the two long-ruling regimes, the May regime, 1969–1985, and the Inqaz, 1989 to the present, were established by two of those post-October personalities: Ja'far Nimeiri and 'Umar Ḥasan al-Bashir. Nimeiri's and Bashir's regimes remain the most violent in the history of the post-independent Sudan. They represent the Janus faces and the doorways, the beginnings and transitions, and maybe the ends of the counter to the Sudanese search for a social contract and a pact of liberation. At the same time, the end of 'Umar al-Bashir's is an end to the postcolonial state and a postcolonial era. Hence, the end of Islamism and the might of the state in the hands of the counter-revolutionaries "goes hand in hand with deciphering the transformed consciousness that must promise and deliver the emerging world."[7]

This proportionately long introduction is meant to situate the central aspect of the void between the twilight of liberation and the counter forces that impeded its progress but diverted into hostilities overbearing the better part of Sudanese post-October history. This multifaceted chain of events includes the collective grievances and the hierarchies of discontent within their violent and nonviolent forms that have been evident for more than half a century. They represents the embedded tension between the quest for changes that derive and embody the October spirit to charter a new Sudan and the counter-revolutionary impulses that act against it. So to understand how the Islamist movement developed into a counter-revolutionary movement in the hands of Ḥasan al-Turabi, one needs to move on two fronts at once. The first is the hegemonic move that came before the establishment of the real subjugation associated with the coup and its first Islamist republic, and the other is the one that followed after that.

7 Hamid Dabashi, *The Arab Spring: the End of Postcolonialism* (London: Zed Books, 2012), xx.

The Counter-revolution Forerunners

The unbroken thread of the post-October story of Islamism and its antagonism toward the Other (*al-ilmanieen* [the secularists]) in general, and the Communists in particular, in addition to the one that they describe as *taifiyya* (sectarian parties) and the traditional political parties, was reformulated. It then escalated with the emergence of Ḥasan al-Turabi as the new leader. It remained closely connected to him and to his renegade disciples who forced him out of power in 2000. It is true that the October 1964 Revolution and its aftermath brought the war between the Islamists and their sworn enemies, the communists, from the open space of university campuses to the public space. This shift led to the curtailment of public space and the deprivation of citizens from all forms of public goods during the first and second Islamist republics. This brings into view the different forms of violence as the dark underside of the Islamist political attitude and mode of governance. The basis and roots for these attitudes and polity can be found in the history of Islamism from its early days and later as one of the strands of Ḥasan al-Turabi's *laïcité* as it redefined its field of action and evolved in different directions that concurred on the attitude but differed in reason and strategy. Perhaps it might be clearer now, at this juncture, when Islamism has run into oblivion and has been subjected to systematic historical critique that even some of its adherents can plainly see how it has acted as a counter-revolutionary force.

After the end of 'Abboud's regime, both the communists and their Islamist rivals claimed the leading role in the revolution while each one was trying to lessen the role of the other. But at a more profound level, this new major fault line over which the battle between the two continued, widened and spilled beyond the university campuses, high schools, and institutions of learning to include the entire Sudanese political landscape. These first started when the Islamists discovered that the communists held more leadership roles in most professional organizations and trade unions and were successful in dominating the National Front of Professional Organization (NFPO)[8] that emerged as the ruling body after the downfall of 'Abboud's regime. The NFPO was established on October 25, 1964, and initially consisted of Sudanese faculty members of the University of Khartoum, Khartoum Technical Institute, representatives from student unions, and representatives of physicians, lawyers, and judges. Almost immediately, they were joined by representatives of engineers, teachers, the Gizera Tenants Association, and the Sudan Workers Trade Unions Federation (SWTUP). After the downfall of 'Abboud, negotiations between different political groups and organizations led to the formation of a transitional government under the premiership of Sir al-Khatim al-Khalifa. Khalifa was known as a neutral person with good knowledge, and he was highly respected in the South "which was hoped would stand him in

8 There were 11 Communists and leftists of the Executive Board of the NFPO, which consisted of 15 members.

good stead in dealing with the southern question."[9] The Islamists claimed that the "communists had for the first time the chance to be the virtual rulers of Sudan"[10] through the NFPO. Although the October government that succeeded 'Abboud's regime was not explicitly threatening because it was of a transitional nature by composition, structure, and mandate. The Islamists were not alone because other political parties and actors felt threatened too. Out of the 15-member government of Sir al-Khatim al-Khalifa, seven were from the NFPO, including Shafi'i Aḥmed al-Shaikh of the SWTUF and Shaikh al-Amin Moḥamed al-Amin of the Gezira Tenants Association. Five members were from the political parties (one each from the Umma Party, the National Unionist Party, the People's Democratic Party, the Islamic Charter Front ICF, and the Communist Party), and two were from the South and what has been considered as strategic ministries. It was clear that the cabinet "represented a number of ideological strands, mainly of the left but by no means all communists."[11] However, the idea of the NFPO emerged as a representation of what the Sudanese perceived as the new or modern political players who made the October 1964 Revolution a success. It presented an attractive alternative to the basic structure of the political parties, or what the Communists described as the old or traditional forces; however, this was not clear at the beginning. But it did not take that long for political groups to enunciate louder what they suspected as a significant latent threat, which turned into a possibility of a new coalition or unified politics that would follow—sooner or later—the ideology or strategy of the Communist Party. It was clear that the animosity that lay beneath this surface of fighting between these parties spawned a new culture war. That sense of threat and its alarming prospects arose less from any NFPO policy during its early days than from when some of NFPO members began to promote ideas that could result in a serious change of political practice that induced terror in the hearts of the main political parties, the Umma Party, and the Unionists in particular. This collective feeling of threat served to bring the Islamist political parties together with other right-leaning parties, especially the Umma party, other political groups in opposition of the NFPO, and those who stood behind it. This culture war escalated even more when the NFPO and the left's arguments started to take an ideological path and a political stand blaming all the ills of the Sudan on what they described as the reactionary forces that came from an alleged a long hibernation rather than a time of clandestine activity. Hence, the left and those who dominated the NFPO perceived themselves as the real revolutionary forces that organized the overt and covert struggle against the 'Abboud regime and mobilized the Sudanese in an unprecedented movement that lead to the downfall of the regime. For these reasons the NFPO began to voice demands for themselves and that their constituencies should have a place and a space not only within the public sphere,

---

9 Peter Woodward, *Sudan 1898–1989: The Unstable State* (Boulder, CO: Lynne Rienner Publisher, 1990), 110.

10 'Abdel wahāb El-Affendi, *Turabi's Revolution*, 73 (see Chapter 3, n. 14).

11 Peter Woodward, *Sudan 1898–1989*, 110.

but a metamorphic role within the legislative and the ruling structure that would accommodate and secure them a place at the state's helm. The political parties and the Islamists perceived one of these demands not only as a threat, but as a direct challenge to their authority and a serious impasse that would lead the ruling system astray; the NFPO demanded that 50 percent of the parliament seats be allocated for the modern forces. The NFPO "proposed special constituencies for workers, tenants, and intellectuals and finally tried to resurrect the old Graduates' Constituencies."[12] In addition, the radical policies that the new government of Sir al-Khatim set out to enact was more alarming for the political parties and their main allies and supporters. These included a collective purge of senior government officials, preparatory plans for dissolving the native administration, and active policies supporting the Arab, Soviet, and international leftist regimes, their organizations, and radical liberation movements. Consistent with that agenda, "branches of the front were being established in different parts of the country, and it seemed possible that the front would engage as one unit in forthcoming elections."[13] Considered in this light, the overall agenda of the professional front, and the Communist Party behind it, was perceived by the political parties as a serious threat to their right to exist. They immediately "realized that such an arrangement would, in effect, perpetuate the status quo and, indecently do away with their political organizations."[14] This development counts not for its particulars or suggestions, but for diverting the discourse of the October 1964 Revolution away from an agreed-upon conversation toward a new covenant. The agreed-upon conversation would have followed the round table modality where—at the very least—citizens would have been involved and motivated by civic virtue that would open the door for innovation for liberating the Sudanese people from tyrannical states and uniting them rather than turning it into a lukewarm monologue uniting only convinced sectors of the population or a return to an absolutist ideology.

In a clear response to the mere content of these claims and actions, the Communist Party and its allies in the left planned, somewhat imperfectly, to phase out other political representations in serious contradiction to the ideals of October. Given such a move from the left, it would have been odd not to expect a strong counter-reaction within these other representations. But, on its own terms, the other side resorted to another route that also diverted from the ideals of October. The expansion of these special agenda structures, when coupled with street violence from one side, turned both sides into a field of counter-revolutionary forces. This had serious consequences, and it critically damaged Sudanese momentum to seize the opportunity to liberate the country from the clutches of the inherited state. Further, these diversions from the spirit and the ideals of October have certainly

12 Peter K. Bechtold, *Politics in the Sudan: Parliamentary and Military Rule in an Emerging African Nation* (New York: Praeger Publishers, 1976), 217.

13 Ibid.

14 Ibid.

overshadowed the political life on a continuous and a regular basis since, and they are likely to do so as long as the current state or one similar is in power.

Over and above this, the added dimension of violence within all its forms and frequencies augmented one further serious tier in this counter-revolutionary development. The enormous implications of this serious step-change have to be sought in the complex formations of discourse and actions that transformed the nature of political responses to the violent takeover of the state. The ideological discourses, effects, and patterns of practice were not necessarily produced by the real superiority of power of either party, as both the left and the Islamists were still at the fringes of the Sudanese field of power. For this reason, each one tried to negotiate terms and pursue an indisputably larger internal power in order to declare a certain victory and advocate for their own sociopolitical, nationalistic, or religious standard for the future society. Here, all groups sanctioned one form of revolutionary or religious violence. For each one of these groups, violence emerged as neither aberrant nor abhorrent.

For al-Turabi it was an opportunity to negotiate terms and pursue a joint encounter against his Communist enemies. He relied on a common cause that other groups with related concerns about the new left agenda that NFPO also acknowledged. As long as these other groups represented an indisputably larger internal power, and they exercised violence, his new strategy would lead to a victory in the name of "saving the country from Communism." The success of this strategy taught him a lesson as a strategist for his new political style of opposition and as a self-reinforcing approach.

On one hand, the window of opportunity availed itself in many curious ways. It took the forms of individual and group campaigns that simultaneously opposed most things in a manner that would pave the way for a self-enforcement. Al-Turabi, instead of criticizing the Front, its associations, and unions or its government and their programs, he launched a campaign against communism itself, its local party, and its allies to underpin concern and opposition to various aspects of any sociopolitical change. Finding himself successful in attracting other anti-Communist groups, he went a step further to organize "the National Front of Parties (NFP) as a counter-weight to the leftist-dominated NFPO and then started a battle over NFPO, aiming to control it or, failing that, to destroy it."[15]

But whatever the case, the most important aspect here is that the Islamists under the leadership of Ḥasan al-Turabi transformed a political event into a religious one to achieve specific political goals. These dissimilar groups found common ground based on their concerns about communism, and they transgressed new complaints to encourage a themed platform to save the country from communism. By taking this approach, the Islamists were able to control and lead these concerned parties "from without," As a result, the NFP was able to apply pressure, and the Umma Party's Ansar brought people en masse from western and central Sudan who demonstrated by "roaming the streets at night and chanting Mahdiyyah war

15 'Abdel wahāb El-Affendi, *Turabi's Revolution*, 73 (see Chapter 3, n. 14).

songs."[16] This evoked recent memories of violent riots on March 1, 1954, that were incited by the Ansar against the visit of Egypt's General Muhammed Najib[17] to the Sudan. The NFPO government of al-Khalifa conceded to the pressure by submitting its resignation. Six days later, al-Khalifa "formed a new government, composed of ministers from the Umma Party, the NUP, the Islamic Charter Front, and the southern Front. The radical experiment was over."[18] Throughout their collaborations, the Islamists depicted themselves as traditional rather than modern as the communists had described them, so the Islamists were able to frustrate the program of their rival. In other words, what al-Turabi's worldview shared in common with what he described as *taifiyya* has typified how the counter-revolution program worked regardless of the prevailing assumptions of al-Turabi and the concepts he used about the divergent interests of these new bedfellows who had been on the opposite end of the political spectrum.

Nevertheless, the impulses and orientations of those who described themselves as modern forces stayed alive in the Sudanese political life. And within their internal reading to an evolving world, they allured the imagination and the support of the left without asking themselves from where and what point of view they operated. Within less than three months, al-Turabi and his emerging young Islamist group "managed to get enough signatures among the 19 or so founding organizations within NFPO to disavow its Communist-dominated leadership. When presented to the government, the prime minister agreed to withdraw recognition of NFPO, and from then on to deal only with representatives of political parties."[19]

On the other hand, al-Turabi, who became the new Secretary General of the Islamists, wasted no time in his stratagem of reappropriation of the Other's comparable political strategies, especially when they proved to be successful as a source of insight to future rebuilding of an Islamist vanguard party and the oversight of the left. This became apparent at a more subtle level regarding how to emulate the Communist Party's vanguard model as a new opportunity and a field of conflict within his own party at the same time. Al-Turabi noted that the Islamist movement was influenced "through competition by numerous communist approaches and ways of doing things such as strict obligation of secrecy, careful

16 Peter K. Bechtold, *Politics in the Sudan*, 219.

17 The riot eruption of what the Sudanese call *awal Maris* (March First) was against the visit of President Najib of Egypt to attend the opening of the Sudanese Parliament that day. The Umma party, who stood against unity with Egypt and called for *al-Sudan li al-Sudaniyyin* (Sudan for the Sudanese), foresaw that visit as a grave danger to the independence of the country. A large crowd of unfriendly Ansar carrying white weapons met Nijab at Khatoum airport and tried to force their way in. A clash with police followed, which led to death and injuries on both sides. The British Governor General declared March law and postponed the opening of the Parliament until March 10.

18 Tim Niblock, *Class and Power in the Sudan: The Dynamics of Sudanese Politics, 1898–1985* (New York: State University of New York, 1987), 228.

19 Ibid.

member selection, and founding of what might look as innocent platforms and intensifying tactics and focus on the strengths of modern sectional organizations."[20] According to al-Turabi, "in 1965 the movement reached another turning-point with the launch of the Islamic Charter Front as an umbrella for the movement's public activities. From then the movement developed very rapidly, to an extent that neither the leadership nor the organization could match."[21] But one could go farther to argue that the most visible sociopolitical properties of the ongoing battles between the Islamists and the communists stemmed out of the Islamists' sense of fear. These most visible properties also caused both parties diverged from the field of liberation and the challenge to each group's own limits. This means that liberation was not just the way in which structural interests of the Sudanese citizens were imminently looming; it was also the action by which the means, ways, and interest of the state and the country conducted themselves. Taking a thoroughly historical approach to study the deeply rooted fear that turned into and continued to comprise and reproduce the Islamists competing program of animosity since the early days of the movement. The success of the communist vanguard model in regard to October 1964 Revolution and the stances adopted in the aftermath of the downfall of 'Abboud's regime compounded their fear and turned the Islamists' performance into a single-issue politic.

It was an eye opener to the Islamists and their new Secretary General that the success of the Communist Party of the Sudan was due to three main factors. First, it was the role they "played over the years as a major campaigner for various social and economic reforms."[22] Second, it was the Communists' ability to build and most of the time infiltrate the leadership of professional associations and trade unions. Even though political parties were officially outlawed during the six years of 'Abboud's military rule, "the communists had continued to function, albeit underground, while all others actually disintegrated as organizations."[23] Third, through their organizational experience, the communists were "able to gain access to, and frequently control of, professional associations despite their own small numbers."[24] Hence, the lesson learned from the Communists Party's effective re-emergence after the downfall of 'Abboud's regime was the means by which it positioned itself as a vanguard and "a proponent of the interests of workers and tenants, whereas the other Sudanese parties generally ignored those interest groups."[25] The vanguard model put the Communist Party, to certain extent, at the fore of a mass-action political movement of the October 1964 Revolution.

---

20 Dr. Ḥasan al-Turabi, *al-Haraka al-Islamiyya fi el-Sudan: al-tatour, al-kasb al-Manhaj*, 2nd ed. (Khartoum: Institute of Research and Social Studies, 1992), 144.

21 Moḥamed E. Ḥamdi, *The Making of an Islamic Political Leader*, 15 (see Chapter 3, n. 22).

22 Peter K. Bechtold, *Politics in the Sudan*, 216.

23 Ibid.

24 Ibid.

25 Ibid.

That experience provided the practical and political leadership that led to close ties between the Communist Party and the Sudanese left, which was clear during the early days after the success of the October 1964 Revolution. This constituted ideological threats to the Islamists, especially when it turned into a generalized political action of the communists in as much as there was apparent sympathy for the party from wide sectors of the Sudanese-educated elite. That sympathy translated into the leading program for the Front and later the victory of most of the Communist Party candidates at the Graduates Electoral College of 1965 general elections. But even before the general elections, the Islamists and their new allies felt that there was something significant at stake. Yet as troubling as such feelings were "the more radical the actions and pronouncements of the Front (NFPO) became, the more vociferous were the demands of the old politicians to change the composition of the cabinet. There was talk of and even genuine concern over 'saving the country from Communism.'"[26] This, then, opened a window of opportunity for the Islamists to act as a counter-revolution. The chance came about not because of their enmity to the Communists and their allies, which had always been there, but more importantly because the Islamists overturned the original idea of dialogue invested in the political public sphere as one of the main ideals of October 1964 Revolution. Thereafter, they assumed a different direction that invested in violent actions as a viable future voucher to politics. Most significantly, and what speaks to al-Turabi the strategist, the Islamists under his leadership increasingly developed two-tier mega and minor institutional frameworks within which internal and external conflicts took shape and were challenged. More to the point, these minor and mega institutional frameworks developed around larger conflicts. These larger conflicts simultaneously grew out of and exploited the political or religious capital of the opposing ends. Al-Turabi defined the opposing ends as Sūfi- or Salfi-oriented groups or an internal power group to be realigned for specific goal while he and his Islamist standing continued to be adamantly partisan both in nature, violent persuasion, and agenda. The mega strategy emerged and was successfully presented by the association and the collective move with what the Islamists and other "ideological parties" described as "the traditional parties." They then banded together with their new Islamists allies to constrain the NFPO and its political program. This move helped the Islamists to rethink their political presence and their program of action over and beyond their traditional anti-communist pursuit. According to their own historian, Ḥasan Mekki, the Islamists were aware, maybe for the first time, that they "did not seem to have made any substantial breakthrough anywhere in the modern sector. … In trade unions, among educated women and in the professional organizations the hold of the left seemed secure."[27]

26 Ibid.

27 Ḥasan Mekki, *Harakat al-Ikhwan al-Muslimin fil-Sudan: 1944–1969*, 15 (see Chapter 2, n. 7).

Nevertheless, the Islamists tried to deploy instead a "from without" mega strategy that would bring together some of the concerned "traditional political parties" and groups to move with violence and speed to meet a specific political goal. It was through this process that the Islamists' political actions, violent reactions, and counter-revolutionary strategies were framed. Whereas this mega strategy succeeded within some limited designates, it was clear from the start that it worked as some sort of "mechanical" rather than an "organic" solidarity in the division of labor between these entities. This is so because there was no way for the Islamists to control these entities "from within." Moreover, because of the different interests and divergent views of each of these groups toward the other, the traditional entities "would then no longer be interested in the support of the modern groups who only represent a tiny minority when it came to votes and national influences. If the traditionalists took notice of these groups at all, then they saw them as rivals."[28] However, the influence that brought about the change in the Islamists party's character after the October 1964 Revolution was al-Turabi's emulation of the Communist party vanguard experience. In one way, looking at that experience is a compelling necessity to meet the challenges and to attain some significant moments of opportunities that availed themselves in post-October era. The Islamism needed to be packaged in different, more modern, attire than the old-fashioned Ikhwan that came to the Sudan with Egyptian schools.

To lead the 2,000 core members of the Islamist movement—composed mostly of students—Ḥasan al-Turabi developed a three-tier strategy. First, he adopted the name Islamic Movement or the Islamic Current—the Islamic Charter Front (ICF)—to replace the name *al-Ikhwan al-Muslimun* that came with an Egyptian package and represented what could be identified as the old-fashioned group of Islamists. Although in essence, the ICF emulated the Communist vanguard idea, the secret veil of the new Islamic Charter Front covered a few *'ulamā'*, some of Wahabi or Ansar al-Suna groups, some members of Sūfi orders, and some of the tribal chiefs. This attempt was neither modern in nature nor progressive in composition. Moreover, those who were part of the Islamic Charter Front had neither a voice in nor commitment to the Islamist program. The main reason behind that could be that the Islamists tried to control the new body. As al-Turabi admitted, they "kept for themselves a majority within the Front not only to keep independent of the front but also to control it."[29] That is why the move did not help much in giving al-Turabi the support that he needed to consolidate his new leadership; eventually it created a state of frustration, as the old guards of al-Ikhwan group of the Islamist movement did not receive the change kindly. According to al-Turabi, several factors led to sharp differences that severely shook the organizational and personal structures of the Islamists. These included deeper disagreements between members of the movement, emerging challenging political stances, and the contradiction held within the new situation itself and

28 'Abdel wahāb El-Affendi, *Turabi's Revolution*, 75 (see Chapter 3, n. 14).

29 Dr. Ḥasan al-Turabi, *al-Haraka al-Islamiyya fi el-Sudan*, 29.

between the Front and Ikhwan.[30] However, through time as al-Turabi continued to fortify his leadership and shape the movement according to a doctrine that made of him a new and different Islamist ideologue, that frustration turned into a rebellion by those who engaged critically in the movement to al-Turabi's strategies. Hence, it later materialized into an outright split. But according to al-Turabi, this change had a functional necessity. Upon reflecting on the history of that period, he claimed that "after the initial stage of its existence, the movement developed a marked sense of self-awareness, positioning itself accurately within its specific time and place parameters."[31] For some sectors of the movement, then, his vocabulary brought a sense of newness and a more modern appearance that made possible a formulation that helped to borrow more from the Communists' vocabulary and strategies of the party as a vanguard.

Related to this was the rise and recognition of a new breed of young Islamists who were graduates of University of Khartoum and/or British university educated, chief among them were Aḥmed 'Abdel Raḥman, 'Uthman Khalid Mudawi, and 'Abdel Raḥim Ḥamdi, who became Ḥasan al-Turabi's main lieutenants for a considerable period of time. As in previous internal conflicts in the Islamist movement, such moves proved to indicate intricate competitions and maybe a rise of a particular bigger group of younger Islamists and the demise of another group, especially those who were Cairo educated or were less educated, older members of the movement. The alternative option, which was provided by that move and the political space that it generated, was a significant change in the leadership and the orientation of the movement. It may well be said that the way and time al-Turabi was elected Secretary General to the Islamist movement deeply affected the functioning and the future of Islamism in the Sudan. Ḥasan al-Turabi's rise to prominence was, in a way, a positioning of the movement within the broader frame of Bābikir Karār's ideological parameters of Sudanization. Al-Turabi's rise also fit the movement within its local ground and field action but without Karār himself at the helm of the organization. Al-Turabi's leadership later merged with an air of modernity that came with the change of his title to *al-Amin al-'ām* Secretary General that replaced the Egyptian Ikhwan title, *Murshid* with its traditional underpinnings.

If history should be considered as an essential part of these changes and the development of Islamism as a phenomenon, we need to trace the genesis of this new formation and how it was different from any previous ones to the post-October Revolution and to Ḥasan al-Turabi as a leader as he concentrated all power in his own hands. At the same time, such a move and the new labels and titles attached to the organization and its leadership positions could be perceived as going hand-in-hand not only with modernization of the party, but as an indication that the Islamists had delinked themselves from the auxiliary status and the stigma

30 Ibid.

31 Moḥamed E. Ḥamdi, *The Making of an Islamic Political Leader*, 14 (see Chapter 3, n. 22).

related to the Brotherhood during the rise of Jamal 'Abdul Nasir and his image as a national leader in the Arab world. Hence, the Islamists joined the crowd who accused communism of being an alien ideology and a foreign import. It was thus left to stay alone as a representation and a product of *al-mabadi al-mustawrda* (imported ideologies) subject to verbal and physical violence. All that had to fit well with the ambition of the young Sudanese Mahdi, who had a Ph.D. from the Sorbonne, while emerging within the ranks of a fairly modern organization and imposing his own *laïcité* against the *'ulamā'*, Sūfi, Salafi, and other Sudanese mainstream social representations of Islamic practice. But if this development arrived from a non-Islamist field, the consolidation of his position as a leader of the Islamists at that critical time had come out of his significant majority win of the electoral seat allotted to the graduates in the first general election after the downfall of 'Abboud's regime. "The Islamists fielded one hundred candidates, including fifteen in the special graduates' constituencies. … [the Islamists] won seven seats of which two (including Tutabi's) were from the graduates constituencies."[32] These steps automatically sidelined al-Rashid al-Tahir and those who followed the Ikhwan of Egypt school—Ja'afar Shaikh Idris, Malik Badri, Ṣadiq 'Abdallah 'Abdel Majid, Moḥmed al-Shaikh 'Umer, and others and who emphasized the *tarbiya* (education) approach rather than politics. In large measure, the formation of the contemporary Sudanese Islamist movement took place and found its growth, most famous and elaborate expression, within that development.

The third tier of al-Turabi's accommodation to the spirit of that strategy and its time can be seen in the rise of an incoming group of the Islamists around al-Turabi replacement of the outgoing group. One of the central characteristics of al-Turabi's strategies to stay in leadership of the Islamists organization was based in his ability to out maneuver those who were likely to secretly challenge his leadership. Now, and from that point on, al-Turabi played that strategy very carefully and successfully in the struggle against his antagonists before they prepared themselves for a confrontation against him. Without a doubt, he stayed conformable for a while in his leadership seat while putting his new team in place.

As referred to above, Ḥasan al-Turabi pursued new strategies that mimicked the methods of the Communist Party in a way that opened the door for adopting not only its tactics and strategies but also some former members of the Sudanese Communist Party. Yasin 'Umer al-Imam, the Islamist's commissar, often reminded his audience that he was once a member of the Communist Party. Another example was Aḥmed Suliamān[33] who was one of the leading members

32 'Abdel wahāb El-Affendi, *Turabi's Revolution*, 77 (see Chapter 3, n. 14).

33 Aḥmed Suliamān (1924–2009) was one of the founders of the Sudanese Communist Party and one of the most prominent members of its political bureau. He and other leading members of the party lead a division in support of Nimeiri's 1969 coup. Even before the coup, in December of the same year, Aḥmed Suliamān wrote in al-Ayyam Daily a provocative and controversial series of articles claiming that the failure of the progressive forces and their system that followed the fall of 'Abboud's regime could be attributed to the

of the Communist party. The Islamists formed the ICF, which was described by al-Turabi as "an umbrella for the movement's public activities."[34] The ICF was an improvement and modification to the formula the Islamists previously tried in 1955 under the name of the Islamic Front for the Constitution. It was the Islamists' way of deploying their party as a vanguard to bring in supporters and sympathizers and to have them rally around a certain message or a loose organization. Al-Turabi utilized this strategy effectively to lead the Islamists from the Muslim Brotherhood (1964) to the ICF (1964–1969), to the National Islamic Front (1985–1989), and on to the National Congress (1998–2000). He argued that "the expansion in the size of the movement itself necessitated reorganization, and forced it to implement large-scale changes."[35] Additionally, since that time and under the leadership of al-Turabi and his team, the movement built on its organizational potentials and embarked on what they thought of as an Islamist project that many within and outside the Islamist movement describe as "al-Turabi's project." Ḥasan Makki argued that the entire Islamists' project in the Sudan was more or less al-Turabi's project rather than the Islamists.' 'Abdullahi 'Alī Ibrāhim argued an inclination among the ranks of the "biographers of Ḥasan al-Turabi … to see his 'fundamentalism' as an expression of the religious traditions of al-Turabis, a lineage of Sūfis, Mahdists, jurists, and clerics that came into existence in the seventeenth century." Such a view, Ibrahim argued "obscures the politics of a shrewd thinker with a great ability to respond to effect change."[36] Whether it obscured the politics of a shrewd thinker or not, al-Turabi's chief innovation was to introduce different forms violence including verbal violence as a mode of operation to the Islamist movement. His longevity as a central and influential figure in the Islamist movement in the Sudan was due to his organizational skills, the mobilization of the movement's political artisans, and his ability to study the strategies of his opponents and to effectively invent and deploy a counter strategy, which was similar to his opponents' strategies. In this way, he was able, with varying degrees of success, to outmaneuver his main rivals' political moves both inside and outside the Islamist movement. Chief among those rivals was always the Communist Party. It is evident that al-Turabi paid close attention to the communists' political strategies and tactics and tried to counter or reinvent similar ones. He developed his notion of Islamism to supplant the communist movement as a first step in his overall program, or

lack of sustained cooperation between these forces and the faction of the army that helped in expediting the downfall of that regime. He added that future prospects of a progressive regime depend on the cooperation of progressive groups in the army and the left civilian movement. Later, he joined the Islamists and played a role in promoting the 1989 coup.

34 Moḥamed E. Ḥamdi, *The Making of an Islamic Political Leader*, 14 (see Chapter 3, n. 22).

35 Ibid.

36 'Abdullahi 'Ali Ibrāhim, "A Theology of Modernity," 195–222 (see Chapter 3, no. 18).

his grand project, the Islamic Front. He built a tightly regimented organization and supplemented it by the rhetorical stance of those lawyers who dominated the leadership of the movement as a close-knit group that apparently stayed around him for the last 40 years or more while in actual fact worked against him. Hence, al-Turabi's biography, vision, political, and intellectual influences warrant investigation. For the left, moving in that direction opened the way for negotiation with the army for a coup and a new despotism as we saw in the May 1969, coup and its totalitarian regime. It is in this sense one can understand Aḥmed Suliamān's advocacy for military coups and why he deserted the Communist Party and joined the Islamists. Aḥmed Suliāman was one of the few civilians in the Sudan who participated in planning for almost the most successful and failed coups in the Sudan except for the 'Abboud one. Before Numairi's 1969 coup he wrote in *al-Ayyam Daily* a provocative and controversial series of articles claiming that the failure of the progressive forces and their system that followed the fall of 'Abboud's regime could be attributed to the lack of sustained cooperation between these forces and the faction of the army that helped in expediting the downfall of that regime. He added that future prospects of a progressive regime depend on the cooperation of progressive groups in the army and the left civilian movement. That led to the sharp disagreement between him and 'Abdel Khaliq Mahjoub and ended in support for the Nemeiri coup and regime. Later, he joined the Islamists and played a role in promoting the 1989 coup. He sold them his theory about a successful coup. He argues that a successful coup is like a banana fruit: you cannot eat neither when it is too raw nor when it is too ripe.

Chapter 5

In Whose Image? The Same Question One More Time

The October 1964 Revolution highlighted the demographic shift in the Sudan that heavily tilted toward a young population. This became an important issue to wrestle with in the social composition of the populace, routes of entry into the community of the state, and other developments that brought change in the country. Expansion in public education, transportation, systems of communication, and other services that the welfare state provided to and placed in new post-independence generations of young male and female Sudanese individuals and groups into comparably favorable situations that helped them assume important places in the state, the politics and culture of an emerging post-October Revolution Sudan. In unprecedented numbers, younger Sudanese students in high schools, universities, and other high institutions of learning inside the country and abroad, grew incomparably since this moment of historical significance. In one of his *Octobariāt* poems, which Moḥamed Wardi—legendary musician and entertainer—popularized, Moḥamed al-Makki Ibrahim[1] described the new dimension and historical significance of that moment. He portrayed it as the coming together of this generation with the previous Sudanese generation of the fathers of independence as a convention of *jel al-bitualt bi jel al-tahadiāt* (the convention of the generation of heroism with generation of sacrifices).[2] Namely, a new relationship between Sudanese generations, transformation, change, and progress toward a Sudanese "good society" became an integral part of that moment in history. The October 1964 Revolution and its legacy gave generations of young Sudanese a sense of their power in what was perceived as a threshold and the drive for changing their world. The distinction of that historic event has gone over and beyond that to endow the people of the University of Khartoum and its faculty, staff, and students in particular, with esteem and higher prestige of an institutional space

1 Moḥamed al-Makki al-Ibrāhim is a renowned Sudanese contemporary poet and ex-career diplomat. He was a senior student at the law school during the October 1964 Revolution. He wrote a number of poems about the Revolution titled *al-Octobriāt* [October Odes]. Legendary Sudanese singer Moḥamed Wardi (1932–2011) popularized most of them. As I mentioned earlier, both Moḥamed al-Makki and Ward remain as icons of the October Civil Religion.

2 Moḥamed al-Makki al-Ibrāhim, *Umatī* (Khartoum: Dar al-Talief wa al-Nashr, 1969), 165.

that regarded that University as the country's seat and flagship of opposition to dictatorship that swept away the *ancien regimes*.

At the same time, the image of the University of Khartoum was and continued to be perceived by its population and other Sudanese as the mainstay of activism and civil political rights in a world of unfolding euphoric reverence for students, young revolutionaries, and the revolutions of the 1960s that exploded almost all over the world. No wonder that Sudanese generation has been depicted in similar ways as their contemporaries in other parts of the world in reference to the serious and multifaceted interrelated political, cultural, and rebellious trends across major world centers. A nascent global civil society was gradually emerging in which non-state actors and groups became more prominent and visible in a time of rising trends in the flow of information via new and more powerful outreach of local, regional, and international media and communication systems and their civic engagements. The Sudanese youth were not only conscious of that political and sociocultural era, but they saw themselves as part of that emerging international phenomenon. In fact, when the Sudanese speak about the 1960s, they remember what the Khartoum civil, public center and intellectual societies experienced. They recall it as a significant change in terms of the intellectual engagement within the regional and international debate in the fields of literature and political thought. And yet, the history and legacy of the October 1964 Revolution and its afterglow is not merely one triumphant event in the life of young Sudanese and an emerging urbanized population of the Sudan. It is also the history of a counter-revolution and a growth of different typologies of violence that turned that triumph into serious conflicts. From there, those conflicts led to the suppression of a new society that could have emerged and to deeper transformations in the fate and destinies of all political and civil representations in general: the state, the public center, the left, and the Islamists in particular.

Moreover, the October 1964 Revolution was not an isolated phenomenon. It is true that it caught the totalitarian and authoritarian regimes in the region, especially Egypt and Saudi Arabia, by surprise. Nevertheless, they both saw this profound change in the Sudan as life-threatening and as a dangerous development to their systems. As a result, they did not wait long to act as a counter-revolutionary force that could check or constrain liberation aspirations and geography that might go beyond an emerging Sudanese "good society." The exact formulas that each of these regimes followed had serious implications and consequences that acted together and separately to torment the Sudanese project of social change. These dynamics promoted a dialogue so distant from the Sudanese discourse of liberation and so close to the prevailing totalizing claims that hid behind the strategies of these regimes.[3] Starting from these premises,

3 On November 16, 1964, Mohammed Ḥasanein Haikal, the editor of *al-Ahram Daily*, who was perceived as the unofficial spokesperson for President Gamal 'Abdel Nassir, wrote a provocative article about the October 1964 Revolution titled: "What is Next in the Sudan?" In that article, Haikal belittled the Sudanese revolution and what the

the Sudanese liberation debate within the public sphere did not go beyond the roundtable conference discussions.

This chapter addresses the Islamist movement and the left by first looking back at its post-October Revolution era as a period of counter-revolution, its subsequent cycles of violent developments that materialized into two destructive coups of 1969 and 1989, and the two oppressive totalitarian regimes that resulted from the coups. The history and manifestation of these developments is by no means linear, but by all means, each had its own dynamic character, coercive capacity, and distinctive nature. Totalitarianism in both cases was a direct result of the counter-revolutionary conditions that worked separately to shape the destructive forms that both regimes and their state took.

A Contour to Ḥasan al-Turabi's Islamism

Both the left and the Islamists representations were born again via the October 1964 Revolution's gestation of a new society. The born-again Islamist movement of the post-October movement is not Islamism in itself or by itself; it is something different. The same thing applies to the post-October Sudanese left. But considered within both groups, the hubris of each, and the acknowledgment of the emergent developments that ended with military coups of 1969 and 1989 and their respective regimes, the two groups paid a high price as their rapacious impulses turned into counter-forces, violence, and totalitarian rule. That, however, has engendered new experiences of a world violated by the requisites of the violence and deviation from the liberation agendas and schemes that the spirit of October inspired and aspired for, but that was vulgarized by the two brutal military coups of 1969 and 1989.

Such as they were, these developments reviewed here seek another compelling explanation of how the Sudanese attempts and dreams of liberation were tempered by the repressions and subjugations of dissimilar multifaceted, interrelated political trends of counter-revolution across local and regional entities. One of these trends was related to the Sudanese Islamist movement within its own time, political practice, and experience. Islamism under the leadership of Ḥasan al-Turabi, came with its own social profile and political culture shaped by al-Turabi's character and his *laïcité* or what I call al-Turabi Islamism. Within the two ends of this development we can see how the boundaries of this phenomenon were stretched time and again and redefined every now and then. So, the terrain of

Sudanese people did. After the 1989 coup, the Egyptian Ambassador in Khartoum sent a jubilant message telling the Egyptian authorities that the coup was theirs. Thus, it should come as little surprise that Nassirite Egypt was behind the1969 military coup, and Sudan later transformed into a pro-Saudi regime after the death of Nassir in 1970. Although the Egyptian regimes, the first to recognize the 1989 coup, were deceived by the Islamists, later both Egypt and Saudi Arabia were able to tame the Sudanese regime.

hostilities and violence, from street and campus violence to the military coup and its state, which has been turned into a repertoire of internal and external violence that dominated over the better part of the Islamists' history, is only the expression of that Islamism and the mode of production of its counter-revolution. Now, not only had Islamism completely lost its character by 2000, but it had in fact renounced its own beliefs, or to be more specific, dug its own grave by the hands of its consumers. The Islamists' route to oblivion leaves no doubt on that matter. But to understand that one needs to look back and place al-Turabi and his Islamism in their objective development. What needs to be discerned on the bases of the Islamist experience is that, in essence, it has never been built on an enduring worldview or a favorable sociopolitical power to base a state upon. In this sense, one would say al-Turabi's Islamism has no essence; although, it has an accidental character. As a result, the Islamists failed to anticipate the failure of their project and could not foresee how thoroughly this failed experience had led the whole scheme of Islamism to oblivion.

How and Why al-Turabi's Islamism Became Possible

That emergent epoch of post-October Revolution enabled Dr. Ḥasan al-Turabi, the young new dean of the School of Law at the University of Khartoum, to develop a new and different construction of himself by assuming the leadership of a movement whose primary constituency at that time were students. His newly constructed self was supported by his win of a significant majority of the electoral seats designated to the graduates in the first general elections after the downfall of 'Abboud's regime. It nearly goes without saying that those who voted for him and his overwhelming victory within that sector of the Sudanese-educated elite represented a nationwide community of the state endorsement for the young Sudanese politician over and beyond the power and numbers of that small constituency of Islamists. However, that does not mean a nationwide endorsement. The Sudanese-educated elite in general, and the population affiliated with University of Khartoum that included faculty, staff, and students in particular, have always felt, especially after the success of the October 1964 Revolution, that they were tricked by the political parties' rhetoric, that they had a mission. Based on their own rhetoric, their mission was to modernize their country, while their role as "vanguards" was always frustrated by what they labeled as "traditional" forces, their parties and regimes.

The real novelty of that situation could be attributed to the spirit of that emergent epoch of the post-October Revolution. At that juncture, one would say that that revolutionary spirit superseded and, to a certain degree, mitigated the intervening differences that already existed, which were taking different forms out of other political commitments or orientations. It was through those young groups and individuals who came of age in a post-October era that commenced a Sudanese time of hope for a new era when human rights could become the political preference for the Sudanese people and the compass that would guide them toward a new Sudan. The formative period of Ḥasan al-Turabi, the new leader of the Sudanese Islamists, was the period when he and that generation of young Sudanese university students needed support from the other. For the university population, he emerged as a representative and a mentor; and from there, he grew his master (teacher) cult. Simultaneously, the support that al-Turabi received from the *khrijeen* (the graduates) at the general elections and from other people at the university led to the perception that the high-achievers and more people with higher education were his constituency and supporters of his leadership. From there, he developed his perception and strategy of life and politics "as a game of chance." At the same time, it was clear that the "old-fashioned" Islamism of the Ṣadiq 'Abdallah 'Abdel Māgid[4] group and its Egyptian Ikhwan school were at risk from what was perceived as the rising tide of the left, other Arab and African nationalist movements and discourses, and the internal struggle for power among the Islamists themselves as explained before. The post-October evolution opened a democratic environment at home and began a rising tide of new secular schools of governance within the region and other parts of the world. It also promoted the need for new interpreters and advocates for Islamism in the absence of an accepted authority in that field. But 'absence' in itself and its different forms opened the door for opportunities to some of the Islamists' younger generation during the absence of their older leaders as will be explained in chapters 7 and 8.

The issue of absence has an equally deeper effect within the universe of Islamism in general, and it is especially important after the oppressive measures taken against the Islamists by the state in Egypt before and during Jamal 'Abed al-Nasser's (1952–1970) draconian measures against the Ikhwan and its members. As Francois Burgat argues, "their members were long confined to clandestine action or, in most favorable cases, to associative or trade unionist institutional outer fringe of political life. The more their capacity for mobilization was asserted, the more the policies of exclusion of the regimes and the ostracism of Western media cracked down."[5] That had frozen Islamism and its Egyptian model to the pre-Ḥasan al-Banna assassination period and shifted the discourse to al-Banna's insubstantial message. Accordingly, those who stuck themselves to that brand of Islamism and to the *Bay'ah* (oath of allegiance) from Ḥasan al-Banna and canonized him as an imam, such as Sadiq 'Abdullah 'Abdel

4 Ṣadiq 'Abdullah 'Abdel Magid took over the leadership of the Sudanese Brotherhood after al-Rashid al-Tahir was forced out of office because of his involvement in a failed coup attempt during the 'Abboud regime. 'Abdel Magid who received his university studies in Egypt during the 1940s, knew Ḥasan al-Banna, and he was one of the Sudanese Muslim Brothers who gave *Bay'ah* to Ḥasan al-Banna. He kept faithful to that up to this day.

5 Francois Burgat, "From National Struggle to the Disillusionments of 'Recolonization' the Triple temporality of Islamism," in *Political Islam: A Critical Reader*, ed. Fredreic Volpi (London: Routledge, 2011), 34.

Māgid found themselves deemed dysfunctional while the Egyptian model of Islamism was perceived as outdated by that time by the rising generations of post-October Revolution. It is surely worth emphasizing that, as Aḥmed Kamal el-Din argues, that *Bay'ah* represented one of the main areas of irreconcilable disagreements between al-Turabi and the local representation of the Egyptian Muslim Brotherhood in the Sudan—Ṣadiq 'Abdullah and his group—and the Egyptian mother organization together with the Brotherhood international organizations. Kamal el-Din argues that for al-Turabi the *Bay'ah* is between a person and his God.[6] Khalid Duran observed that "there is a predominant urge [for the Sudanese] to keep their distance from their Northern cousins [the Egyptians], at least in the sense that they resent playing the role of eternal vassals to a center of the North."[7] Especially the Sudanese Islamists had been accusing their communist adversaries of playing such a role. Duran added that al-Turabi, with his double doctorate (Oxford and Paris) and felicity of language in Arabic and English, had little difficulty in rising to higher pan-Islamist prominence than the Egyptian Islamist of his days. The aging and ailing 'Umar al-Tilimsāni in Cairo was no match for him."[8]

At the same time, the Sudanese Islamists were warned against Sayyid Qutb's ideas. They were told that the "conclusions that he arrived at on collective excommunication, based on the *jahilīyya* [ignorance of Islam] and *'uzla*,[9] are intellectually erroneous and practically dangerous."[10] It was explained to al-Turabi's Islamists that their position should stem from "their regard for the characteristics of the Sudanese society, their involvement, and functioning within a multiparty political system, and from the distinct ideological perspective and independent organization that they began to develop from the early 1960s."[11] Hence the new post-October situation in the Sudan and its open democratic environment created the desire and the need for the production of an authority and leadership different from that old-fashioned Egyptian model, its leadership, Sudanese followers, and the intellectually unsound Qutbism. That extraordinary situation brought al-Turabi to the leading edge for not only a precipitous political experience but also for an ideological Sudanese innovation that might fill a glaring gap in terms of its local imports.

---

6 Aḥmed Kamal al-Din in an internet interview, March 2012.

7 Khalid Duran, "The Centrifugal Forces of Religion in Sudanese Politics," *Orient*, 26 (December 1985): 587.

8 Ibid.

9 Qutb coined the term *al-'uzla al-shu'uriyya* and *al-Mufāṣalah al-Shu'uriyya* to indicate a psychological separation from society by feeling and consciousness as opposed to actual or physical separation.

10 Eltigani 'Abdelgadir Ḥāmid, "Islam, Sectarianism and the Muslim Brotherhood in Modern Sudan, 1956–1985," Ph.D diss. Department of Economics and Political Studies, the School of Oriental and African Studies, University of London (1989), 138.

11 Ibid.

Given the sociopolitical conditions that prevailed during that time, al-Turabi wasted no time in introducing his new strategy of attack to other Islamist and non-Islamist political and religious representations while investing heavily for the future of his leadership. Simultaneously, he invested heavily on his Islamist movement—shaped by his *laïcité*—while banking on an opportunity that availed itself within the power relations that underlie that new emerging epoch and its emerging young educated groups. More students from rural Sudan, especially Darfur, equipped with temperament and a cultural capital that would likely make greater numbers of them lean toward whoever would call for Islam, strengthened the Islamist student population, the movement's infrastructure, and the new leader who acted as the center of gravity for the emerging movement. Since that time, al-Turabi became the producer of the ideological and political direction of the movement, and the movement became equivalent with what the leader had done, did not do and what he would do and say.

It was a historic moment for the new Secretary General and the former dean of the law school to look at the University of Khartoum where growing numbers of students were drawn toward a non-threatening political orientation, different from communism, with a modern sugar coating that could be accepted, to a certain extent, by the conservative side of the Sudanese culture. Some families might argue with their young family members who advocate a Communist politics but the same families might take it easy or even feel happy noticing those family members observing their religious duties and they might not question their relationship to Islamism. Having done so, al-Turabi's Islamism, served for some groups and individual students, the Islamist solidarity as a functional conformity with home. Moreover, and to a certain extent, it acclimated itself with a new religious and cultural affiliation within the Sudanese's emerging civil and political spheres in what that could be perceived and described as a novel way. Having done so, this novel way had to specifically reject communism, it orientations, and its conduct conceptualized by progressive liberal values. Consequently, this impulse developed not only as a complete rejection of Communist and liberal orientations and values only, but it grew as a totally hostile and violent entity toward the Other including other Muslim representations, such as Sūfi, Salafi, *'ulamā'*, and Maḥmoud Moḥamed Ṭaha Islamism, as well as al-Banna or the Egyptian Brotherhood model. This hostility toward the Other actually represented the core of al-Turabi *Islamism*. Hence, as the center shifted from the Brotherhood and its underpinning Salafism to al-Turabi'sIslamism, this new phenomenon became the master signifier of that brand of Sudanese Islamism. At the same time, al-Turabi—who immediately turned into the Secretary General of the organization and later in a gradual process into *Shaikh* Ḥasan by his followers—ascended through his personality cult into the new *Mahdi* of an emerging Islamism and became its axial point.[12] When the decision was made by al-Turabi the new

12 See 'Abdel Raḥim 'Umar Muḥi el-Din, *Al-Islamiuoon fi l-Sudan*: *Drasat ta Tour wa al-fikir al-Syasi 1969–1985*, p. 127, for a quote about young al-Turabi: "al-Turabi, his

Islamist Secretary General to abolish the Brotherhood and to bring its members into the *Jabhat al-Mithāg al-Islami* (the Islamic Charter Front (ICF)) in 1964, his *Islamism* became the Islam and Islamist signifier for those who followed him together with those who sympathized with him or joined his camp. But this major transformative move did cause serious conflict. As el-Tigani 'Abdelgadir reported, "in the inner circles of the Ikhwan, *Jabhat al-Mithaq al-Islami* [ICF] was seen as victory for the school of 'modernizers' over their conservative colleagues."[13] But al-Turabi was especially challenged by those who were not willing to move from the Muslim Brotherhood's school of thought. Those who challenged al-Turabi most vigorously included Moḥamed Ṣalih 'Umar, Ja'far Shaikh Idris, Moḥmed Yousif Moḥmed (for a short period), and Moḥamed Yousif Moḥamed, attacked his leadership possibly because, according to al-Tigani, he was "an innovator who wanted to destroy the Ikwan and change its *Salafi* ideological basis." Mahmoud Burat, who was then one of al-Turabi's supporters, argued at the Majlis al-Shura, which was convened to deliberate on this serious issue that "an ideological split has taken place within the Islamic *da'wa* (the Ikhwan).There [are] now two groups and may (or may not) co-exist. Al-Turabi's group, Turabi represents an ideological current. As for Ja'afar and Moḥamed Saliḥ 'Omer, they stand for disciplinary ethics."[14] It would be too simplistic to explain al-Turabi's Islamism or Islamism in Sudan in general as a mere after-effect or a consequence of a radical saga with communism as some of its own historians advocate. As has been explained before, al-Turabi's Islamism, which had always been dismissive of all other political and religious representations including Egyptian Islamism, began to float away independent from or delinking itself from the mainstream and the specialized knowledge embedded in the Sudanese Muslim culture, intellectual discourse, and ideologies of other religious and political representations.

Within this development, al-Turabi became the "leader" in the Stalinist sense. Out of this, the seeds of the totalitarian impulse started to grow within the Islamist movement. The organization perceived itself as a novel movement led by a dynamic leader who provided for all members a sense of security and political and religious thought and guidance toward a brighter future as an outcome of the growth and development of the movement. Hence, it would be incumbent upon the members to follow him in the same way students follow their professor and mentor, believe in him the same way they would believe in their religious *Shaikh*, and meekly serve him as they should serve the leader. It was long overdue to remind Ḥasan al-Turabi as Aḥmed 'Abdel Raḥman did later, that he "turned

---

yearning to remote horizon where looming assurances of prophethood and good tidings of God's promise of succession."

13 Eltigani 'Abdelgadir Hāmid, "Islam, Sectarianism and the Muslim Brotherhood in Modern Sudan, 1956–1985," Ph.D diss. Department of Economics and Political Studies, the School of Oriental and African Studies, University of London (1989), 104.

14 Ibid.

the Islamist movement into a Sūfi *ṭariqa* and you became its *Shaikh*."[15] In actual fact, that took place long ago, and that is why the Sudanese Islamist movement within more than a half century has produced only one thinker or ideologue; because the ideology and its production became attached to one single "Leader." The rest became disciples, operatives, and "artisans." The relationship of the foundational conservative commitment and the political agenda that came with it was negotiated through the emerging personality of the new young leader who combined the image of the "brilliant professor," a Sorbonne Ph.D graduate, and the descendent of Wad al-Turabi. This very special physiognomy of al-Turabi's Islamism began to attract more committed and non-committed students to the new political star and sometimes to the newly reinvented party. For those who hoped to gain entrance to the community of the state al-Turabi, with his elegantly tailored full suits and his eloquent though sometimes-aggressive style, became a magnet for growing numbers of even non-Islamists as he was a frequent public speaker at the University of Khartoum Students' Club. The public speeches of al-Turabi at students' clubs continued to draw increasing numbers of students from the University of Khartoum, from other learning institutions, and the Capital three cities as well.

This of course was not the time when Islamism began in the Sudan. It was the time in which Islamism was born again in its new form and started to gain some prevalence across the public and political spaces. Then it started to draw more diverse groups of young Sudanese who came to the University of Khartoum and other institutions of higher learning. As it happened, many of those who helped define al-Turabi's Islamism and gave it a fairly modern face—different than the traditional rigid Ikhwan appearance—were the University of Khartoum graduates and United Kingdom-educated members who congregated around al-Turabi. They included Aḥmed Abdel Rahman, 'Uthmān Khalid Mudawi, Mohammed Yousuf, 'Abdel Raḥim Ḥamdi, and others. It follows that what al-Turabi himself has said, "the students who were at the center of the entire Islamic movement [while] chapters of the community outside the institution were only external branches of the movement in the University."[16] The deeply buried social and mental structures of that situation created an emerging social universe with the University of Khartoum at its core. Within this social universe, it became an incentive for the new recruits to al-Turabi Islamism to adopt the posture of their new iconic leader who was presented as a role model *par excellence* in his field of studies. The qualities that defined this social universe were complex as it emerged as a master signifier that structured a new and different brand of Islamism, which Ḥasan al-Turabi represented in all forms, ideological orientations, and strategic planning. It was an Islamism that did not fall either into the ideological essentialism,

15 'Abdel Rahim 'Umar Muhi al-Din, *al-Turabi wa al-Igahd: Siraa' al-Hawa wa al-Hawiya* (Khartoum, Maroe Bookshop, 2006), 180.

16 Dr. Ḥasan al-Turabi, *al-Haraka al-Islamiyya fi el-Sudan,* 132 (see Chapter 4, no. 18).

theological imports, the international aspect, nor the cultural particularism of the Egyptian Brotherhood. T. Abdou Maliqalim Simone noticed that al-Turabi "in the past always down played the international aspects of *Ikhwan*."[17] In fact, it was more than that. Al-Turabi, as stated in chapter three, perceived the Egyptian Brotherhood as "traditional" and never mentioned a belief or an intimate relationship with the Muslim Brotherhood as practice or common values. That explains why he abolished the Sudanese Muslim Brotherhood entity when he issued his first communiqué as the ICF's Secretary General in 1964 in which he "declared that all Ikwan public activities would henceforth be conducted through ICF channels."[18] For that reason, al-Turabi Islamism or *laïcité* has been used here as a metaphor to describe a Sudanese development in the field of political Islam that emerged following Ḥasan al-Turabi's assumption of leadership for the movement in 1964. That explains his claim of "novelty" as one of the main characteristics of the Islamist movement in the Sudan. At the same time, it reflects the controversial presence of al-Turabi's ideology in the Islamist and non-Islamist market of ideas and how it was received with acceptance from some and rebuffed and severely criticized from others. Later, in a series of interviews with Moḥamed E. Ḥamdi, he reflected on this important aspect of his Islamism. He recalled that the movement "is very much aware of its own history. It might in early days have assumed the form of Egyptian experience, which in turn emulated an earlier model of Islamic life, mainly characterized by education and reform. Within a short time, however, and after the initial stage of its existence, the movement developed a marked sense of self-awareness, positioning itself accurately within its own specific time and place parameters."[19]

This key moment of al-Turabi's Islamism that characterizes the historical past of the movement, which could be found reiterated in the narrations of the different generations of Islamist scholars and politicians, was consistent in the way it reconstructed the history of the movement as a unique and self-made organization that came from nowhere. By promoting such an instructive method for their own social construction and historical interpretation of the movement, al-Turabi and his Islamists chose two initial approaches to systemize the distinction between them and their surroundings. They did so by locating themselves within a place, space, and scope of events, which they determined.

---

17 T. Abdou Maliqalim Simmone, *In Whose Image? Political Islam and Urban Practice* (Chicago, IL: the University of Chicago Press, 1994), 162.

18 'Abdel wahāb El-Affendi, *Turabi's Revolution*, 76 (see Chapter 2, no. 63).

19 Moḥamed E. Ḥamdi, *The Making of An Islamic Political Leader*, p. 14 (see Chapter 3, no. 22).

An Islamist Hubris

Ḥasan al-Turabi and the oral and scholarly historians of the movement have long been so preoccupied with their attempts to locate the movement as it presented itself apart from the territorial bounds of other Sudanese and other Islamist movements in the region. They employed a variety of means to create what could be considered as self-defining constructions for categorizing their movement as a movement apart. In 1971, the Sudan Islamists were asked to give *Bay'ah* to *al-Murshid al-'Āam* , which is what some consider as the mother organization of the Muslim Brotherhood of Egypt in accordance of the 1948 bylaws of *Jam'iyaat Al-Ikhwan al-Muslimeen* (the Muslim Brotherhood). Al-Turabi refused to do so. Consequently, Ḥasan al-Turabi and the Egyptian *Murshid* Ḥasan al-Hudiabi held a meeting in Saudi Arabia in 1973.[20] The Sudanese Islamists explained in that meeting their disagreement with *al-Bay'ah* model of incorporation in the mother organization "and proposed, instead, a formula of cooperation but that has never materialized. Ever since, the Sudanese have retained their autonomy, the Egyptians have resented that relations between the two have remained sore and sensitive."[21] Such an attitude involved a sense of superiority that reflected itself in the polity and practices of the movement, which led to tension and sometimes open conflict with internal and external Islamist and non-Islamist entities. While this wholesale character of the movement has always been overlooked by those who have been studying the Islamist movements in the Sudan and their political behavior, this attitude that denies the historical relationship to the place and all other territorial bounds has its meaning. What stands out is that such a breaking away from the surrounding traditions and cultures as Roy elucidates "leads to a fundamentalist-type assertion (a demand to return to explicit religious norms and only to these) or integralist (i.e., every aspect of my private life must be governed by my faith, even if I don't impose it on others)."[22] By such an attitude, the Sudanese Islamists have tried to convince themselves, their sympathizers, and their detractors that their legitimization does not come from the past as it does in other religious representations in the country. This is especially the case with the Ṣūfi orders, which they despise, the *'ulamā'* whom they deride and ridicule, or the

20 Ḥassan al-Hudaybi (1891–1973) was the second *Murshid* of the Egyptian Muslim Brotherhood. He was chosen for that position after the founder of the organization Ḥasan al-Banna's assassination in 1949. He was arrested in 1965 in the crackdown against the Brethren by President Jamal 'Abdel Nasser (1952–1970), but he was later released from prison in 1971 with other Brotherhood political prisoners held by President Anwar al-Sadat (1970–1981).

21 Eltigani 'Abdelgadir Ḥamid, "Islam, Sectarianism and the Muslim Brotherhood in Modern Sudan, 1956–1985," Ph.D diss. Department of Economics and Political Studies, the School of Oriental and African Studies, University of London (1989), 105.

22 Olivier Roy, *Holy Ignorance: When Religion and Culture Part Ways* (New York: Columbia University Press, 2010), 9.

related contemporary offshore or neighboring experience like the Communists or the Ikwan of Ṣadiq ʻAbdullah ʻAbdel Magid.

This impulse to delink and create autonomy from culture, history, place, and space has its deeper effects and future consequences on the different generations who joined the movement before and after al-Turabi' Islamism was in place. For the older generations of Ḥasan al-Turabi's followers or those who joined the movement before 1964, such as Aḥmed ʻAbdel Rahman, it has been clear they continued to reflect on the fact that they broke away partly or wholly from a surrounding Sūfi and *ʻulamā'*, as well as their mainstream cultural norms and traditions. Yet, they continued to share certain aspects of their local and regional culture with their surroundings. Subsequent younger generations, such as ʻAlī ʻUthmān or the "kittens who ate their father," who joined during or after the period of al-Turabi's ascension, grew up and matured with the conviction that they were part of a novel sociopolitical culture or "al-Turabi Islamism" that perceive life and politics "as a game of chance."[23] These two different routes to al-Turabi's Islamism and their different groups that evolved each within its own field and cultural productions have created a very complex situation; studying it could provide us with an opportunity to understand the internal conflicts within the movement and later the Islamist regime. More importantly, as these "kittens" developed their ideological, political, and cultural religious beliefs from an insider and in relation to al-Turabi's notion of the political scheme (which many perceived, including some within the movement, as opportunistic, totalitarian, and self-serving) it is important to look at their engagement with the Islamists in power since 1989 and how that led Islamism to oblivion. Chapters 7 and 8 explain the rise of ʻAlī ʻUthmān and his "new class" as a dominant group but also as part of the determinants of that system.

Starting from this premise, it is important to note that most of al-Turabi's leading Islamists from the older generation spent years in prison and exile. Al-Turabi himself spent seven years in prison during the May regime. Some of the post-October generations matured within the thin line between exile, life, and death. Later, they turned from barefoot, educated individuals into a propertied middle-class group. The absence of leadership in prison and exile was an opportunity to some of the younger generation to assume advanced positions in the organization. Later, after the reconciliation with the May regime and transformation of the Islamist movement into a corporation[24] with national and international scope hiding behind the Islamic economy, its banking system, and their Islamist managers and workers, some quickly climbed the economic ladder. This change of status and fortune strengthened the deep-rooted individualistic spirit instilled by the public

---

23 It was attributed to the late John Garang, who was well-known for his biting humor. He jokingly said to ʻAlī ʻUthmān during their first meeting that "we have heard of the mother cat that eats its kittens but we have never heard of the kittens that eat their father" referring to what ʻAlī ʻUthmān and his group did to their political leader, Ḥasan al-Turabi.

24 See ʻAbdullahi A. Gallab, *The First Islamist,* 77–96 (see Chapter 1, no. 1).

education and continued to grow since their early days as operatives or artisans in the organization. The result that focused on what they called *al-tamkeen* and grew into a reward-driven culture that nurtured envy and greed over empathy and faking religiosity and self-constraint and tugging governance and position toward excessive self-indulgence, trickery, and meanness. The relevance of this for the Sudanese population can be seen within the satire literature (oral and written) that describes the Islamists and their regime. The literature illustrates them in the likes of deceit, intrigue, and greed, which is exemplified by their moral deficit that showed itself and has continued since their first day of presenting their coup to the world via a big lie that set a moral standard for them. Such patterns of behavior led to a decisive lack of integrity structure, which later clearly surfaced in the way al-Turabi and his Islamists deliberately misled the Sudanese people about the true nature of the coup and in the way al-Turabi never apologized for the deception. Al-Turabi himself was seriously committed to that great lie by denying for more than a decade any involvement in the 1989 coup. He only claimed to have played a leading role in every step of its planning after his fall from power in the year 2000. He later disclosed that, as stated earlier, he "went to prison and ordered al-Bashir to go to the Palace." Everybody kept asking where, then, is the Islam in the regime's Islamism? While in its actual practice of Islamism, Islam and its state[25] metamorphosed into a dreadful system of violence and deceit as it was practiced by that younger generation, "the kittens" of al-Turabi's Islamists. For its idealism, this practice was even incompatible with what they advocated before or what other Sudanese citizens, whether Muslims and non-Muslims, thought of the Islam's religious ideals. It was also inconsistent with an Islamic rule that would promote the kind of commitment to political ethics, social justice, and civil liberties to which a Muslim political and humanitarian project might comply with or aspire to.

The second direction that al-Turabi and his Islamists chose as an initial approach to systemize the distinction between themselves and their surroundings was to locate themselves within a place, space, and scope of events that was determined by the way they described themselves. It goes without saying that a clear Islamist political thought existed before 1964. It is only after al-Turabi assumed the movement's leadership position that Islamism began its transition to a counter-revolutionary force. It is true that his rivalries in the left always accused him of being *rajee*, but they never made their point clear on how reactionary he was or could be. Different generations of the Sudanese Communist Party repeated their demonstrations against the Islamists: *al-Ikhwan jihas fashisti* (the Muslim brotherhood is a fascist instrument). Al-Turabi's Salafi enemies accused him of being *'ilmani* (a secular person), but they failed to prove that. Moreover, all these dice were cast without capturing the depth and breadth of al-Turabi's hubris or the intoxication of mind that imbedded the assumptions within the movement that it was the one and the only valid path to Islam, its state, and to the true existence,

25 When the Islamists came to power, their main motto was *hia li allah la lil sulta la lil jah* (it is for Allah it is neither for power nor prestige).

while others are inevitably true or false according to al-Turabi's own verdict. Based on this premise, he and his disciples felt compelled to act verbally and physically violent through the state coercive apparatus, and they later destroyed all possibilities of existence whom they considered false, including their former *Shaikh* and those who were '*ikhwa fi al-Islam*' (brothers in Islam), as a means to further their plans. Thus, soaked in political and religious correctness, al-Turabi's Islamists turned the movement into a counter-revolutionary entity that bred systematic violence. However, what turned the movement into a counter-revolutionary entity had nothing to do with all that. The founding of the Islamist movement in its post-October phase and the personality of its leader are thought to have been determined by Islam. And although adopting Islam could be perceived as a positive thing within a Muslim society, by itself it did not qualify such Islamists, or any other group, to perform the functions of the Islamic movement or the leadership as it has been limited within its Islamist confines.

In fact, Islamism in power has created its own counter-revolution. It is not by accident that the idea of Islamism threatens the existence and future of the Muslim institutions of the *'ulamā'*, who gained and solidified their legitimacy from an institutionalized religious knowledge that qualified them to functions as judges, imams, and teachers who issue *fatwa* in matters relating to Islamic specialized knowledge and Muslim life. At the same time, Islamism has fueled attacks on the Sūfi orders and its leaders in a way that threatens the existence and future of Sūfism that gained and solidified its legitimacy from an institutionalized religious practice of purifying the self from its blameworthy attributes while invigorating, instead, the self with what is praiseworthy by following *ṭariiq al-Qowm* (the path of pious community: the saints of Sūfi orders). Accordingly, as long as the Islamists are not and will not be the ones qualified to open up the *'ulamā'*s' corpus, they choose to denounce the *'ulamā'* and nominate themselves to be thinkers, rather than *'ulamā'*, and stand out as self-proclaimed spokespersons of Islam as *din wa dawla* (religion and state). On the other hand, as al-Turabi has always described himself and his movement as being modern, he continued to condemn Sūfism, its saints, and its practices as "relicts of the past" and as anti-modern. At the same time, he and his Islamists created their counter-revolution here as well. They stepped out of modernity and further denounced it by telling their secular competitors that as long as they acted like the epitome of modernity, then al-Turabi and his Islamist group represented a special identity, whose compact with modernity was evident in their rhetoric of authenticity, rhetoric that provoked the idea that the threat of modernity is thus so dangerous. In 1997, al-Turabi attempted to raise the modern aspect of his movement when he told his American audience of Islamic and Sudanese Studies in Florida that "Islam is the only modernity, because if the modern sector in our society represents modernity, then the modern sector is dominated by

Islamic currents."[26] But this attitude that hand picks or fences in "the students and university graduates" as the sole representatives of modernity, he designated them as well, "as the only current which exercises any measure of *ijtihād*."[27] This discourse and its "inherent reinvention of difference" that separates the Islamists' ascribed authenticity and its self-made identity sets in motion a problematic political, cultural, and religious process that might be very difficult to evaluate. This is so, especially if we consider that each *mujtahid* (i.e., the jurist conducting *ijtihād*) arrived at the truth following that extensive relativism that gave rise to the famous tenant that 'every *mujtahid* is correct,' "a maxim that proved operative and became sanctified."[28]

While a great skepticism arose about al-Turabi's assertion regarding his followers' capacity to exercise *ijtihād*, it would be interesting to see what would have happened if Islamist leaders including al-Turabi opened the door of *ijtihād* to their followers. Up to this moment, none of these organizations had created a research center or forum for conducting *ijtihād*. As political or religious thought is not that important for the Islamists, *ijtihād* remains a one-man show. If it occurred, it might have been only within its own characteristics, and where it has been entrapped, it might or could be questioned. First, of course that situation raises the issue of competing understandings of both Islam and modernity that could only have been resolved in al-Turabi's mind. Second, as long as these essentialist definitions of the Other were not agreed upon, then all the consequences of such objectification could have been alarming, especially when it came from a position of power and authority. It follows, finally, that all other religious representations, including Sūfism, the 'ulmā's orthodoxy, Moḥamed Moḥamed Ṭaha (who was debunked with apostasy), the other Islamists described as "traditional," the Communists, and the left, who were labeled as unauthentic in relation to modernity, would not be embraced in the vision of common humanity, worth, dignity, and equal membership in the polity that they might assume.

Here is where al-Turabi's *Islamism* resides. That is to say, his Islamism and later his state would function and impose themselves as a "moral *et enseignant*" (moral and teaching agency). In order for his Islamism and the state to keep no religious or other political obligations, both his Islamism and the state had "*une morale independente de toute* religion" (a morality independent of all religion), and they enjoyed "*suprématie morale*" (moral supremacy) in relation to all religions.[29] The basis of this supremacy is al-Turabi Islamism. This confirms that the essence

26 Arthur L. Lowrie, ed., *Islam, Democracy, the State and the West: A Round Table with Dr. Ḥasan Turabi* (Tampa, FL: The World & Islam Studies Enterprise, 1993), 18.

27 Ibid.

28 Wael Hallaq, *The Impossible State: Islam, Politics, and Modernity's Moral Predicamenti* (New York: Columbia University Press, 2013), 58.

29 See Charles Taylor, Why we Need A Radical Redefinition of Secularism, in Eduardo Mendieta, (ed.) *The Power of Religion in the Public Sphere* (New York: Columbia University Press, 2011), 34.

of Islamism in general and al-Turabi's Islamism in particular, had an accidental character that was more about a violent totalitarian *dawla* (state) than *din wa dawla*. As stated earlier in chapter three, this of course went hand-in-hand with and became inseparable from al-Turabi practice of always placing himself above individuals, colleagues, organizations, the nation, and the state. Accordingly, and within such dominant principles of such classification and order of things, we find ourselves in front of a personality that floats above history. However, it is both of these issues that made al-Turabi possible; it is him who made his Islamism and its counter-revolutionary productions of violence and corruption possible too. But as an accidental character as all these developments worked with and without him.

From Where Does the Counter-revolution Come?

The counter-revolution, as a functioning phenomenon within this development, brought about a complex set of inventions of the self-imaging of the leader, the group, and the strategies that had underlain al-Turabi's Islamism, their discourses and the group's violent and nonviolent actions all through his life. At the same time, the conditions that created these complex inventions of such self-imaging and narrations of the movement's history have an enduring impact on the mode and politics of the movement and its mission to violently destruct the Other. When the Islamists' were planning for the 1989 coup, Yasin 'Umar al-Imam suggested that the first thing they should do after the success of the coup is liquidate all of what he called the "traditional" leadership of the Sudanese political parties and "to free the country from the endless conflicts between those big families who did not contribute anything of value to the progress of the country."[30] It is true that the Islamists did not liquidate any of those political leaders, but their new regime took an active policy that developed into a systematic selection and development of different forms of violence and extermination of human beings. That policy started in December 1989, with the execution of three Sudanese individuals who were accused of acquiring foreign currency. It was a well-known fact then that *tujar al-Jabha* (the Islamist merchants) were the main dealers in foreign currency in both the black and white markets. Those three people were selected as the launch of a gruesome systematic selection policy. Those three Sudanese were Magdi Maḥgoub Moḥamed Aḥmed, a member of a well-known financial and intellectual family, Gergis al-Qus, a civil aviation pilot of a Christian Coptic origin, and the southern Sudanese student Arkinglo Ajado who was preparing to leave the country to study in a neighboring nation. In the case of Magdi Maḥgoub, "whose one-day trial inside a military compound ... witnesses reported that Major Ibrahim Sham el-din, a member of the Revolutionary Command Council, attended the trial and influenced the judge to order the defendant's lawyer to leave the

30 'Abdel Rahim 'Umar Muhi al-Din, *al-Turabi wa al-Igahd: Siraa' al-Hawa wa al-Hawiya* (Khartoum: Maroe Bookshop, 2006), 180.

military compound where the trial was taking place, a serious violation of due process."[31] Not only that, but it has been reported that "on the day the sentence was carried out, December 14 (1989) Maj. Shams al-din was seen outside Kober prison awaiting confirmation of the execution. Contrary to the regulations of the General Administration of Prisons—whereby executions are carried out immediately after Dawn Prayer, about 3:00 am—on this day the sentence was executed at thirty minutes past midnight. This speed in execution was possibly an effort to avoid any last minute review of the case or clemency."[32] Other selective killings included Dr. 'Alī Fadl (medical doctor and an activist), Dr. Mamoun Moḥamed Ḥussian (Head of the Medical Association), al-Taya 'Abu 'Aāgla (student), and advocate Ḥamdan Ḥasan Kuri to mention very few. Did it take the Islamist a long time to create a multifaceted system of selective elimination of human beings that included the "ghost houses," the military defense force, *dababeen* (tank bombers), and the Janjaweed, which was a system that utilized coercion as a prime mover of social engineering and dehumanization.[33] The regime that they installed represented a massive reaction against the spirit of every aspect of happiness and optimism that the Sudanese people had dreamed for since they gained independence in 1956. This stands at the heart of the Islamist counter-revolution, as violence was a common denominator of the movement even before assuming power through the military coup, which is in essence a violent act. Then the centrality of violence as a source of political authority and a mode of governance started from the first day of the coup and continued unevenly across the country, as they put faith in violence and perceived coercive measures to be the most effective, if not the only, mode of governance and social control. Starting from this premises one can say how al-Turabi Islamists by default and by design positioned their Islamist model on violence. This long episode has been a complicated saga not only against the Other but also against former fellow adherents and their supreme leader. This trend of violence and its glorification by the movement's members and later the regime has its own cipher or encryption code and curious particularity that is inherent in the grandiose theory of Islamism and its mission, which needs to be deciphered to make understanding this phenomenon possible. This mode that put faith in violence has opened the way for a remorseless and never-ending war against all shades of the Muslim and non-Muslim Other–being citizens or former fellow Islamists who all have been perceived as ephemeral. For al-Turabi's Islamists, violence is neither aberrant not abhorrent, and in a broader perspective, their inventions of self-imaging and the reproduction of violence, which has been rooted, performed,

---

31 Jemera Rone, *Behind the Redline: Political Repression in Sudan* (New York: Human Rights Watch, 1996), 106.

32 Ibid.

33 Ḥasan al-Turabi claims that a member of a Darfur investigation committee told him that al-Bashir said to the committee members at his meeting with them that "any Darfuri women should feel proud for being raped by a J'ali person."

and celebrated by the Islamists, has three important developments in the life of the movement.

First, T. ʻAbdou Maliqalim Simone was one of the very few, if not the only, sociologist who spent "nearly two years as both academic and consultant to the Islamic movement in Khartoum."[34] Simone's book and the basic question that came out of his serious first hand experience with the Islamists, their regime, and the state is *In Whose Image?*[35] did political Islam and its urban practices emerge. Of course, there is more than one image that includes, the self-image of al-Turabi Islamism, the image of the state of their dream, and the image of the rhetorical stance associated with both. The Islamist self-image, as explained before, defends "the essence or experience itself rather than promote the full knowledge of it and its entanglements and dependencies on other knowledges."[36] In this sense, al-Turabi Islamists sought to "demote the different experience of others to a lesser status."[37] At the same time, they never reflected on their violent obsessions and conduct that produced an unprecedented death toll, misery, and destruction everywhere in the country for almost a quarter century.

Second, the Islamist basic theory and belief that ignores the social, economic, and political conditions meant to delink them from other cultural milieus within which other Sudanese communities existed in its diverse religious, cultural, and social settings and histories. But this provided them with such a powerful and vicious ideology, which they used to "purge" Muslim societies in different parts of the country—primarily Darfur—and incite jihād against Sudanese citizens whom they labeled as the "impurities" and *hasharat*[38] (insects) and turn the world of Ḥasan al-Turabi and his followers upside down.

Finally, the most important aspect of this discourse and its historical narration is that it makes the Sudanese Islamists a self-sufficient political association rather than a religious movement. Ḥasan Mekki, as noted before, described that as al-Turabi's own project. Through this medium of excellence cult to which both educational and political institutions conformed, grew a complex situation that has shaped and constrained—at the same time—the Islamist movement ever since. This situation has revealed other worlds that were long in the making. The first one became clear by strategically promoting some new student members to stardom within the movement according to each one's academic success, which I call "the new class." This promoted a deeper sense of individualism and continued to be the invisible hand behind negative attitudes of jealously, selfishness, viciousness, and

34 T. Abdou Maliqalim Simone, *In Whose Image? Political Islam and Urban Practices in Sudan* (Chicago, IL: University of Chicago Press, 1994), ix.

35 Ibid.

36 Edward Said, *Culture and Imperialism* (New York: Vintage Books, a Division of Random House, Inc., 1993), 32.

37 Ibid.

38 That is how ʻUmar al-Bashir described al-Haraka al-Shabiyya (the SPLM) as *al-Hashara al-Shabiyya.*

finger pointing that developed later through the modes of competition as they bred into conflict, character assassination, and identity management and engineering. The contemporary individual and factional internal wars within the ranks of the Islamists were not just expressions of different opinions or attitudes; they were deeper than that. And they emerged after the culmination of the comprehensive peace agreement that would have incorporated the different visions for the new Sudan and the collective demands of the Sudanese for rebuilding their nation, their state, and sociopolitical order. But, the Sudanese can only succeed if they can see now, in this unhappy hour, that their long and complex experiences of failure and success do point to matters of considerable weight. These things can also enable them to draw upon a deep repertoire to make sense of a history of experiences, values, and complex inheritances. All of this has yielded a variety of responses that shaped their lifeworld and endeavored to constrain their social sphere. These have been combined with violent actions and reactions that the state, along with the enterprises they involved themselves in, caused either to further certain agendas or to use its power to subjugate each other. Yet they can see through the thin line separating things; they have the potential to reconstruct a civil society. A new generation of Sudanese citizens and a new order are emerging. They can see them "emerging from the outer shadows of these 'zones of waiting' unprecedented"[39] social life within which they can create a space where active and peaceful engagement is vital over the long term. This could be achieved by building up their inner resources to construct their state to meet their all-encompassing self-definition.

But at the same time, counter-assertions and reactions to the October 1964 Revolution and the meanings and the content of this emerging phenomenon have acted, galvanized, and amplified in the counter-revolution where everything is perceived as a threat. Such counter-activist discontents—emerging from a different, bipolar extreme of playing out imagined threats—are explored in ways that may degrade the revolution's content and substance. Already, scholars, pundits, journalists, and think tanks are producing publications, panels, and blogs and are initiating conversations addressing various facets of this "revolutionary spring." These proliferations of that phenomenon, in their elementary form, point to the first impulse toward fundamental change, its complex conversations, and its supporting discourses. The October 1964 Revolution and its legacy gave generations of students a sense of their own power and continued to endow them and the university with the esteem and prestige of an institutional space regarded as the country's seat and flagship of opposition to dictatorship and a mainstay of activism for civil and political rights.

Whereas the student unions operated openly, state terror had erupted from time to time subjecting the leaders of these unions and student activists to harassment and imprisonment. As a result, that phase of the Nimeiri period

39 Jean-Francois Bayart, *Glabal Subjects: A Political Critique of Globalization* (Cambridge: Polity Press, 2007), 268.

provided the Islamist movement with a new generation of party members and activists whose life experiences were shaped and deeply influenced by two conflicting dynamics: the special status of the university and state terror perpetrated by a regime that viewed itself as threatened. Another important dynamic to consider was the mutual violence that both the regime and its opponents exercised against each other and the mistreatment of political opponents combined with the hardships that characterized the Nimeiri period, which opened the door for a culture of violence. This culture of violence was demonstrated in the students' lives by al-Ṭayib Ibrāhim Moḥamed Khair, nicknamed the Iron Rod or Sikha, who was notorious for the use of such a rod against political opponents. Sikha's violent assaults on students at campuses stand as the example and the symbol of the conformation between the Islamist students at institutions of higher education and their opponents, especially the Communists and the Republican Brothers. From the late 1960s through the 1990s, these Islamist students resorted to violence in order to intimidate their opponents and advance their causes. Many students lost their lives in these campus wars. Later, Sikha played a key role in the execution of the coup and afterwards has been an important member of the regime.

This brand of hard violence was complemented by a softer but perhaps more pervasive form of violence. With the tremendous rivalry and antagonism among the Islamists and other political groups, a group of university students among the ranks of the Islamist activists promoted written violence. These students provided campus wallpapers with a language and expressive hostility that complemented Sikha's violent pursuits. This violent style evolved over time to become one of the Islamists' ways of attacking, intimidating, and sometimes assassinating their opponents' characters. As the movement progressed, these unruly students matured with it, and they began to import their tactics from campus wallpapers to newspapers like *Alwan*. Among these students turned journalists were Hussein Khojali and the late Moḥamed Ṭaha Moḥamed Aḥmed, who was kidnapped from his home by unknown kidnappers on September 6, 2006. His body was found decapitated in a remote area of Khartoum. Ṭaha's aggressive style of journalism that the Islamist movement incubated, nurtured, and utilized against its enemies turned against al-Turabi, his son, and the NCP before Ṭaha's tragic death.

That went in tandem with al-Turabi's grand strategy to significantly change the balance in favor of the Islamists, especially after the gains the Communist Party had achieved in the aftermath of the October 1964 Revolution. The fact that the Communist Party "virtually ruled the Sudan in the early post-October months and scored a decisive win over Ikhwan [the Islamists] in the graduate constituencies made Ikhwan even more wary."[40] This happened at a time when the forces of the left appeared to be making progress throughout the Arab and Muslim and in Nasser's Egypt in particular. What the Islamists needed to do "was to fight communism"[41]

---

40 'Abdelwhahab El-Affendi, *Turabi's Revolution*, 76 (see Chapter 3, no. 14).
41 Ibid.

so as to alter that balance. To achieve that goal, the Islamists needed an organized cadre of party artisans to rally the Muslim sentiment in the country behind an Islamic constitution and to work diligently on "the unmasking of the treacherous elements represented by the Sudanese Communist Party."[42] Within such a strategy of reductionism, the Islamists initiated or participated in major violent acts against all shades of what they perceived as part of the Communist other. Hence, violence by the Islamists and their rivals claimed the lives of many students and thousands of other ordinary Sudanese citizens and has continued to blemish the image of the Islamists, as well as other groups that have collaborated with them ever since.

42 Ibid.

Chapter 6
Al-Turabi Islamism and its Webs of Ironies

It was once said, that "believing, with Max Weber, that man [and, presumably, woman] is an animal suspended in webs of significance he [she] himself [herself] has spun, and the analysis of it to be therefore not experimental science in search of law but an interpretive one in search of meaning."[1] One might add that it is not only "man" or "woman" but also human beings and things that create these "webs of significance," and that the meanings generated out of them come with their ironies too. By all means, what has been going on in the Sudan in the field of Islamism, in particular, in the last three decades and the resulting transformations are not isolated phenomena. The way the Islamists assumed power in the Sudan in 1989 through a military coup has provided its own ironies as well; but it has been hardly an issue that would satisfy many, including the Islamists themselves who seek an answer to the difficult question that must be asked again and again: who killed who?—Islamism, religion, or the state? Each one of these has its own identity not only in terms of origin but also in context and field of power. And each has been suspended in their webs of significance and entanglements that mark their places and the way they work within the particular and general Sudanese experience. It is true that the political expectations of the Sudanese populace, from the first day of the coup, were rather modest

Most of the Islamists and some of their leading elite, such as 'Abdel wahāb El-Affendi had higher hopes for a more measured approach to governance that was similar to that of 'Umar ibn 'Abdel 'Aziz, as stated earlier. But they ended up in resentful loud cries: "where is my Islamist dream?" For the Sudanese Islamist experience, this and other kinds of questions, their aggregate of answers and enthused results, and the debate generated out of all the discourses that emerged would lead us to adequately understand why the Sudanese Islamist project in particular heralded toward oblivion a long time ago while other Islamist projects elsewhere were heading the same way. This is not based on comparisons; but rather by looking at the particular extents of the phenomenon's changes that affected the field of production within each one's sociological reality and might define each one's difference. It is true that internal and external changes and the initiative of transformation owe their independent causal and dynamic factors to new modes of thought, and it seems that each century is a gravedigger of one or more "isms." If the nature and causes of the transformation of the

1 Clifford Geertz, *The Interpretation of Culture: Selected Essays* (New York: Basic Books, 1977), 5.

Sudanese experience from disintegration to oblivion are easy to see now, then such projection for the fate of other Islamist experiences may also be easy to observe, whereas rudiments of degeneration of the other ones are grounded in and asserted by each one's field of action. Neither the decline of the Sudanese experience nor the projection for the fate of other Islamisms can be attributed only to the Sudanese people's determination to get rid of Islamism. It also cannot be ascertained that the decline was only a consequential effect of the gradual encroachment that has triggered social change as an integral part of the Sudanese populace's everyday life and the effects of the "quiet encroachment of the ordinary"[2] as people of different classes struggled to survive within their social worlds. The reasons could be external factors related to social space that invoked significant persistence of specific forms and processes of mechanistic causalities inherent in encroachment and sometimes impingement factors that intensified degeneration and debilities of the system itself. In addition, it is the idea that Islamism and its encounter with the state from within as the only ruling regime in the Sunni Muslim world, not from without as an opposition group as happened with other Islamist representations in other Muslim and Middle Eastern countries that might help us to understand the phenomenon and its future. The significance of such an example and the production of different vistas that emerge out of that experience with or without their lessons, values, and conventionality could transpose that discourse and appropriate it for such a projection.

The withering of Sudanese Islamism, therefore, also projects the end of similar forms of Islamism, and our observations of this might help us to conceive a new type of investigation into what might arise to outmode "passé" Islamism, profoundly transform it, and in both cases push it into oblivion or the past. By seriously addressing these issues, this chapter explores the Sudanese Islamist experience within the ironies that came out of its webs of significance.

Mapping and Qualifying These Ironies

The Local

The dramatic event of the 1989 Islamist coup encouraged more scholars to seek a genuinely new framework to study Islamism and the Islamists' thoughts and plans for assuming power. From here comes the big irony suspended in the military coup and its webs of significance. The modern military profession is, by all means, "expert and limited. Its members have specialized competence and lack that competence outside their field."[3] It seems that the Sudanese civilians who

---

2 Asef Bayat, *Life as Politics*, 14 (see Chapter 1, n. 12).

3 Samuel P. Huntington, *The Soldier and the State: The Theory and Politics of Civil-Military Relations* (Cambridge: The Belknap Press of Harvard University Press, 1957), 70.

collaborated, or thought that they might use the military to initiate a coup as a short cut to assume power, never learned the simple lesson that "the task of the military man is to view all problems in terms of fighting efficiency. The moment he finds himself being forced of this clear line on the vagaries of political argument he will be in danger. He will begin to lose the confidence of the politician, who wants his military advice, and he will be false to fighting services, who look to him as their professional leader."[4] Hence, it is incumbent that "the military command must never allow his military judgment to be warped by political expediency."[5] Military institutions of any society "are shaped by two forces: a functional imperative stemming from the threats to the society's security and a societal imperative arising from the social forces, ideologies, and institutions dominant within the society. Military institutions which reflect only social values may be incapable of performing effectively their military function."[6] Moreover, "it may be impossible to contain within society military institutions shaped purely by functional imperatives. The interaction of these forces is the nub of the problem of civil-military relations."[7] Using the coup as a system for change is not only an acceptance to go with the violent logic of the state and one of its institutions—the army—but it is also a restoration of an open project of unmitigated disposition for advancing the cause of violence over all other causes of governance from day one. In this sense the Sudanese Islamists and their leader, by initiating the coup, abandoned their project—*al-Islam hwa al-hal* (Islam is the solution)—and replaced it with another project that says: violence or militarism is the solution.

The web of irony here has many different faces. First, according to ʻAlī al-Ḥaj when Ḥasan al-Turabi came from Paris to Sudan "in June or July 1964, he found members of the Islamists *Haiat al-Shura* council on weeks long deliberation over the viability of a military coup option against the ʻAbboud regime and how to do that."[8] Al-Ḥaj remembers that there was an agreement among the members of *Haiat al-Shura* council on the coup option, and some even suggested robbing local banks for money to finance the coup. Al-Ḥaj, a member of the secretariat team of *Haiat al-Shura* at the time recollected that al-Turabi, who attended his first meeting—as he was immediately included in *Haiat al-Shura*—argued forcefully against the military coup idea, and he successfully won the debate by convincing all members of *Haiat al-Shura* against the military option.

But it seems that al-Turabi had not come to such views from a life of isolation. It appears likely that al-Turabi's peak performance began to spark and sprout. He "was impatient with the constraint imposed on Ikhwan by the elitist organizational

---

4 General Sir Richard N. Gale, "Impact of Political Factors on Military Judgment," *Royal United Service Institution, Journal*, 99 (Feb/Nov 1954): 37.

5 Ibid.

6 Samuel P. Huntington, *The Soldier and the State*, 70.

7 Ibid.

8 ʻAli al-Ḥag Moḥamed, interview by author, audio recording, Bonn, Germany, July 24, 2012.

framework inherited from Egypt, and had been pushing for opening up the movement, either transcending the movement itself and turning it into a pressure group with access to parties, or by joining the other big parties in a united front."[9] And so the web of significance and its ironies that relate to military action might have started to show their trickery ways and different roads in relationships, opportunities, and consequences to ascend up the organization and make himself more visible within the Sudanese political scene. In the course of the anti-coup strategies during the time of rising hate for the 'Abboud military regime, it might have been the smartest way to challenge that distinct enemy by expressing such negative views and attitude against the idea of a military coup. That is what worked perfectly well for al-Turabi later when he was invited to speak at a different setting in the panel organized by the Social Studies Society at the University of Khartoum in 1964. As explained in previous chapters, that brief speech did not take up the Islamist organization alone, but gave him nationwide attention.

Thinking deeply about the coup option might bring us back not only to the Islamist web of violence, but also to the entanglements of the entire weave of al-Turabi's ascendency to power, his downfall, and where these ironies hold each one's yarn. In his book, *al-Ḥaraka al-Islamiyya fi al-Sudan: Dairat al-Ḍow wa khiuot al-Dhalam* (The Islamic Movement in the Sudan: The Light Circle and the Threads of Darkness), al-Maḥboob 'Abdel Salaam argued that it was the circumstances that accompanied al-Nimeiri military coup of May 1969, and the detention of al-Turabi before other main political party's leaders that made him rethink his position on the military coup. Al-Maḥboob, the secretary of external relations for Ḥasan al-Turabi's Popular Congress Party and one of al-Turabi's very erudite disciples, claims that it was Yasin 'Umar al-Imam who tried and failed at an earlier time to persuade the Islamist leadership to plant cells for the movement in the army. However, according to al-Maḥboob, when Ḥasan al-Turabi the Secretary General of the movement and the Islamic Charter Front, found himself to be the first one to be detained in the morning of May 25, 1969, coup "even before the Prime Minster and the minister of defense, although he was a Secretary General of a small party that had not had more than two members in the constituent Assembly [the parliament], he got convinced by the correctness of logic of [Yasin] the Islamist leader of a Marxist background and the falsehood of the logic of the academic members of the party"[10] who opposed the idea of the coup before. In this sense, the 1989 coup that the Islamists chose as a platform for government or what they called *Thawarat al-Ingaz* (salvation revolution) is not revolutionary at all. Of course, calling it salvation does not make it so; nor does calling something a revolution make it so. It is a counter-revolution and a substitution to the promised and advocated statement: *hiya lil allah* (it [the state] is for God). Further, the Islamists have turned their Islamist republic and governance experience into a

9 'Abdel wahāb El-Affendi, *Turabi's Revolution*, 75 (see Chapter 3, n. 14).

10 al-Mahboob 'Abdelsalaam *al-Ḥaraka al-Islamiyya fi al-*Sudan, 24 (see Chapter 1, n. 6).

colossal beast of coercion immediately after their violent takeover of the Sudanese state through the coup. It follows that the first distinction between the two lies in the "lack of legitimacy, that is to say, their [military regime] lack of a moral title to rule,"[11] which invited challenge by other citizens of the country who did not choose the Islamists or favor their regime to rule over them. And if "force creates right," wrote Rousseau, "the effect changes with the cause. Every force that is greater than the first succeeds to its right. As soon as it is possible to disobey with impunity disobedience is legitimate; and the strongest being is always the right, the only thing that matters is to act so as to become the strongest."[12] No wonder the role and pursuit of that state and its ability to invent different types of violent means, or violence as a political project, that included but was not limited to the ghost houses, massive purges of government officials, jihād against its own citizens, and counter-insurgency on the cheap such as the Janjaweed,[13] has become and has been preserved as the institutional framework germane to such practices. As a consequence, what continued to be and consisted of "a nonlinear processes [of violence] in which every effect is a cause of yet another outcome in a complex and endless array of"[14] was the mode and actualization of an innovative inter and intra violence as the symptom and the temperament of the Islamist state and its true normative essence. 'Umar al-Bashir continued to say every now and then "we took it by the gun and who would like to take it from us have to take it by the gun."

Thus, it is not as though the inadequacy of religion and the state remains universally valid. It is also the model of Islamism in itself and by itself—from the first day of the Sudanese Islamists state and within every day of its development—that has been parading Islamism and its path toward oblivion. That is to say that the model of the Islamist state became detached not only from Islam but also from the spirit of a good society, which led to the failure of both the Islamist governance (if there was any) and a nation-state—not based on citizenry—as a political project. That is why, as failure has shown itself at all levels, the Sudanese satire has been very accurate in describing the five pillars of *al-Inqaz*[15] regime as: "*bunia al-Inqaz ala khomsin, ḥalat tawāri, ḥirāst kabāri, noum ijbari, mashi kadari, and banzeen tijari li man istata aliyhi sabelan*" (the five pillars of *al-Ingaz* are as follows: state of emergency, guarding bridges, forced asleep, walking

11 S.E. Finer, *The Man on Horseback: The Role of the Military in Politics* (Boulder, CO: Westview Press, 1988), 12.

12 J.J. Rousseau, *The Social Contract,* Book 1. Chapter 3. Quoted in S.E. Finer, *The Man on Horseback*, 12.

13 See Alex de Waal, "Counterinsurgency on the Cheap," *Review of African Political Economy* 31, no. 102 (December 2004), 716–25.

14 James N. Rosenau, *Distant Proximities: Dynamics Beyond Globalization* (Princeton, NJ: Princeton University Press, 2003), 12.

15 The Hadith says that Islam has five primary obligations, or pillars of faith, that each Muslim must fulfill in his or her lifetime. The Sudanese satire contrasts that by claiming that the regime has five obligations forced upon people which are the fundamentals of the regime.

barefoot, and commercialized petrol for those who could afford it). Later, as the violence of the regime escalated, another version of these pillars circulated: "*ttakul ma tashb'a. telbas maraq'a, tmshi al-Janoob ma targ'a, 'indak ma 'indak tdf'a, taftah khashmak 'einank tatl'a*" (you do not find enough food to eat, you wear rags, you go to the South of the Sudan to die, you have to pay [taxes] whether you have money or not, and you will suffer if you open your mouth). The second distinction between the two also lies in the absurd conviction that led to the Islamists idea of society as one and that the whole society should share one belief system or should be coerced or forcefully organized to do so. This is how the Sudanese Islamists found and organized a common ground with all the shades of *takfiri*[16] groups including Osama bin Laden and Aymen al-Zawahiri and their jihādists whom they hosted, and who exported terror on behalf of the host Sudanese regime to neighboring enemies or Sudanese pro-Saudi Salafis inside the Sudan. Later, and especially after the *mufāṣala*, the ruling Islamists found it useful to encourage a counter-insurgency on the cheap by unleashing some of the neo-Salafi *takfiri* groups against some of the regime's enemies particularly, Ḥasan al-Turabi, al-Sadiq al-Mahdi, and the Sūfi representation. This also sheds some light on why the Islamists before and after the *mufāṣala,* throughout the lifetime of their first and second republics, played the jihādists and global jihād card to secure their position by intimidating their neighboring states and far away enemies in an attempt to force them to submissively collaborate by kneeling before the Islamists in power. In both ways, nothing in the political market including human beings, belief, and the natural world has moral value; but these things could be manipulated, exploited, and taken advantage of until they crumble or subside. The Islamists, in the first instance of their regime, tried to show the world that the theory and practice of their political program could be well advanced through their slogan: *sa nahzim al-Amrican wa Ḥusni al-jaban wa nagiem al-Azan fi al-Vatican* (we will defeat the Americans and coward Husni [Mubārak] and we will call for prayer in the Vatican). However, it would be artificial to explain the Sudanese Islamists' rhetoric on its face value. Looking deeply in their rhetoric within its web of significance and practice one could clearly see the irony of how the two mutually falsify one another.

The Local II: The Great Lie: Withholding of Moral Trustworthiness

The second irony is the result of al-Turabi sending himself to prison the first day of the coup and 'Umar al-Bashir to the Palace. This key moment in the history of the Sudanese Islamists' experience and their state has been viewed with irreverence and turpitude. Regardless of the ploy behind that incident and/or the oversimplifications or misinterpretation of the meaning of that sinister act as recounted by the Islamists, that action by its result and by the way that it was done

16 *Takfir* is declaration to a fellow Muslim to be a disbeliever; while Takfiri groups are those who issue statements to that effect.

gave a practical endorsement to the state and a license for it to turn violent logic into a rule and wreak havoc on human beings. Hence, they laid the groundwork conditions that made the state's violent disciplinary conduct not only possible but it made it the governance on behalf of God. This most ungodly representation of God became an indelible mark that continued to ring true of the vile conduct of the Islamist state. By enduring, however, such sequences of dealings, the Islamists have initiated and legitimized using the state monopoly of violence, its disciplinary apparatus, and the use of force to curtail human rights rather than to preserve them.

The Local III: The Prison

The third irony is that the prison that Ḥasan al-Turabi sent himself to during the first coup of 1989 as a ploy to save himself and his dreamed-of Islamist state from repercussions was the same prison his disciples sent him to when they ousted him during the 1999 palace coup. But this time it was for real and repeatedly as sequel of removing him from power and to shield the same state from what they considered as his vice. Hence, the palace coup against Ḥasan al-Turabi on December 12, 1999, was similar to the 1989 coup, as both radically changed the political environment in the Sudan and to a lesser extent in the wider region by giving an "added value" to the state as "a morally empty space, a set of lifeless procedures, and culturally alien institutions that could be given life"[17] through such violent acts. Both developments gave rise to an uneasy feeling among most Sudanese citizens and political groups, who vigorously debated whether or not the palace coup was merely another ploy or a game the Islamists were playing that was similar to the events of June 30, 1989, when al-Turabi sent himself to prison as a cover-up. However, the resulting developments out of that occurrence exhumed memories of past events not only as a tragedy but also as "a farce."[18] More information about the prison and occultation as an opportunity is provided in chapters 7 and 8.

It was a reminder of December 1965, when al-Turabi, as the principal figure, expelling the 11 elected members of the Communist Party from the parliament and banned the Communist Party altogether. Such a ban was impossible before when "Yahia al-Fadli failed to achieve with the help of the first regime of the parties [1956], and what Abdalla Khalil was, agonizingly, reluctant to do without the advice of his Attorney-General."[19] On December 9 of the same year, a law was enacted that banned the Communist Party and confiscated its property. The Communist Party "decided to take the matter to the Supreme Court and got a ruling

17 Thomas Bloom Hansen, *The Saffron Wave: Democracy and Hindu Nationalism in Modern India* (Princeton, NJ: Princeton University Press, 1999), 50.

18 One of Marx's most quoted statements that history repeats itself: "the first as tragedy, then as farce."

19 Mansour Khalid, *The Government They Deserve: The Role of the Elite in Sudan's Political Evolution* (London: Kegan Paul International, 1990), 222.

against the ban, but the Government decided to ignore it."[20] The same happened when al-Turabi raised his case against the state in 1999.

The second tragedy was the moral dearth of the Islamist regional parties and personalities who hurried to Khartoum in at attempt for reconciliation and mediation between the two warring camps of Sudanese Islamists. Those regional Islamist parties and personalities remained silent through the years when the regime of the Sudanese Islamists was slaughtering, torturing, and annihilating its opponents and waging wars against Sudanese people all over the country. Did the Sudanese reign of terror seem contrary to what those regional Islamists were subjected to in the past? It could not be so; it might be even more. Nevertheless, those high-level Islamists from abroad gave no attention to the decade-long, sharp accusations that continued to fill the regional media and that soon focused both local and international minds on the reality of the situation in the Sudan. It soon became clear that not only the conflict was real, but also the route to the Islamist second republic lacked legitimacy and moral authority the same way the first one did. However, the course of the Islamist movement and its politics, the human beings, the things that created the web of significance, the meanings generated out of railing the movement toward the dethroning of Ḥasan al-Turabi, and directing Islamism toward oblivion started a long time before the first and second coups in 1989 and 1999 respectively. It evolved about four decades before now out of changing patterns and internal and external shifts in the balance of power that provided for new, young actors to emerge. However, we cannot understand that unless we carefully follow the route of the social commotions from which all that emerged, sometimes unnoticed, sometimes by luck, and sometimes by careful calculation. But in most a momentous way, certain groups of younger Islamists claiming no particular intellectual or ideological loyalty expanded in place through time. Most of them were well educated but lived by the dormant value of their individual ambitions and the nature and nurture mindset that Ḥasan al-Turabi taught them. In the ultimate paradox, they deposed him while they continued to maintain his style and follow his conduct.

The Regional

The fourth irony relates to the other political Islam or the emergence of the neo-Salafi Islamism and its love-hate relationship with al-Turabi Islamism. Perhaps the two inexplicable sets of ironies are those that stemmed from the rise of Salafism and Shi'ism, each within its own terms, together within each one's sentiment toward the other, and within the Sudanese socio-religious field of action in relation to al-Turabi Islamism, its Islamists, and their political practice. The irony is that we cannot tell who belongs with whom within these warring groups and for what purpose. As a general rule, many have felt that the Salafi tradition within its different representations as a nonmovement was

20 Ibid.

without a clear political program. Hence, as alliances between or collaborations among different parties are experiences of willed association, Salafist groups are expected to shy away from becoming involved in the political fray. With the shifting relationships between al-Turabi Islamists and the neo-Salafi Islamists, that is no longer the case. The second irony is that Sudan for its entire history has been perceived a Shi'a-free zone. That is no longer true for the post-Khomeini political Shi'ism. The third irony was that, since its early days, al-Turabi's Islamism rejected Salafisim and Shi'ism within their different orientations. Simultaneously, none of these orientations was known for its history or relationship with or sympathy for Sudanese Islamism and especially Ḥasan's al-Turabi who never hesitated to denigrate both and consider them as relics of the past.[21] Given the importance the system of meaning in the Sudan, until very recently, the terms Salafi and Salafiyya were associated with Ansar al-Sunnah or Wahabi groups and individuals. As a general rule, Ansar al-Sunnah or Wahabi in the Sudan were known for spreading their messages through *al-dawa* (preaching) and leading severe attacks on the Sufiyya, their rituals, and their religious practices. That is why, however, a great sector of the Sudanese Muslim community and, in particular, the Sufiyya have been often suspicious of the Ansar al-Sunnah and consider their agenda as a deviation from the Islam that they knew if not offensive to what the majority of Sudanese Muslims follow. Al-Makawi, the most famous of the Samaniya Sūfi *ṭariqa* bards, accused the Salafiyya of ingratitude in his very famous *madha* (poem), which he dedicated for his Shaikh Abdel Mahmoud Nur al-Diem. He describes such a person as *jaḥid al-fadul shin basu* (what is significance of the thankless).

The Islamists in power after 1989 presented a situation where the two religio-political representations, the Salafiyya and the Sufiyya, the nemeses to the Islamists and their state. Hence, they were involved in bitter institutionalized struggle against each other The Islamists in their new state waged a war of words on the Wahabis. They described their king as *khainan al-Haramien instead of khadim al-Haramien* (the traitor instead of the custodian of the two Holy Mosques of Mecca and Medina). They also described the Saudi royal family as *Yahood Yahood Al Saud*, meaning that the Saudi royal family members are Jews in disguise. The Ansar al-Sunna groups in the Sudan became very strong in their opposition to the regime while their benefactors in Saudi Arabia set their sight on Ḥasan al-Turabi whom they accused of not only being secular but also being an apostate as explained here before. Moreover, a new alliance between the Sudanese Wahabi group and al-Turabi's sworn enemies from the Muslim Brothers was forged around the opposition to the new Islamists regime. Ansar al-Sunna's mosques in Khartoum became the preferred platforms for Muslim Brothers preachers, such as Dr. al-Hibir Nour al-Diam, who attracted more and more audiences not only for prayer but also for listening to bitter attacks on the regime. With such

21 See Ḥasan al-Turabi, *Islamic Fundamentalism in the Sunna and Shia Worlds* (London: The Sudan Foundation, 1997).

antagonism and tremendous rivalry between the Sudanese and the Saudi states, a more controversial development took place in 1991 when the Khartoum regime gave refuge to Osama bin Laden as a prominent guest after he fell out with his Saudi ruling royal family over their support for the United States during the US's first Gulf war against Saddam Hussein. The presence of Osama bin Laden and his collaborators, including Ayman al-Zawahiri and their jihādists from the Afghan Arabs, turned the Sudanese field into a place for an open war waged by proxy between Saudi Arabia represented by its Wahabi followers and the Sudanese regime represented by its ally Osama bin Laden.

Another development that coincided with arrival of bin Laden, the Afghan Arab jihādists, and others to the Sudan was the deportation to the country of some the Sudanese Sururi Salafi individuals from Saudi Arabia and other neighboring Gulf Arab countries. The Sururis, or *al-Sururiyyyun* in Arabic, are named after their founder, the Syrian ex-Muslim Brother Moḥamed Surur Niyaf Zayn al-'Abidin who belonged to one of the groups that emerged with the broader social movement in Saudi Arabia and some Gulf countries called *al-Sahwa al-Islamiyya* (the Islamic Awakening). The Sururi *jamaa'ah*, or group, that introduced a new generation of Saudi public intellectuals during and after 1980s, most notably including Salman al-'Awdah, Aid al-Qarni, Safar al-Hawali, and Nasir al-'Umar, emerged as a *takfiri* and developed later into a dissident jihādist group that mixed forms of Sayyid Qutb Islamism while remaining within the confines of the Wahabi Salafism. The Sururi, in particular, and the other *Sahwa* groups directed their hostility first toward what they depicted as secularists. They relied "on a substantial library of ideological texts inherited from early theorists such as Moḥammad Qutb and 'Abd al-Rahman al-Dawsari and consistently developed by contemporizes like Safar al-Hawali."[22] The Sayyid Qutb ideas and the ideology behind it and the Saudi educational system were behind the generation that called itself *jil Al-Sahwa* (the Sahwa generation). This generation made this ideology "operational in the late 1980s. Under its tutelage, the Sahwa generation soon saw itself as the collective victim of vast 'secular-Masonic plot.'"[23] The Sururis brought in their intellectual group via their publication, *al-Bayan*, "non-Saudi thinkers," which demonstrated the extension of the Sururi network beyond the kingdom's borders. Among them were "two substantial figures, the Egyptian Gamal Sultan and the Sudanese Ja'afar Shaikh Idris, both Islamists were critics of the Muslim Brotherhood in their respective counties because of their stronger adhesion to Wahahabi precepts."[24] In fact, Ja'afar Shaikh Idris was not a critic of the Muslim Brotherhood in the Sudan, but rather a sworn enemy of Ḥasan al-Turabi and his Islamism as previously noted. Within the tremendous rivalry and antagonism among the born-again Sudanese

22 Stėphane Lacroix, *Awakening Islam: The Politics of Religious Dissent in Contemporary Saudi Arabia* (Cambridge, MA: Harvard University Press, 2011), 152.

23 Ibid.

24 Ibid.

Sururis, who lived in Saudi Arabia, the *takfir*[25] of Ḥasan al-Turabi took shape in publications and continued in different forms of venomous verbal and written attacks ever since. Another old enemy of Ḥasan al-Turabi was Zayn al-'Abidin al-Rikabi, who "turned over the faculty of *D'awa* and Communication of Imam University ... [into a place] where the Sahwis had an overwhelming majority."[26]

By 1989, the year the Sudanese Islamists assumed power through a military coup, things began to change in all directions for Sudan and Saudi Arabia, especially after 1991 and the Gulf War. Chief among these developments were the Sudanese Islamists' establishment of their first Islamist republic (by hijacking the state) in the Sunni Muslim world. This event coalesced and grew with the presence of Osama bin Laden in the Sudan "hijacking the *Sahwa* protest and its symbols,"[27] to initiate the ideology of global jihād. By that time the al-Sahwa movement itself "was running out of steam in Saudi Arabia ... primarily to state repression";[28] and the Sudanese Sururi preachers in Saudi Arabia and the Gulf were deported to their country. Top among those deported was Moḥamed 'Abdel Karim, the former imam and preacher of Al-Kawthar Mosque in Jeddah, who was deported in 1993. Others included 'Abdel-Hai Yusuf, the former imam and preacher at the Moḥamed bin Zayed Mosque in Abu Dhabi, who was deported to Sudan the same year, and Mudathar Aḥmed Ismail. All of those Salafi jihādists studied in Saudi universities, graduated, and worked there or in the Gulf countries before being deported to Sudan. To the surprise of many academics in the Sudan, Moḥamed 'Abdel Karim, 'Abdel Hai Yusuf, and 'Ala' al-Din al-Zaki were offered important positions in different departments at the University of Khartoum. They held positions at the university with other religious scholars who graduated from Islamic universities in Saudi Arabia and publicly carried out missionary and political activities through formal networks of charity organizations, such as *Mishkat* Charity Organization.[29]

25 The term *takfir* is derived from the Arabic Qur'anic term *kufr* and *kafir* (to accuse), or it refers to the practice of one Muslim declaring another Muslim an unbeliever or *kafir*. The term is reinvented to describe a situation of excommunication of a group or an individual. Such individuals and groups who excommunicate others are labeled as *kufar* or *kafiroon*. The term gained currency in the public discourse and the Arabic and later the international media after 1970s in connection to Sayyid Qutb ideology and, in particular connection to, the Egyptian Islamist Shukri Mustafa and his group *Jama'at al-Muslimin*, which became labeled by the media as *al-Takir wa al-Hijra* [excommunication and exile]. Specific Sunni Islamist groups in Egypt and neo-Salafi groups in the Sudanese are described as *takfiris*.

26 Stẻphane Lacroix, *Awakening Islam*, 44.

27 Ibid.

28 Ibid.

29 For more about their different activities, see a report written by Dr. Einas Aḥmed, *The Rise of Militant Salafism in Sudan:* http://www.cedej-eg.org/IMG/pdf/Einas_Aḥmed_-_The_Rise_of_Militant_Salafism_in_Sudan.pdf.

Despite what might look like similarities between these neo-forms of what could be called jihādi Islamism and al-Turabi Islamism, there is a divisive difference, and as explained elsewhere here, that difference is crucial. The most important similarities between Islamism and jihādism in general is that they "share a common premise, namely that Islam and politics are one and the same; they both believe that their receptive programs represent paths that are distinct from and independent of the religious and political establishments; that unlike the later, the Islamic principles that Islamists and jihādis live by are uncompromised by the ephemeral interests."[30] If that is part of the irony, the similarity on which one can see the emerging relationships among neo-Salafi Islamists, al-Turabi Islamism, and their first Islamist republic is their mutual enmity to the Saudi regime and its official council of *'ulamā'*. But beyond the very principles of similarities and dissimilarities among these groups, the foundation of any form of political connection among them was called into question. Nevertheless, once settled in Sudan, Moḥamed 'Abdel Karim, in addition to the university position, was given access to the Sudanese government-owned TV to preach in public nonpolitical Salafi ideas. At the same time, he began to gather young Sudanese at his mosque in al-Kalaka, whom he organized as *al-Jabhat al-Islamiyya al-Musalaha* (the Armed Islamic Front).

About the same time, what emerged then, by the rise of the Sudanese and the bin Laden's *takfiri* Salafism in Sudan were different forms of violence and new lines of conflict together with fissures within each one of these groups. *Takfiri* hostilities toward each group not only surprised the Sudanese society, but it alarmed its urban members. The first violent act from what the Sudanese described as the local *al-Takfir wal-Hijra*[31] took place in the al-Gezira region in a place called *Compo* (camp) 10 about 250 miles south of Khartoum. At the end of 1993, declared contemporary Muslim rulers as *ṭawāqhit* (tyrants and apostates) and the state as *kafira*. They also proclaimed that the acceptance of government-issued documents such as passports, citizenship cards, identity cards, and the use of paper currency as manifestations of *bid'aa* or heresy. Hence, 'Abdel Karim's young followers planned their *hijra* by walking on foot to distance themselves from that society and settling in that place which is called Compo 10. Upon their

30 Nelly Lahoud, *The Jihādis' Path to Self-Destrucrion* (New York: Columbia University Press, 2010), 106.

31 Generally translated into English "Excommunication and Exodus," but most of the time as "excommunication and emigration." It is the popular name given to a radical Islamist Egyptian group who call themselves *Jama'at al-Muslimin.* It was founded by Shukri Mustafa in the 1960s as an offshoot of Muslim Brotherhood inspired by Sayyid Qutb's ideas of *'uzla*. Although the group was crushed by Egyptian security forces after its members kidnapped and murdered the Egyptian minster of Islamic Endowments Moḥamed Hussian al-Zahabi in 1977. Today, it is believed, *Takfir wal-Hijra* has members or supporters, not related to Egypt, in several other countries including Sudan allied to Al-Qaeda.

arrival there, some of the village, most of the follow al-Tiganiyya Ṭariqa, residents reported to the authorities the presence of an armed group in the village. The local authorities demanded the group to surrender their arms. Following their view that obedience to the state police is a heresy, they refused. A clash ensued, which led to the death of the group's emir, 'Awad Jumm'a Sayla, and a number of his followers, along with the death of some members of the local police force. Jumm'a Sayla was one of 'Abdel Karim's close disciples. 'Abdel Karim was arrested after that event and charged with illegal acquisition of arms hidden at his al-Kalakla Mosque.

The next year in 1994, a group of Arab Afghans under the leadership of a Libyan jihādist and one of Osama bin Laden's personal bodyguards, 'Abdul Raḥman Al-Khulaifi, carried out a massacre of 'Ansar al-Sunnah members in Omdurman. A similar event happened in a Wad Madani Ansar al-Sunnah Mosque as explained before. Even though these Salafi jihādists claimed they were not organized within political parties or militias, their video and cassette recording, as well as their mosque speeches reflected the skill and military experience of the Afghan Arabs who came to Sudan, and their militaristic activities escalated. As a result, Sudan witnessed several cases of bloody violence among the Salafis themselves, which later extended outward toward other groups. Moḥamed 'Abdel Karim and his disciples, together with his other Sururi Salafi jihādists, introduced a new form of violent fiery speeches at their mosques where they emphasized religious fervor rather than *d'awa* or education that traditional Ansar al-Sunnah of Shaikh al-Hadiyya were known for. In addition to the mosque, they used old and new communication and media systems including cassette and video tapes recordings, YouTube, and other social media. In their speeches, they emphasize *fatwa*s of *takfir*, that denounced high-level personalities and organizations as apostates and heretics. One of the most famous cases in this field was the statement Abu al-Dardaa al-Ṣadiq Ḥasan issued in which he called for killing some of the Sudanese journalists and opinion writers whom he accused of being apostates. In 1995, Moḥamed 'Abdel Karim distributed a cassette-recorded tape entitled "*Farfarat Zindeeq*" (a convulsion of a hypocrite) in which he declared Dr. Ḥasan al-Turabi a heretic and demanded his execution. Shortly thereafter, other *fatwa*s were issued declaring the heresy of anyone who joined or had already joined the Sudan People's Liberation Movement led by the late John Garang. Moreover, these *fatwa*s continuously produced to demean other political personalities, secular political parties, trade unions, and civil society organizations. Paradoxically enough, they accused the ruling NCP of being secular. Moreover, they issued a *fatwa* that declared participation in the country's elections as a heresy because democracy for them was *bid'aa* (an innovation) and accordingly elections were considered *haram* (forbidden) or a heresy. In 2006, the jihādists were accused of killing journalist Moḥamed Ṭaha Moḥamed Aḥmed whom they denunciated with blasphemy.

After *al-mufāṣala*, both 'Ali 'Uthmān and the Sururi Salafis looked for a nemesis as a rallying point. They both rallied around a common enemy, and al-Turabi was that common enemy. The escalating armed and a civil opposition to the regime eroded the power of the Islamist state and its rhetorical stance. That was when the Salafis began to gain more political momentum as its leaders started to get involved in a series of violent acts, or they instigated violence by making speeches or issuing *fatwa*s that led to such acts. Such activities included *fatwa*s that declared the Shi'a as heretics and asked the Sudanese government, in a press conference, to shut down the Iranian embassy and the Iranian Cultural Center in Khartoum. Some *fatwa*s also asked the Sudanese government to collect and burn Shi'a books on display in a wing of the 2006 Khartoum Book Fair, as some of these books were considered, by the Salafi spokesperson as disparaging to Prophet Moḥamed's companions and his wife 'Aisha.

In in a much-publicized case in November 2007, the Salafi imams denounced her during Friday prayers and lead angry demonstrators across Khartoum to demand the execution of British teacher Gillian Gibbons. Miss Gibbon, an English teacher in the Sudanese Unity High school, was accused of insulting Islam and his Prophet for naming a teddy bear Moḥamed.

They renewed their denunciation of Ḥasan al-Turabi of heresy because, he said in one of his public lectures, women could lead both men and women as imam in group prayer. Moḥamed 'Abdel Karim publicly called for implementing *hud al-Rida* (apostasy capital punishment) on him. Moḥamed 'Abdel Karim and other Salafi jihādists issued another *fatwa* declaring Sadiq al-Mahdi, leader of Umma Party and Imam of the Sudanese Ansar, an apostate for his unorthodox views regarding women's equal right in inheritance. Other violent acts committed by the jihādists included the vital shooting of the US diplomat John Granville and his driver by a young *takfiri* group on New Year's Eve in 2008. The four men sentenced to death for Granville's murder escaped from prison in 2009. In September 2009, during the opening ceremony of the Communist Party headquarters in Khartoum, some of Moḥamed 'Abdel Karim's followers barged into the inaugural event and clashed with the gathering audience. Later, 'Abdel Karim declared members of the Sudanese Communists as heretics, and he asked the government to ban the party and stop off its activities.

One of the recent violent acts attributed to the jihādists was the clash that took place between them and a group of Sūfis during the *mawlid* (birthday of the Prophet Moḥamed) celebrations on January 31, 2012. Many bystanders were injured before the Sudanese police arrived to stop the fighting. As Salafi groups became more politically involved, 'Ali 'Uthmaān took his relationship with them a step further. In 2004, the first international conference for the Islamic *dawa* was convened in Khartoum under his sponsorship. The conference, which brought together member organizations of Salafi jihādists from different parts of the globe, was followed by the establishment of *Majlis Ahl al-Qibla* (Council of the People of the Qibla [direction that should be called when Muslim pray]). This new Salafi-jihādist Comintern is a reminder and may be an alternative of Ḥasan al-Turabi's defunct *al-Mu'tamar as-sh'abi al-'Arabi al-Islami* (the Popular Arab-Islamic Conference [PAIC]). The conference was followed by the establishment of *Haiat 'ulamā' al-Sudan* (The Sudanese Bureau of *'ulamā'*) to add to already existing structures; 'Abdel Ḥai Yusuf became its deputy secretary, and 'Abdel Karim was its member. The Bureau became the regime's scarecrow that distributed *takfir fatwas* against whoever the regime wanted to scare or intimidate. At the same time, this new body added to other state structures that include senior Salafis in its boards. These bodies include, "the College of Islamic Jurisprudence, *Mujamm'a al-Fiqh al-Islami*. Dr. 'Abdel Kareem is a member of the Consultative Committee for the minister of Religious Affairs and Properties. Dr. 'Abdel al-Hai Yousouf is a member of the College for Islamic Jurisprudence, Dr. 'Alaa al-Din al-Zaaki is a member of the Committee for Drafting the Curriculum in the Ministry for Higher education."

In so arguing, both sets of government manipulation appeared to be important policies for intimidating its enemies through *takfir* and the jihādist feeling of success in establishing the new Comintern as Moḥamed Sarur Bin Nayif Zayn al-Abidin. The founder of Saruri Salafist orientation became a regular visitor to Khartoum, and he was hosted by his former Sudanese disciple Moḥamed 'Abdel Karim. These developments may explain the speculations that within the growing political, economic, and security challenges that there might have been a window of opportunity for the neo-Salalfi Islamists to emerge as an alternative Islamist party that could have contradicted the program that the rebels, liberals, and secular groups adopted to provide an Islamic opposition that could have inherited the regime of President 'Umar al-Bashir.

The Global

Through the better part of the lifetime of the first Islamist Republic, from 1989 until 2000, events graphically illustrated that the impulse and rhetorical stance of the Islamists and their state went far beyond a mere ideological rage. In many cases, there were efforts toward what some perceived as instigation of a global jihād or open hostility toward what they described as *al-istikbar al-'alami* (the international arrogance) in a direct reference to the West and the United States in particular. Every now and then, the Khartoum official media reminded the Sudanese population that *Ameryca qud dana 'azabouha* (America's suffering will come soon).

But the Khartoum global jihād era and its web of significance had its ironies too. Mansoor Ijaz[32] has written about the role he played between the Sudanese

32 Mansoor Ijaz (1961–) is an American-Pakistani businessperson, an investment financier, and founder and chairperson of Crescent Investment Management LLC, a New York investment partnership since 1990. His firm's partnership includes retired General James Alan Abrahamson, former director of President Reagan's Strategic Defense Initiative. Between 1993 and 1996, he was part of a select group who claimed to have been "friends of Bill" Clinton. He wrote extensively about his role as a broker between the Sudanese Islamist regime and the American government. He claims that his role was supported by the American Ambassador in Khartoum, Timothy Carney, 1995–1997. Moreover, it has

Islamist regime and the American government. He has also testified on the issue before the Judiciary Committee of the United States House of Representatives and at congressional hearings, and he appeared on TV shows. In his 1996 testimony before the US Congress, Ijaz submitted a then recent letter sent by President 'Umar al-Bashir to Representative Lee Hamilton (D-NH), the ranking Democrat on the House Foreign Affairs Committee at the time. In that letter, al-Bashir stated that "we extend an offer to the FBI's Counterterrorism units and any other official delegations which your government may deem appropriate, to come to the Sudan and work with [us] in order to assess the data in our possession and help us counter the forces your government, and ours, seek to contain."[33] That might be in reference to the extensive files on al-Qaeda that the Sudan gathered during the time bin Laden stayed in the Sudan. Ijaz claimed that he discussed the letter with Secretary of State Madeleine Albright, Clinton National Security Advisor Sandy Berger, and Susan Rice, who served as President Clinton's Assistant Secretary of State for African Affairs, but he had no success. According to the *Christian Science Monitor*, Ijaz provided a paper with what appeared to be copies of letters from Dr./*Shaikh* Ḥasan al-Turabi, who was considered then the real power behind the Islamist regime in Sudan, offering President Clinton a bid to extradite bin Laden to the US to back his assertions. In more details, Ijaz, wrote about his discussion with Qutbi al-Mahdi, Former Head of the External Security Organization. Ijaz claimed that the purpose of his meeting with al-Mahdi was "to see if we could glean any insights into the data Sudan has on those who have been attending the Popular Arab & Islamic Conference meetings convened by (Sudan's theological leader Ḥasan) Turabi." Ijaz quoted Qutbi telling him, "as you recall, during our August meeting, I told you I thought this data could be invaluable in genuinely assessing terrorism risk from Sudan and neighboring countries." Ijaz explains that, Qutbi's "central contention is that Sudan is prepared to share data on those people attending the conferences and belonging to banned groups, such as Hamas, Hezbollah, Egyptian Islamic Jihād, al-Jamaah Islamiyah, and others, if we are prepared to genuinely engage and incent the Sudan away from its present course." Qutbi al-Mahdi, according to Ijaz, complained bitterly about repeated efforts to communicate with the administration, which are as I understand it, being blocked at very low levels because of what he called "blind spots." Ijaz claims that al-Mahdi showed him "some files in which the data seemed pretty compelling—names, bio data like dates and places of birth, passport copies to show nationality, recent travel itineraries in some cases, and a brief description of each individual to delineate which groups they claim loyalties to." Ijaz maintained

---

been understood that Ijaz has had ties with the CIA and its former director James Woolsey. Many media reports say he negotiated as a private citizen with the Clinton administration in April 1997, when the Sudan offered to share intelligence data on al-Qaeda, bin Laden, and other terrorist groups.

33 http://www.historycommons.org/entity.jsp?entity=madeleine_albright April 5, 1997: US Again Not Interested in Sudan's Al-Qaeda Files.

in short, "it seemed to me everything we discussed in August was available. I strongly suggest we test the Sudanese on the data, perhaps even try to get at the data on an unconditional basis."[34] The irony here is that the Sudanese Islamist state, the first and only Islamist regime in the entire Sunni Muslim world, gave global jihādists the opportunity to build an infrastructure and operational base, but it is also put them, Islamism itself, and their actors on sale.

It is further ironic that global jihād can be seen both in the web of significance of Islamism and its intangibleness with al-Turabi's Islamist grand scheme of the civilizational project, its external extension, and its open market for sale, with its salesmen and brokers. That market was not open only to the United States, but it was open to Britain, France, Saudi Arabia, and who knows what others. In April 1990, *mutamar f'āliyat al-Umma* (The Congress for the Umma Events) was inaugurated in Khartoum in front of a big attendance of Islamist leaders, leaders of liberation movements, activists, and other political leaders from different parts of the world.

But even before inviting other Islamists to an Umma Congress or an "Islamist Comintern," al-Turabi jubilantly shared his vision with other Islamists worldwide that the demise of that brand of communism coincided with what he believed to be the promise of an emerging new Islamist order that would liberate the entire human race "from the clutches of all kinds of material, political, occult, or psychological control."[35] After the first phase of secret battle between him and his disciples who kept him in prison for more than the time agreed upon under house arrest after that, al-Turabi began touring the world advocating the Sudanese Islamist state model would act as a launching point for "pan-Islamic rapprochement … proceeding from below."[36] He argued that that model "would radiate throughout the Muslim World."[37] Hence, al-Turabi's laborious work in which he diligently spent time and effort explaining might not have been synonymous with the model he left behind at home. He argued that "if the physical export of the model is subject to Islamic limitations in deference to international law, the reminiscence of the classical Khilāfah and the deeply entrenched Islamic traditions of free migration (*hijra*) and fraternal solidarity would make such a state a focus of pan-Islamic attention and affection."[38] This

34 Mansoor Ijaz, "The Clinton Intel Record: Deeper Failures Revealed," *National Review Online*: http://www.nationalreview.com/articles/206745/clinton-intel-record/mansoor-ijaz#.

35 Moḥamed E. Ḥamdi, *The Making of an Islamic Political Leader*, 14 (see Chapter 3, n. 22).

36 Dr. Ḥasan al-Turabi. "Islamic Fundamentalism in the 'Sunna' and 'Shia' Worlds," Part One: Press Conference Given by Dr. Turabi in Madrid August 2, 1994 (Religion File No. 6, The Sudan Foundation, 1998). Available at http://www.sufo.demon.co.uk/reli006.htm.

37 Ibid.

38 Ibid.

is because Ḥasan al-Turabi, the "present growth of Islamic revivalism means a sharper sense of inclusive-exclusive identity, a deeper experience of the same culture and stronger urge for united action, nationally and internationally."[39] What was that formative period for, which he further referred and elaborated that "once a single fully-fledged Islamic state is established, the model would radiate throughout the Muslim world."[40] He did not mentioned that in name or implicitly.

But when and how does that become sufficiently possible to generate the momentum toward that state? Whatever such a situation might indicate, al-Turabi made some attempts toward a tipping point in that direction. By its inadequacies, al-Turabi transformed the Sudanese new state and its capital Khartoum into a hub and base of operations for receiving, training, and providing a sanctuary for a network of radical individuals and groups from different parts of the Muslim world. Osama bin Laden, his four wives, children, Ayman al-Zawahiri and his Tanzim al-Jihād[41] group, and more than 1,000 Afghan Arabs who chose Sudan "for two main reasons. First, the restless, radicalized veterans of the Afghan war were unwelcome in most Arab countries but Sudan left its doors open. Second, bin Laden liked Sudan's politics."[42] On the other side, the official account of the justification of that situation was that "the Sudanese accepted bin Laden as an investor."[43] It might be true that he was an investor and a business person in the Sudan. However, he "had never really ceased running his terrorist networks."[44] CIA Director George Tenet of the CIA later commented in his book *At the Center of the Storm: My Years at the CIA* that "the then-obscure name 'Osama bin Laden' kept cropping up in the intelligence traffic. ... [the CIA] spotted bin Laden's tracts in the early 1990s in connection with funding other terrorist movements. They didn't know exactly what this Saudi exile living in Sudan was up to, but they knew

---

39 Ibid.

40 Ibid.

41 Tanzim al-Jihād or al-Jihād was formed in 1980 from a merger of two clusters of Islamist groups: a Cairo branch, under the leadership Moḥamed 'Abd-al-Salaam Faraj, and an upper Egypt branch under the leadership of Karam Zuhdi. Faraj wrote the 1980 short book titled *al-Faridah al-Ghaiba* (The Neglected Obligation). He coordinated the assassination of the Egyptian President Anwar al-Sadat in 1981.

Ayman al-Zawahiri and his Egyptian contingent fled to Pakistan and Afghanistan to help the *Mujahideen* there and escape persecution at home after they were released from prison. They became the brain trust of al-Qaeda. Bin Laden, al-Zawhiri, and their jihādists moved to Sudan after the 1989 coup. Later, al-Zawahiri became the second person of al-Qaeda and later its leader after the death of bin Laden.

42 David Rose, "The Osama Files," *Vanity Fair* (January 2002), http://www.vanityfair.com/politics/features/2002/01/osama200201.

43 Ibid.

44 Richard Miniter, *Losing Bin Laden: How Bill Clinton's Failures Unleashed Global Terror* (Washington, DC: L. Regnery Publishing, 2003), 15.

it was not good."[45] Bin Laden "rented a number of houses and bought several large parcels of land that would be used for training."[46]

Ayman al-Zawahiri and his Tanzim al-Jihād were already in the Sudan. He bought a farm north of the capital. The neighbors began complaining about the sound of explosions coming from the untilled fields. Bin Laden was being explicit when he brought "bulldozers and other heavy equipment, announcing his intention to build a three hundred-kilometer road in eastern Sudan as a gift to the nation. The leader of the Sudan greeted him with garlands of flowers."[47] But he was implicit when he brought and used "an $80,000 satellite phone and al-Qaeda members used radios to avoid being bugged."[48] Based on testimony of former bin Laden aides in the United States during the trial, especially that of Jamal Aḥmed Al-Fadl,[49] "bin Laden appears to control a sophisticated international network of operatives and has developed links to other terrorism organizations around the world."[50] The London Times, however, claimed that "Bin Laden is mistaken in his belief that satellite phones cannot be monitored; a satellite phone he bought in 1996 will be monitored as well."[51]

But there were divergences, convergences, and several consequences that flowed from that grand scheme that translated into new policies by al-Turabi and the Islamists' regime in the Sudan and bin Laden and his al-Qaeda "government" during the time he was in the Sudan. While the regime continued granting Sudanese citizenship to anyone who might not meet the eligibility conditions. This provision was said to have been intended to help solve the problems of

45 George Tenet, *At the Center of the Storm: My Years at the CIA* (New York: HarperColins, 2007), 100.

46 Lawrence Wright, *Looming Tower: al-Qaeda and the Road to 9/11* (New York: Knopf, 2006), 164.

47 Ibid.

48 History Commons, http://www.historycommons.org/context.jsp?item=a98saifchechnya.

49 Jamal Aḥmed al-Fadl is a Sudanese member of al-Qaeda. He testified for the prosecution in in 2001. He was recruited to bring money for the *mujahideen* in Afghanistan, as he claimed in his testimony through al-Farouq Mosque in Brooklyn in US in the mid 1980s. He was sent to Peshawar, Pakistan, to become a "senior employee" of al-Qaeda. He worked for Maktab al-Khidmat, the Services Bureau, which was run by 'Abdallah 'Azam and Osama bin Laden, to help new recruits when they came to Afghanistan. Al-Fadl became a business agent for al-Qaeda in the Sudan when bin Laden moved there, but he resented receiving a salary of only $500 a month while some of the Egyptians in al-Qaeda were given $1,200 a month. In his testimony, he admitted that he had embezzled about $110,000 from bin Laden. When discovered, Fadl then defected and became an informant for the United States.

50 See court transcript: http://www.pbs.org/wgbh/pages/frontline/shows/binladen/bombings/trial.html.

51 *History Commons*, http://www.historycommons.org/context.jsp?item=a020598sudanletter.

prominent Islamic activists who were persecuted in their own countries and were needed by Sudan. By 1994, the *la e lahila ila Allah* (no God but God) passport was deliberated on by the parliament regarding what action to take toward more than one million Africans, most of whom were Muslims, living in the country but who were not eligible for Sudanese nationality. The Chairman of the Legal Affairs Committee in the National Assembly, Ḥasan al-Beli, stated that "our nationality and passport under Shari'a is *la ilaha illa Allah* 'No God but Allah'[52] and Sudan is an open country for all Muslims especially those who fight for the Islamic state and those who are persecuted in their own countries and who look to Sudan as a safe haven."[53] This went hand-in-hand with the developments of emerging strategies fashioned out of the policy of the regime which expected to work in coordination with the host global Islamist allies as they expected to work together and to draw support from each other. The Sudanese Islamists under the direction of al-Turabi, Secretary General of PAIC, established a new international organization that claimed the leadership of the world Islamic movement. After April 1991, al-Turabi organized PAIC in Khartoum and called for its first meeting, which was attended by about 500 delegates. According to the British news magazine *The Economist*, the PAIC "was the culmination of a quarter–century of study, political activity, and international travels by Turabi during which he had met with the Islamists of the Muslim world where his rhetoric and ability were acknowledged in the exclusive fraternity."[54] The delegates at these meetings represented various Islamist groups from around the world, hoping to promote the Sudanese capital as a major center in the Islamic world and to claim the leadership of the world Islamic movement. According to al-Turabi, the PAIC represented a radical alternative to the Organization of the Islamic Conference (OIC) "led by intellectuals and not reactionary traditionalists." On the other side, Osama bin Laden and the pan-Islamic brigades who came to Afghanistan from different parts of the Muslim world had returned to their countries after the defeat of the Soviets and their allies in Afghanistan. This first generation of Arab Afghans who received training in warfare techniques in Afghanistan and forged through their experiences an Islamist ideology of global jihād based on armed struggle, found in the Sudan a base—which I call the federated al-Qaeda—for spreading this ideology. I call it federated because it acted as an autonomous entity with a high degree of independence from the Sudanese state. The strategic location of the Sudan made it an ideal place for the nascent al-Qaeda to build a power base and start to operate in a certain manner so as to influence change in the Arab and Muslim world. The Sudanese regime gave shelter to Osama bin Laden, Ayman al-Zawahiri, and global jihādists to use the Sudanese territory as their base of operations. This new kind of activism and the politics that emerged out of it had

52 That indicates that for Muslims, no passport is needed to enter the Sudan.

53 Quoted in Ali Dinar's *Sudan News and Views*, 4 (1994).

54 Arthur L. Lowrie, ed., *Islam, Democracy, the State and the West: A Round Table with Dr. Ḥasan Turabi* (Tampa, FL: The World & Islam Studies Enterprise, 1993), 55.

invoked feelings of fear at home and alarm and frustration abroad, especially when the Sudan's Arab and African neighbors started accusing the Khartoum regime of deliberately acting to destabilize the region by battling these countries through the infiltration of "trained terrorists" and by giving different types of assistance to internal radical Islamists groups actively engaged in the undermining of the security of governments in these countries.

The PAIC consolidated al-Turabi's position as the leader of and spokesperson for the revolutionary global Islamist movement. According to al-Turabi, the quick success of this global Islamist movement has turned "the Islamic phenomenon into a mass movement." He elaborates, that "it is no longer Islamic movements; it is now Islamic masses who have taken over control." This expansion of global Islamism territorially and ideologically introduced an alternative to the traditional Islamist Brotherhood, both local and international bodies, which had always been at the center of al-Turabi and Ayman al-Zawahiri's criticism and scorn. Al-Turabi argued that "many Islamic movements are now completely outflanked. It is not only the governments that are being undermined by this massive movement of Muslim people, but it is the Islamic movements themselves; the Jama't Islami and the Ikhwan Muslimun for example. They have to go popular or perhaps perish."[55]

For the Sudanese Islamists, the PAIC represented "'the most significant event since the collapse of the Caliphate' and the 'first occasion where representatives from mass movements from all over Muslim world came together in one place' to represent an alternative to the timidity and acrimonious backbiting between the Arab League and the OIC."[56] In this instance, the Sudanese Islamists and their benefactors inside and outside the country had expected the emergence of a model that could reinstate a certain version of political Islam as an alternative ideology and act as an example after the collapse of the Soviet Union and the demise of Eastern European socialism. Hence, it did not take bin Laden that long to confide to his friends "'this man [Ḥasan al-Turabi] is a Machiavelli ... He doesn't care what methods he uses.' Although they still needed one another, Turabi and bin Laden began to see themselves as rivals."[57] As for the Islamist regime and its government who called bin Laden "the moving bank," they had "squeezed him for all they could, demanding bribes, kickbacks, and especially 'loans' to pay for roads, airports, and other infrastructure projects. When it was time for bin Laden to pack (with profit), the government pled poverty and compensated him with money-losing, state-run enterprises."[58]

Considering these ironies together might lead us to see the internal evolution and progression of the disintegration processes of Islamism by adding to other factors that collectively dipped it into oblivion. These processes and factors are

---

55 Arthur L. Lowrie, ed., *Islam, Democracy, the State and the West*, 56 (see Chapter 2, n. 44).

56 Ibid.

57 Lawrence Wright, *Looming Tower*, 166.

58 Richard Miniter, *Losing Bin Laden*, 103.

always contingent on conditions and on what sometimes looks as cooperative processes that Islamists themselves created individually and collectively. We may say that most of these factors were not predicted, neither their end results nor the consequences that lent to fermenting violence and streams of blood which were not addressed adequately. The coming chapters will so much give shape and meaning to all that.

Chapter 7

‘Alī ‘Uthmān Moḥamed Ṭaha: When the Hurly-burly’s Done (1)

The peculiar mixed feelings with which the Sudanese Islamists and the local and international political communities reacted to the December 1999, events that dethroned Ḥasan al-Turabi from power would have given one person more delight than any other in the Sudan had it not been for his unconventional personality. It might have been due to his very secretive nature; he made it difficult for the most acute observer to watch and report about that person’s feelings that day. At the same time, it is difficult to understand the scale of that person’s ambition without looking carefully into the events before the coup and how he reached the pinnacle of the Islamist movement and its state.

‘Alī ‘Uthmān Moḥamed Ṭaha was an obscure figure who was extremely reserved, calculated, controlling and ruthless. And he always acted as a very humble person in his manner and his quiet demeanor. The December 1999, events made his indignant Islamists colleagues—who never accepted the palace coup on the fourth day of the fasting month of Ramadan—describe him as *as-Samiri* (the Samaritan) who led the Israelites astray during the absence of Moses and persuaded them to worship the golden calf. That day, the most indignant person was Ḥasan al-Turabi, the Moses of the Islamists, who led the Sudanese to the desolate Sinai Desert of the first Islamists republic through the coup of 1989. In this peculiar allegory, ‘Alī ‘Uthmān assumes the role of the happy magician, the false prophet, or he has been called, *as-Samiri*, while the golden calf is ‘Umar al-Bashir. The Qur’an describes how the golden calf is hollow and how the wind passes through it producing a loud sound. However, for historical Moses who regained his leadership of the Israelites, who purged themselves, the meaning is different to that of latter-day Moses—Ḥasan al-Turabi—whose Islamist disciples acted belligerently and cold-heartedly. They stripped him not only of his prophethood but also of all other worldly positions. ‘Alī ‘Uthmān and his golden calf, who both survived that experience, have continued to lead Sudanese Islamism astray and into oblivion since that day.

There are at least three ways related to this particular development that might help us address the significance of this event as a landmark in the withering of Islamism in the Sudan. The first has to do with ‘Alī ‘Uthmān Moḥamed Ṭaha as a person. The second has to do with what I call “the opportunity of absence” as ‘Alī ‘Uthmān, in particular, and others of the younger al-Turabi Islamists, climbed the movement’s ladder by taking advantage of the absence of their leaders while they were in prison or exile. The third one deals with the “pathology” produced and the community created out of that pathology. All that makes the wilting of Islamism in the Sudan a unique experience with nothing to compare it to, as no other Islamist group has ever assumed power the way the Sudanese did. In this sense, such developments have made the Sudanese Islamism a "one-item set" in the society in which it occurred. Nevertheless, it sheds light on and adds a lot to the study of the essence of Islamism at large. It is most likely from this view that one can understand one of the routes to the end of Islamism in the Sudan.

Who is 'Alī 'Uthmān?

It might be extremely difficult for the best chronicler of the Islamist movement in the Sudan and its personalities to write two pages about 'Alī 'Uthmān Moḥamed Ṭaha (1948–), the former first vice president[1] of the republic. Many of those who know him very well describe him as *katoom* (very secretive). Others will describe him as an insular militant, intellectually archaic, and politically brutal. It has been understood that 'Alī 'Uthmān was the "architect-in-chief" of planning and execution of the June 1989 military coup. 'Alī 'Uthmān's ascent to power started even earlier than the last the National Islamic Front (NIF) general conference in 1987 when he was elected as the deputy Secretary General of the party. However, it was hardly difficult to find anybody within the political field or even among the Islamists who tried to expose 'Alī 'Uthmān's character or the nature of his behavior and to show how they both or individually relate to an ambitious though discrete political player who climbed the ladder of power through co-optation rather than election. For that and other reasons, before the 1999 palace coup 'Alī 'Uthmān was always associated with Ḥasan al-Turabi and was described as his most loyal, trustworthy, and obedient disciple. The French paper *Jeune Afrique* described him as *un homme de confiance* (a man of confidence). He has always been perceived by most Sudanese observers as a political bureaucrat that Ḥasan al-Turabi handpicked and trained. Although relations of patronage—articulated or perceived as nepotism of kinship, preferentialism of friendship, peer relationship, or religious favoritism—may have played their role in building networks and suggesting some sort of solidarity is of no great significance. However, opportunistic and Machiavellian relations and temporary collaborations would and could also have taken advantage of justifiable and unthinkable opportunities.

One of the very few non-Sudanese who wrote about his character was Hilde Johnson, the former Norwegian Development Minister (1997–2000). Johnson

1 'Alī 'Uthmān resigned from his position in government and his deputy chairmanship of the ruling National Congress Party (NCP). His resignation was announced by President 'Umar al-Bashir on December 7, 2013. 'Alī "will voluntarily step down" as he did in 2005 following the signing of the CPA peace agreement according to al-Bashir. Speculations and rumors are rife in Khartoum that he was either purged or forced to out of office over irreconcilable differences with al-Bashir's inner circle.

was one of the international personalities who played an important role in the 2005 Nivasha peace negotiations. She stated that 'Alī 'Uthmān's "aura of quiet authority derived from his role behind the scenes of government and the Islamist movement."[2] She described 'Alī 'Uthmān as "rather withdrawn. Resolute when he wanted something done, he was a careful political planner and had stamina and staying power. He did not take risks, was never in a rush, and preferred to pull the strings and lead from behind. Reflective by nature, "Alī 'Usman was a very good listener; he gave people space, preferred to hear people out, assessing them, before saying anything himself. An intellectual, he saw issues from different angles, discerning what were possible and what was not, he was a pragmatist."[3] So it is clear that peculiar situations do not merely express the complexity and the diversity of odd and unorthodox relations, but most of the time they create them. And in this way, they might have created 'Alī 'Uthmān as the person who has been perceived by many Islamists as the embodiment of whoever was keeping and maintaining the power in the politics of Islamism by holding all the keys of power in his hands and affirming that position at each turning point. Meanwhile, Ali's own low-key style, which is a mixture of opportunism and astuteness, in addition to his child-like features and deceptively quiet demeanor, allowed many people to overlook his manipulative, conniving, and ruthless character. But these qualities that made of him an obscure figure on one hand prevented him, on the other, from being an ideological leader with any intellectual capital that could make him appear as the studious heir or even a close champion or possible competitor to Dr./ *Shaikh* Ḥasan. Many would argue that as one of the main reasons that al-Turabi kept him so close to him.

Most parts of 'Alī 'Uthmān's life are not known to the public or even to his Islamists colleagues, even though most Sudanese know what makes them feel proud, or sometimes sarcastic or ashamed, of their past and present political characters, celebrities, religious, and even historical leaders. Those who feel that they have a duty to inform the public about 'Alī 'Uthmān's background as one of the Islamists' political leaders are among his sympathizers, antagonists, and enemies, and they speak about his modest upbringing and background. However, such an issue in the Sudan, a country where most of its elite came from a similar, if not more modest, social background. Yet most Sudanese within similar situations do not feel shy about it; most likely feel proud, as if they "made it" the hard way. That may have been forefront in 'Alī's 'Uthmān's mind, and this perspective helped guide his swift ascent to power. Although the Islamist scholars and writers are not the only interpreters of the "myth of origin" and development of the Islamist movement, most of their writings very rarely mention 'Alī 'Uthmān, his persona, his role, and particularly how these characteristics or developments were cultivated. 'Alī never helped himself by writing anything that could attest to the

2 Hilde F. Johnson, *The Waging of Peace in the Sudan: the Inside Story of Negotiations that Ended Africa's Longest Civil War* (Brighton: Sussex Academic Press, 2011), 13.

3 Ibid.

development of his thoughts or reflect his "insights as well as his blindness." But if one looks at this within a broader and more thought-provoking exploration, one might entertain an interesting idea that might give that peculiar situation a political sense, as his rise to power was rather based on objective factors contrary to his supreme leader Ḥasan al-Turabi who built a personality cult that ensured his political capital. It is thus possible that this anti-hero image worked very well for him when he assumed possession of power in the state and the movement from al-Turabi after the year 2000 as humble person who had not planned for it. All these issues cannot be disregarded. Yet, when recognizing the existence of such counter-insightful observations or developments in the life of 'Alī 'Uthmān, one cannot disregard such broader propensities in the realm of the Sudanese public culture. Hence, 'Alī 'Uthmān's story needs to be approached and written down in its own perplexity and encryption, which has to be deciphered to make an understanding of that character possible.

To speak of 'Alī 'Uthmān's ascension to power is to speak of the complexity of the backstage of al-Turabi's Islamism in practice. Erving Goffman has pointed out that "back regions are typically out of bounds to members of the audience."[4] This, in a sense, represents parts of the political circumstances the Sudanese society, in general, and the Islamist community, in particular, experienced after the October 1964 Revolution, which played a role in shaping developments that could by now be considered, for some Sudanese, a distant past. But to another extent, for some, this adds to what could be described as embedded capacities of what the Sudanese describe as *makr* (scheming). The backstage behavior worked very well for 'Alī 'Uthmān for a while with 'Umar al-Bashir where he could "regularly derogate the audience in a way that is inconsistent with the face-to-face treatment that is given to the audience."[5] It could, however, also be a strategy that consciously 'Alī 'Uthmān followed, which enables us to account for the processes that he ascribed to during his political career. 'Alī al-Ḥaj and al-Maḥboob 'Abdelsalam confirmed that al-Turabi and 'Umar al-Bashir met without a third-person audience only after the Husni Mubārak assassination attempt in Addis Ababa in 1995. But some of these backstage developments became front stage scenes performed at will when required. But sometimes the performances provided a chance for al-Turabi or 'Alī 'Uthmān to gain favor during the absence of the other. Some of the present-day manifestations, one would assume, might be the contemporary carriers of political tumors that asserted relationships to the underground politics (backstage) that derive from the style and time of the Islamists' way of doing politics. 'Abdelgani Aḥmed Idris states in his book, *al-D'awa lil Dimocratiyya wa-l-Islaḥ al-Siasi fi-l-Sudan* (Call for Democracy and Political Reform in Sudan),

4 Erving Goffman, *The Representation of Self in Everyday Life* (New York: Anchor Books, 1959), 124.

5 Ibid.

that 'Umar al-Bashir confronted his previous security chief, Ṣalah 'Abdulla Gosh,[6] and said to him "your tribe has a deceitfulness mentality; and that he, al-Bashir, benefited from that one day during the election for the presidency of *Shura* council."[7] Al-Bashir was referencing 'Alī 'Uthmān who conspired with him [al-Bashir] against al-Turabi for the position and for his own nomination instead. Al-Bashir is as hollow as the *Samiri* golden calf and the wind passing through it would not produce a sound. But the strategy of absence would not have assumed the significance we now give to it had there not been significant developments related to it with 'Alī 'Uthmān's rise to and stay in power.

Absence as an Opportunity

The most meaningful of the Islamist occurrences in connection to 'Alī 'Uthmān is the emergence of al-Turabi Islamism, its relationship to the University of Khartoum, and its community from one side and the military coup of Ja'afr Nimeiri and his regime from the other. As explained in Chapter 5, the University of Khartoum became not only an antecedent to and the originator of a prestigious position within the community of the state, but it also became endowed with sociopolitical status, symbolic value, and an image as the main

6 Major General Salah 'Abdalla nicknamed "Gosh" is the former Presidential National Security Advisor (2009–2011). Prior to that he was the former head of internal security, and then the director of Sudan's National Intelligence and Security Services (NISS) for the period 2004–2009. Ṣalah 'Abdalla Gosh, graduate of the Faculty of Engineering Department of Civil, University of Khartoum. His relationship with the Islamists security system and spy work started when he established an "information bureau" to provide the movement's leadership with intelligence on political activity within the university. After the Islamist coup of 1989, Gosh devoted himself purely to intelligence work, acquiring the position of director of operations in the new regime's security bureau. It was in this position that he collaborated with Aymen al-Zawahi, other jihādists resident in Khartoum, and other Islamists groups based within the wider Middle Eastern region. It was also in this role that he helped to provide Osama bin Laden with the economic and military infrastructure to make Sudan an early base of operations for al-Qaeda. He later came to be known by the Americans as "our man in Sudan." It seems that under Gosh the contribution of the NISS to the "War on Terror" was more substantial. In 2005, a state department official told a reporter from the *Los Angeles Times* that the information provided by NISS was "important, functional, and current."

He is one of the power group around Vice President 'Alī 'Uthmān Moḥamed Ṭaha. Wikileaks cables released in 2011 showed that as early as 2008 Gosh had been considering exploiting the International Criminal Court indictment against Omar al-Bashir to enable 'Alī 'Uthmān Ṭaha to displace him and take power himself. He was arrested along with 12 other top army officers in November 2012, over a suspected coup attempt, which the government described as "plot" to destabilize the country.

7 'Abdelgani Aḥmed Idris, *al-D'awah lil Dimocratiyya awa al-Islah al-Siasis fi al-Sudan* (London: Sinar Publishing House, 2012), 80.

citadel of al-Turabi's Islamism. Underlying the endorsement of that combination of reproduction and promotion, the ideology and image of Islamism within the ranks of expanding numbers of younger, second-generation, Islamists at the University of Khartoum, in particular, reflected the growing belief in al-Turabi's personality cult, which followed his defiant and violent style of conversation as its manifesto and took pride in disseminating the news of the growing numbers of his disciples.

The military coup of 1969 altered the whole political scene in the country. The new regime banned all political parties, arrested the political and trade unions' leaders, and nationalized the press. Some of the political activities and most of the activists who were not imprisoned went underground. At the same time, the coup was a test that uncovered another face of some of the October revolutionaries—both civilian and military—and their sham belief in the "October Creed," or *mabādi October* (October ideals), as they revoked what was considered not long ago a mission of the nation as a whole. Within the left, a conspiracy and collaboration among some left groups within the Sudanese Communist Party, some factions of pan-Arab Nassirites, and similar groups in the army brought another military rule to the country.[8] The coup decisively strained the public and private spheres.

Ja'afar Nimeiri who seized power in 1969 in a military coup and who "promised 'everything must change' … for sixteen dramatic years he lead Sudan on an extraordinary political dance which reached every corner of the political spectrum, from close alignment with the Communists, to aggressive secular developmentalism, peace with the south, embrace of the conservative sectarian parties he had deposed, an eccentric version of radical Islamism and—in his final days in power—the hint of yet another twist."[9] Furthermore, Nimeiri "in his time in power, espousing [the] Nasserite revolution, Nimeiri savagely crushed the Ansar and Muslim Brothers, then turned on his former Communist allies, and survived repeated coup attempts and invasions."[10] Within the back stage of the Sudanese political theater, the University of Khartoum, its students, and some of

8 In his memoirs, *Mayo Sanuat al-Khasb wa al-jafaf* (Many Years of Fertility and Drought (Khartoum: Markaj Moḥamed 'Umar Bashir lil Dirasat, 2011), Zain al-Abdien Moḥamed Aḥmed, a military officer who played a key role in the 1969 coup and a member of the Revolutionary Command Council of what was called the May Revolution, claims that the leader of the coup, Ja'afar Nimeiri, met with 'Abdel Kahliq Mahjoub, the Secretary General of the Communist Party, and members of his general secretariat the morning of the coup to seek the party's collaboration by backing in the coup and its regime. According to Moḥamed Aḥmed, Mahjoub's refusal to accept that request lead to a major split in the Communist Party as a faction led by Mouawia Sourij and Aḥmed Suliamān to collaborate with Nimeiri and his new regime.

9 Alex De Waal, "Late Jaafar Nimeiri—Reflections on His Life" (*African Arguments*, 2009) http://africanarguments.org/2009/05/31/reflections-on-the-life-of-the-late-jaafar-nimeiri/.

10 Ibid.

its faculty were able to a certain extent to protect their turf. Thus, a new situation arose in which the university became a signifier whose meaning was expressed by its ability to protect and preserve part of its freedoms within its campus and campus life. Once emerged, it was congealed by the spirit and the legacy of October 1964 Revolution. Within the underground politics of that period, that development directed and indicated something beyond the campus as a field in itself into a field by itself. As its picture emerged, so did the university develop into a launching pad for opposition to the regime. Al-Turabi's Islamists, while waiting for their Secretary General who was in "occultation"—away in prison for seven years—formed an important opposition body of the Students Unity Front.

Within that environment, between 1969 and 1971, 'Alī 'Uthmān was a law student at the University of Khartoum. He was elected as the president of the University of Khartoum Students' Union in 1970. This, to a certain degree, opened up new fields of possibilities that might lead us to examine the significance of an absence as an opportunity. In the absence of al-Turabi and the top leadership of his Islamism, the young Islamists at the University of Khartoum were uplifted to show defiance. Although, that standoff was perceived by some as the ideological Islamist right against the left-leaning regime of Nimeiri in so far as the left was on the wrong side of history and far away from the spirit of October and what the University—the citadel of October—stood for. It was said that 'Alī 'Uthmān, as the Islamist president of the Students' Union, vainly placed himself up to the occasion; nevertheless, the Islamists hailed him as part of their victorious defiance to the regime.[11] That was not only an ideological phenomenon; it was a political phenomenon, too. Since that day, we have witnessed all the cues and provocations by which the "militant" young Islamists placed themselves as an opposition group and the ways they began to utilize the campus as space to reconstitute a national field of resistance to the regime.

After graduation, 'Alī 'Uthmān was appointed a judge in the judiciary. After that, he started a private law practice and then entered politics where he has worked ever since. At the same time, he assumed responsibility of the Islamist party's student sector. During the absence of most of the senior Islamist leadership, when they were either in prison or in exile, 'Alī 'Uthmān not only inherited the authority of Secretary General in that field, but he also found himself deeply seated at the heart of one of the most dynamic political groups of young Sudanese struggling to find their route to the Sudanese community of the state and their way within the groups who opposed Nimeiri's regime.

It is important to note that several important aspects of the students' sector at that time gained prominence in the underground and overground arenas of major political conflict in the country. One of the major aspects of that is the opposition to the idea of the coup and the totalitarian system that came out of its regime. It is only against that background that one can see an emerging important

11 'Ali al-Haj claims that al-Turabi confided to some of his confidants that 'Alī 'Uthmān showed some cowardice at that situation.

phenomenon that made overt political activities more difficult on a national scale, except on campus. At the same time, it made covert activities more important countrywide except in the university zone. Aḥmed Kamal el-Din described his first secret lecture at one of the university halls. It was 1978 and the speaker was 'Alī 'Uthmān. In his speech, he said "it was for the first time I felt that I joined a secret organization with open activities."[12] This situation made the university and its students, in particular, a very important political community that both the regime and its opponents beheld very seriously.

In addition, the country witnessed patterns of rural to urban migration, improvements in transportation and communication, the introduction of free higher education, opportunities for higher and graduate education in Britain, Egypt, and the US, and undergraduate education prospects in the Soviet Union and other Socialist countries were among the most important developments in the postcolonial setting and during Nimeiri's early period. By the 1970s, "a large number of Muslim Brotherhood supporters had become teachers in Western provinces (Kordofan and Darfur), and consequently there has been major support for the Brotherhood amongst Sudanese pupils. When they then went to the university, they dominated students' politics to such extent that until this year (1984) the Muslim Brotherḥood's candidates had swept to victory in all union elections."[13] 'Alī al-Ḥaj added that some high school students from Ḥantoub and others who studied in Egypt, who were government employees in Niyala, also participated in recruiting some local children to the brotherhood from an early time.[14] Such developments provided more new opportunities for many students, including those from the periphery or marginalized parts of the country, such as Darfur, Kordofan, Southern and Eastern Sudan, and the lower and middle classes. These higher education opened the entire Sudanese landscape for new social groups from different parts of the country to gain noticeable degrees in upward mobility.

The overground campus environment at the University of Khartoum and other university campuses provided an additional value to their political, journalistic, and intellectual activism. Notably, this growth of university students that multiplied every year corresponded to the emergence of a new breed of Islamist student leaders of a similar variety who came from different regions. Most likely due to age factors and similar educational experiences, the impulse for togetherness among these young Islamist student leaders and 'Alī 'Uthmān as their leader had gone beyond mere ideological affinity. Through time, the political structure and the atmosphere of togetherness became very important.

While there were many elements out of which the togetherness of the 'Alī 'Uthmān phenomenon was consolidated among the younger generations of educated Islamists, the increasing presence of younger Islamists who migrated

---

12 Dr. Aḥmed confided that to author in a personal email conversation.

13 Charles Gurdon, *Sudan at the Crossroads* (Kent: Menas Press, 1984), 69.

14 'Ali al-Haj Moḥamed, interview by author, audio recording, Bonn, Germany, July 24, 2012.

to Saudi Arabia and Gulf countries, in particular, after graduation for work added another dimension to the phenomenon. It came at a time of the vast rise in oil prices of the 1970s and the steady decline of the Sudanese economy. The high increases in revenues of Arab states and private beneficiaries provided for unlimited resources in the hands of these entities and through them some of the Sudanese Islamist expatriates. At the same time, these new conditions came with new transformative makings and productions in the Arab counties and in the Sudan in particular. As these Arab counties continued to get richer, some of the ramifications of that situation kept Sudan and the Sudanese poorer primarily for geographical factors, bad luck, and wrong policies. These policies included the military coup and the plunder contained within its resulting regime. By the beginning of the early time of Nimeiri's regime and its acceleration through the 1970s, high numbers of Sudanese left the country as an outcome of intended and unintended consequences of that plunder. It is impossible not to notice the deep effects of that period in the history of the Sudan. These effects are reflected in the *hijra* (migration) to Arab countries, its concurrent development of underdevelopment in the Sudan, and of its participation in development of development in the other parts of these Arab countries.[15]

Islamists of all ages and qualifications migrated to Saudi Arabia and some of the Gulf States in order to find a temporary refuge from what they perceived, experienced, or feared an oppressive communist regime. The first groups of Sudanese Islamists, such as 'Uthmān Khalid Mudawi[16] who fled the country, confirmed to King Faisal (1904–1975), the Saudi authorities, and other Arab rulers that not only Nasserism, Baathism, and other secular ideologies, but also an imminent communist threat was sneaking in through the Saudi back door. The anti-communist stance of the Sudanese groups afforded them easy access to positions of rank and responsibility in Saudi Arabia and other Gulf states. Thousands of young Islamists together with other Sudanese expatriates crossed the Red Sea by air to Saudi Arabia and other oil-producing countries. It is in this connection through the 1970s and 1980s that the Sudanese economic problems of hard currency started to come to the fore as a serious preoccupation for the state, the private sector, and the ordinary citizens.

At the same time, migration turned from a gain into a serious brain drain that took its toll on every aspect of the Sudanese life. In 1979 "the figures estimated suggest that migrants constituted 10% of the male population between the ages of 20 to 34." Moreover, in "1985, it was estimated that two-thirds of Sudan's

15 One of the stories that could summarize this situation was of the Saudi ambassador, which has circulated for a long time. The ambassador, after getting fed up trying to find a good plumber in Khartoum to mend his water supply, sent for a plumber from Riyadh, who turned out to be Sudanese.

16 'Uthmān Khalid Mudawi, a lawyer, a business person, and an Islamist who played an important role in the external opposition to Nimeiri's regime.

professional and skilled workers were employed outside the country."[17] As a result, we can say that Islamists expatriates' money and experiences served the consolidation of a new emerging economic structure and transformation of the party and some of its members. For example, "the policy makers and advisors were hoping to find compensation through the injection of migrants' remittances and savings, [which] were expected to bail Sudan's economy out from its growing indebtedness and balance payments deficits," but it went elsewhere to Islamist party and its new commercial and money-exchange units.[18] However, "through the years which followed the *mughtaribin*[19] boom, the fall of Nimeiri and after, the Sudanese governments conspicuously failed even to approximate this goal. Instead the country's socioeconomic situation continued to deteriorate from bad to worse."[20] As the economic retreat of Nimeiri's regime continued, the Islamist party showed itself to be financially prospering. Three of the most consequential aspects of this development shaped an emerging Islamist party and the situation of 'Alī 'Uthmān as one of the persons not only firmly connected with young Islamists at home and abroad but also as one of the few people who were holding the reins of the reality and the evolution of this new development.

The first consequence was that the Sudanese Islamists in Arab countries accomplished a significant break with the traditional thinking of the *hijra* and other Sudanese *mughtaribin*. In their newfound refuge, they created new networks, discovered new forms of inter and intragroup solidarity, and achieved political and financial empowerment by collecting and channeling money to the other end of the Islamist private (black or white) money market at home, which became a daily routine. These networks grew into the Islamist *maktab al-Mughtaribin* (the Mughtaribin bureau). Later when severe famine affected the Sudan in 1984, a number of relief organizations were established. Both the Bureau and the relief organizations, according to al-Tigani 'Abdel Gadir, were left to those who administered them with capitalist mentality.[21] By the 1977 national reconciliation between Nimeiri and the opposing political parties including the Islamists, these networks were operational. By channeling money from the oil-rich Arab countries, the Islamists became the most important underground and overground group dealing in money in the country. This situation clearly represented and presented a set of practices where the money-exchange dealers and dealerships established new habits and consequences similar to the IMF [The International Monetary

17 'Abdel Salam SidAḥmed, *Politics and Islam in Contemporary Sudan* (New York: St. Martin's Press, 1996), 195.

18 Ibid.

19 The Sudanese expatriates and workers who migrated and temporarily stayed in Saudi Arabia and the Gulf countries because of employment there.

20 'Abdel Salam SidAḥmed, ibid.

21 Al-Tigani Abdel Gadir, *'al-Rasimaliyoon al-Islamiyoon, mada yafaloun fi al-Harka al-Islamiyya'* (The Islamists Capitalists: What do They do With the Islamic Movement?, Khartoum: *al-Sahafa Daily*, December 12, 2006).

Fund] recipe of devaluation of the local currency. With the decline of local currency, the hard currency became a high-demand commodity with unfavorable terms. The same became true of the value of the Sudanese *mughtarib* in the Saudi and Arab labor markets, as it had been subordinated to the requirements of markets that demanded a cheaper commodity. This commodity was none other than human beings themselves of which every human community, society, or nation consists. Hence, under the *kafeel* (sponsorship) system[22] and its conditions that turned labor almost into a feudalist system, the devaluation of local currency deeply affected those who were already subjected to the market mechanism or those who were subordinated to the dreams of a better life, which was the requirement to join al-*mughtaribin* in the land of plenty. So, in both situations of the Sudanese money and human resources as commodities, "the desire to make a profit by buying low and selling high could easily shade into various forms of sharp practice ... closely associated with the common view that the act of exchange itself, expressed through trade, was morally dubious, since one party always seemed to come better than the order in any purely instrumental exchange."[23] Hence, this phenomenon created its own universe and form of Islamists' accumulation, which was represented by its new riches who were primarily active in currency dealings, such al-Tayib al-Nus, Shaikh 'Abdelbasit, and others.

The second fundamental point that possesses critical normative, political, and economic dimensions and that needs to be added here, which became one of the greatest elements of the empowerment of the Islamists in the Sudan, was the growth and the consequences of a new phenomenon of Islamic economics and its financial institutions. Equally important, people behind that phenomenon strove to make the argument that it was the alternative to other forms of economy. They worked hard to make the Sudan the main example for the implementation of the new economic system. The earliest debate about this issue took different forms in different parts of the Muslim world. However, "the efforts of Indian Muslims, beginning in the 1930s, to create a Muslim state on the former territory of British

22 The *Kafalaa* or the *Kafeel* system is used in many oil-rich Arab countries with the exception of Bahrain. According to this system, foreign workers are allowed to come into any of these countries only when sponsored by a national employer. The worker's visa remains entirely in the hands of the employer who acts as the visa sponsor and who can withdraw permission at any time from the employee if they quit the job or leave the country on vacation, and the employers use the visa as blackmail.

The *Kafeel* system which has been criticized by the International Labor Organization, governments, and human rights organizations, has been responsible for creating a foreign workforce in these countries that is repeatedly abused and overworked, blackmailed into working for little pay, long hours, and no benefits. Many sponsors do not allow the transfer of one employee to another sponsor.

23 Charles Tripp, *Islam and the Moral Economy: Challenge of Capitalism* (Cambridge: Cambridge University Press, 2006), 106.

India following Britain's withdrawal gave rise to intense debates about an Islamic system for an Islamic state."[24]

Later, there were two basic influences underlying the resurrection and the growth of the issue anew: (1) the first of these influences was related to the growing numbers of Islamist scholars like Khurshid Aḥmed, N. Naqvi, and N. Siddqui who dominated the International Center for Islamic Economics at the King 'Abd-al-'Aziz University, Jeddah. What was of more significance here was that the Islamists "grafted their political interests onto the Saudi pipeline, even though Kuwait offered them greater freedom of movement than they enjoyed in the Kingdom."[25]

(2) The second of these influences, by the mid 1970s, young Islamist economists and groups of businessmen in Saudi Arabia and the Gulf started the first Islamic Banks in Dubai, Sudan, and Egypt. Moreover, other Islamic economic institutions began to grow to cover areas of investment, business, and finance, in addition to relief and *da'wa*. In relation to the *da'wa*, "Saudi policy is determined by a powerful clerical machinery, such as the Muslim World League with its sheer number of organizations and institutions. The Islamist wing of Saudi foreign policy is likewise fond of Sudan, although for different purposes. Sudan was to be the matrix of an Islamist network meant to bring African popular Islam in line with fundamentalism, or at least, orthodoxy, and then to spread it out to the rest of non-Muslim Africa."[26] It was not Nimeiri and his regime who received "considerable political and financial backing from such powerful vested interests,"[27] but it was the Islamists who did. All that led to a major transformation of the Islamist movement by turning some of its members from barefoot intellectuals into a new propertied middle class. This new middle class was made of a new breed of merchants called *tujar al-jabhah* (NIF merchants) and other white-collar professionals who emerged from the new Islamic banking institutions, and organizations that generated the opportunities, motives, and means for the change of status, which was distinguished by viewing the image of wealth as symbol of success. When the Islamist movement was bloated with money, it successfully transformed into a corporation.[28] Al-Tigani 'Abdel Gadir described that development by recalling that "the market mentality and the capitalist groups that started to become active and expanded until they were about to 'swallow' what was remaining from our

---

24 Volker Nienhaus, *Fundamentals of an Islamic Economic System compared to Social Market Economy* (Berlin: KAS International Reports, 2010), 75.

25 Akbar Aḥmed, *Discovering Islam: Making Sense of Muslim History and Society* (London and New York: Routledge, 2002), 201.

26 Khalid Duran, "The Centrifugal forces of Religion in Sudanese politics" *Orient* 26 (1985): 572–600.

27 Ibid.

28 See more elaboration on the transformation of the Islamist movement into a corporation in Abdullahi Gallab, *The First Islamist Republic* (see Chapter 1, n. 1)

Islamic organization which we did not join in the first place except for running away from wild capitalism."[29] Another view point that still persists is even more critical of this "market mentality." He called it *Uhud mentality* referring to the Uhud battle, which was fought in AD 625 between a force of the small Muslim community of Madina and a force from Macca, the town from which many of the Muslims including Prophet Moḥamed emigrated in AD 622 after years of persecution. During that battle while the Muslim force had been close to victory, some of the Muslim force, especially the archers, breached Prophet Moḥamed's orders and rushed to collect Meccan spoils. That move allowed for a surprise attack from the Meccan force, which caused chaos and disorder within the position of Muslim forces. Many Muslims were killed, and even Prophet Moḥamed himself was badly injured. Such a rush to collect the spoils was described in the Sudanese satire *al-habaro malu* as reinventing the relics of an old famous Sudanese Sūfi verse that refers to those who rushed toward piety and gained their rewards from God to mean the opposite, scramble for the spoils of the state. Another form of an assault or scramble for the spoils of the state was described by 'Abdel Gadir who exemplified "our *gubsh* [barefoot] brothers who used to eat with us fava beans and lentils [poor people's food] and reside with us in *Um Dirawa wa al-Droushab* [poor neighborhoods], those wretched of the earth became ministers and governors. We felt at first that was a good omen … as we felt that we found a rock that would close the gate for corruption and blocks the road to brokers and mafias and turns toward the poor and disadvantaged." But that was too great as some of them turned to look only to what was around them and built only their high buildings and spent only on their entourage and closest clan. Such provocative arguments might have started and continued as part of the younger generations residue of a legacy of resistance to the older generation and Ḥasan al-Turabi's agreement to reconcile with Ja'afar Nimeiri's regime in 1977. For those younger Islamists who joined the Sudanese National Front, an armed opposition groups in Libya, and who participated in the military operation against the regime in 1976,[30] the reconciliation was a big betrayal to those who gave the most in fighting against the regime. In their memos, many

29 Al-Tigani Hamid 'Abdel Gadir, *al-Rasimaliyoon al-Islamiyoon, mada yafaloun fi al-Harka al-Islamiyya* (The Islamists Capitalists: What do They do With the Islamic Movement?).

30 On June 2, 1976, one of the bloodiest confrontations between the Nimeiri regime and National Front—the opposition group led by the Umma, Unionists, and Islamists—took place as "one thousand fighters from the Ansar and fifty from the Islamists" who had military training in Libya were sneaked into the country from their training camps in the oasis of Kufra and launched a surprise attack on the capital. The operation, which Nimeiri labeled as *murtazagh* (mercenaries) attack, was led by retired army colonel—Moḥamed Nur Sa'ad—failed. Some of the participants including Sa'ad were captured and killed, and others were tortured and imprisoned. A few found their way back to Libya while al-Sadiq al-Mahdi, al-Sharif al-Hindi, and other ringleaders of the failed attack were sentenced to death in absentia.

of them were bitter, and with increasing frequency, those fighters blamed their Islamist leadership who accepted the reconciliation with the regime for never visiting the fighters in their camps in the Libyan desert, or consulting with them in such a serious and dangerous matter.

Before the evolution of these developments in 1969, almost everything of significance in the Islamist movement lay within the control of Ḥasan al-Turabi. But during the absence of Ḥasan al-Turabi in prison, these developments became integrated and grew within a new organized system that matured under the direct control of ‘Alī ‘Uthmān and to a certain extent ‘Alī al-Ḥaj.[31] However, ‘Alī ‘Uthmān was the organizational nucleus of the most complex emerging group of the younger Islamists, as they were transforming into a new middle class and later undergone a serious transformation through identity management into some kind of civic patronage. As they say, “it is impossible to understand the magic without the magic group.” Most of the younger Islamists began to look at their relationship with al-Turabi Islamism as activists positions rather than an ideologically based roles. The separation between ideology and activism prompted all other factors including religion, ideology, and ethics to distance themselves from Islamism, Islam, and any Sudanese creed. Hence, every attitude toward the other could be hostile and violent. That explains why violence has been the modus operandi of this group before and after they assumed power in 1989.

In the wake of the national reconciliation, the younger Islamist group intensified its activities due to certain developments. First, the growth that occurred in this internal system within the front stage of the students of the University of Khartoum in particular and other schools of higher education in general. Second, the clear effect of the increased numbers of *mughtaribeen* and the way the movement channeled their remittances to strengthen the movement’s economic might. Third, those who were in the United States and Western Europe with graduate degrees from different universities returned. Fourth, the return of the Islamist fighters who came from the Libyan Desert added to the diversity and strength of the group. All that had an important transforming result on the democratic composition and the internal discourse within the back stage of the Islamists movements and its underground tributaries. All that held back to put ‘Alī ‘Uthmān as the deputy Secretary General in the first general conference for the movement when the movement went overground. The general conference, when the movement came overground, opened a new field for the nascent middle class formed by ambitious younger groups of al-Turabi Islamists to gain recognition by ascending the upper echelons of the organization. That move caught some of the old guard of the movement by surprise. These new Islamist middle-class people were themselves the bearers of their own interest. And they were not necessarily whole-hearted believers in al-Turabi’s Islamism or happy with the control of the older generation over leadership positions in the movement since 1964.

---

31 According to Ali al-Haj in his interview with the author in Bonn in July 2012, he was responsible for the party affairs while Ḥasan al-Turabi was in prison after 1969.

Many observers were caught by surprise that 'Alī 'Uthmān was elected to the position of the deputy Secretary General of the Islamist movement. Later, Moḥamed Ṭaha Moḥamed Aḥmed (killed in 2006), a Sudanese Islamist journalist and the editor of the *Al-Wifaq* who was known for his violent approach to writing, reminded his readers and 'Alī 'Uthmān as well that they were the ones behind his rise to deputy Secretary General. In a sense, that conference was a condolence meeting for a certain aspect of al-Turabi's Islamism and some of its leaders. The emergence of 'Alī 'Uthmān and his new young Islamist middle class as a paradigm case was not only a subversive Other of the older generation of the Islamists but in essence of al-Turabi and his Islamism in the first place.

We might need to look at this phenomenon not within the growth and development of al-Turabi's Islamism and its political party but as a distinctive creation that involves a parallel form of power, status, and authority relations. For a considerable period of time, this phenomenon had three levels of complexity: (1) it continued to grow as a self-sustaining movement of *a new class* moving to gain new grounds; (2) the Islamist movement field was a predominantly underground system of identity management differentiating die-hard believers (mostly from western Sudan) from pragmatic non-believers (primarily revarians); and (3) showing belief in either Ḥasan al-Turabi, or his Islamism, was a functional necessity as long as that would help endow the core group with all the privileges and the way for upward mobility.

In an interview with al-Tigani 'Abdel Gadir he argued that al-Inqaz "turned over the page of political parties as well as the Islamist movement that elevated to governance."[32] Of course, many see the growth of that development the way el-Tigani saw it, as a new element in the life of Sudanese Islamism that came with and as an outcome of the coup. Later Sudanese Islamism linked to the state as a practice to the exclusion of other groups, their behaviors, and the benefits of those other emerging groups. In reality, that could be true, but the real thing might be different. That impulse started to sprout and gradually emerge as Ḥasan al-Turabi started to turn his Islamism against his surrounding political culture, its old and new representations, and dead and alive personalities. As an outcome of the gradual replacement of most of the old dominant strata or what he called the traditionalists before his imprisonment in 1969, he started systematize how this new class reproduced and maintained itself before and after his release in 1977. From the perspective of those who watched al-Turabi's very closely early on, one can easily see the rise of this new class not as conflicting but rather providing a better picture of how al-Turabi's style became the brand and the *vade mecum* or the referential book that 'Alī 'Uthmān in particular and his group adopted, learned by heart, and followed with great caution. This was the case at least for a while

32 Osman Naway Post: al-professor al-Tigani 'Abdel Gadir, al-Inqaz kant Inglaban Muzdawagan alaa al-Ahzab wa alaa al Haraqa al-Islamiyya (al-Inqaz staged two coups at the same time. The first was against the political parties while the second was against the Islamists movement, http://osmannawaypost.net/?p=6427.

because they could never succeed in distinguishing themselves from him. By the time they disconnected themselves from Ḥasan al-Turabi, certain characteristics of this new class started to surface. One of these characteristics was greed. As more of these groups began to comply with the values of the city, the more that different forms of unchecked or controlled wilding developed. Such behavior was bred by selfishness and indulgence in pleasures of all things worldly, including multiple marriages[33] and what Ḥasan al-Turabi describes as *fintant al-mal* (lust for wealth), that incapacitated the virtues and integrities of public, social, and religious life. This situation involved a separate synchronized form of deploying the state and its violent apparatus to secure the savage separation of religion and state. It also helped the construction of the group routed in certain economic relations coming from essential functions related to the way that the group used its new status to accumulate wealth as a primary characteristic of this newly constructed group. The system that they developed and perfected was described by Sudanese as *fasad* corruption. The international community perceived Sudan as extremely "corrupt, and all available data and country reports indicate persistent, widespread, and endemic forms of corruption, permeating all levels of society."[34] According to Transparency International's Corruption Perception index, Sudan now stands at 173 out of 174 compared to 177 out of 182 in 2011. Turkmenistan and Uzbekistan moved ahead of the East African nation since last year. But this guarded *fasad* which the Islamists describe as *tamkeen* and *kasb* warrants serious consideration. The most noticeable aspect of this is the violent forms of using the state power for unequal distribution of resources to complement and perpetuate an emerging social stratification and differentiation of power, prestige and wealth. Corruption which has been one of functional necessities and one of the tools of a regime assisted system for upward mobility should not be understood in moral terms. The processes of the rise of Sudanese Islamists from rags to riches, viewed as a whole, could well be regarded as a proper management through violence and coercion that has been set in motion where its effectiveness works to enhance forms of differentiation and social stratification the Islamists designed and exercised by using the state and its coercive force for unequal distribution of rewards among themselves. For example, 'Umar al-Bashir "has taken the No. 1 spot on *People with Money* Magazine's top-highest politicians for 2014 that 'al-Bashir is the highest-paid politician in the world, pulling in an astonishing $46 million between 2013 and February 2014, a nearly $20 million lead over his closest competition.'" That does not include his brothers, wife Widad and other family value.

However, different opportunities of absence provided many of those young Islamists with most opportunities to act slowly and sometimes discreetly to climb up the organization before the 1985 conference and with a faster pace after the

33 It became almost a state policy to encourage the Islamists to marry more than one wife. 'Umar al-Bashir married a second wife and continued to encourage his fellow Islamists to follow suit.

34 Transparency International, U 4 Expert Answer, p. 4.

general conference. But absence neither keeps normal hours nor this formula, and its rules were established by the party. Most importantly, when such an occasion occurred, a person, a number of individuals, or a group moved up and would be recognized as if they were chosen through a legitimate process of selection or election. It has given rise in and of itself to the symbolic capital that is augmented and amplified with the degree and the status of the positions and to a certain extent the reputation or the background of the group so established. Be that as it may, these opportunities of absence should not conceal how these younger generations started to create their own networks for the democratic process and the impatience of some of them to find a shortcut to power through a military coup. These unusual and sometimes peculiar developments can only be explained if we realize that the social enterprise and consequences of the positioning persons or groups into higher levels are most likely blurred by similar peculiar circumstances as the ones explained earlier. Thus, we will see in the next chapter how 'Alī 'Uthmān climbed into a situation not governed by roles that go beyond tyranny itself; this could be called "savage inequalities."

Chapter 8
'Alī 'Uthmān Moḥamed Ṭaha: When the Hurly-burly's Done (2)

The joint formation of specific events of absence and the rise of 'Alī 'Uthmān dwarfed most, if not all, members of the three groups of leadership and any potential leaders of the Islamist movement, including those who supported Ḥasan al-Turabi at a crucial time. This process represented an important part of the serious developments that led the Sudanese Islamist movement from disintegration to oblivion. In one sense, the story of 'Alī 'Uthmān's rise to power and the long and peculiar way he achieved it represent the path of the degeneration for al-Turabi Islamism. This saga can be better understood—as partly explained in the previous chapter—against the topography of the specific front and backstage developments accentuated in the post-October Revolution, as it was these developments that resulted in the production of a complex postcolonial situation in which the new Islamist generation were considered by most as supporting actors. However, the political rise of young Islamists was obscured for a time because although the growth of this "new class" within and under the shadow of al-Turabi Islamism was incessant, the Sudanese Islamist and non-Islamist older generation put the younger Islamists and their mounting leadership in a different location. For the generation of older Sudanese politicians, the younger Sudanese Islamists and non-Islamist class was a typical representation of what we could view as a "Sudanese Peter Pan." To the older generation, this Sudanese Peter Pan would have spent his never-ending childhood serving elders of Sudanese political leadership. Peter Pan condition rarely, if ever, sees developments and mobility in the political field and their own political organizations as something that a better informed and a greater relative power offered generously to some of members of a younger generation.

A better example of that is the prevailing argument that 'Alī 'Uthmān is *Ṣani'at* (made by) Ḥasan al-Turabi, or he has been solely made by Ḥasan al-Turabi who handpicked, groomed, and favored him to other older members to acquire such a high position in the party. Some the members of the Islamists older generation, like Yasin 'Umer al-Imam, claim that it was their idea to give the younger generation of the party a chance to climb up the ladder of the movement as an institutional arrangement to renew and energize the movement.[1] Others attribute 'Alī 'Uthmān's fortunes to the role played for his

1 Yasin expressed this idea on several occasions in interviews with him. He expressed that idea to the author in a recorded interview at his home in al-Thoura district in Omdurman, January 3, 2006.

favor by the obscure Islamist personality Moḥamed Yousif Moḥamed.[2] Such a recurring approach to reading social phenomenon makes it difficult to answer the serious questions raised by the rise of the personality at issue or any other social or political development. To achieve a better reading and understanding of the rise of the person at issue and his class, it is necessary to consider, in this chapter as in the previous one, the historical chronology, the settings, and the contexts within which the phenomenon of absence turned into or provided opportunities for 'Alī 'Uthmān and his political class. This development is therefore one of the major condition of reference against which this study is undertaken. Moreover, the point at issue becomes more worthy of our inquiry when we realize that al-Turabi's struggle with this class was ineffective because he failed to see the complexity of this free-floating development not only as similar to but also as an integral growth emerging out of and counter to his own Islamism. Hence, we can more clearly understand the rise of 'Alī 'Uthmān and his class in relationship to what Ḥasan al-Turabi followed and perfected as some sort of a norm-aberration pattern of free-floating Islamist political pursuit. If so, then we can also begin to recognize that the maneuver followed from one situation to another, the way in which one could see the tangible relation at work within "absence" and the opportunities it provided, as explained in the previous chapters. More or less, both experiences of Ḥasan al-Turabi and 'Alī 'Uthmān in this field reflect different responses to forms of exculturation[3] that signifies different moves beyond and outside of the culture that Ikhwan Islamism—in al-Turabi's case—and al-Turabi Islamism in 'Alī 'Uthmān's case—helped form over the years but at different times. Needless to say, the question that might arise from such an inquiry deviates or appears to have ebbed from the local, regional, and the planetary discourse about Islamism. Is it possible to think of Islamism in its different transformations as a free-floating praxis within a norm-aberration pattern? A search for an understanding of such a pattern and its hidden effects that might be essential for coming to terms with that unfolding

2 Moḥamed Yousif Moḥamed (1932–2010) was one of the six students of Gordon Memorial College who founded *Harakat al-Tahrir al-Islami* (Islamic Liberation Movement) in 1949 under the leadership of Bābikir Karār. He assumed a leading position in the Islamist movement through time and its transformations and changes. He won the second seat for the Islamist in the Graduates' Electoral College in the elections that followed the October 1964 Revolution. He assumed the position of the speaker of the constituent assembly from 1986–1989 after the national democratic elections that followed the downfall of Nimeiri regime in 1985. 'Alī 'Uthmān received his first training as a lawyer after graduation from the University of Khartoum at Moḥamed Yousif's legal firm and maintained a close relationship with Moḥamed Yousif and his family.

3 Exculturation is a term created by the French sociologist Daniele Hervieu-Leger in her study of Catholicism: *Catholicisme, la fin d'un monde* (Catholicism: The End of a World) Paris, Bayard Presse, 2003). The term, according to Hervieu-Leger, indicates a situation of terminal decline when believers no longer identify with the surrounding culture, and when the cultural ethos are diminished or no longer in conformity with religion.

saga (which we have been addressing here as part of the developments of the present Sudanese or al-Turabi's Islamism as it has been entangled within 'Alī 'Uthmān and his class's web of significance) drives us to answer the question in the affirmative. The answer becomes worthy of our attention as more cumulative evidence confirms what exercises the mind and what lies everywhere. For as we look deeper into the genealogy of the diverse form and transformation within other Islamist experiences, the path of Islamism to oblivion is mapped, and investigations in this field of inquiry encompass similar or all-embracing relevant situations. To explain this better, let us illustrate this point from the case at issue.

Different Forms of Absence and Peculiar Routes to Power

During the first seven years of Nimeiri's rule—when most of the leaders of the Islamist movement were either in prison or in exile outside the country—the size, demography, and internal balance and unbalance that represented previous accord and kept the Islamist group within an accepted harmony were changed, if not clearly upset. The significance of this new development in Sudanese sociopolitical life was illustrated in the previous chapter. Yet, how that development established a very significant paradigm shift within the progression of al-Turabi Islamism has hardly been explored or even referred to by the Islamist scholars or those who have been studying Islamism in the Sudan. The exculturation of al-Turabi's Islamism took its first step with this shift. But what paved the way for a closed-ended, unfolding development of that phenomenon was that 'Alī 'Uthmān and his new class had been expanding numerically and directly or indirectly in their generational groups, political experience, and activities while being profoundly conditioned by that prevailing situation to transform the movement into a civic patronage of sorts. However, al-Turabi's prison years, long as they were, were not by any means similar to Antonio Gramsci or Sayyid Qutb's prison life, which were rich with intellectual achievement, as recorded in Gramsci's prison notebooks or Qutb's *M'aalim fi al-Tariq* (*Sign Posts*) and *Fi Zilal al-Qur'an* (*In the shade of the Qur'an*). The single prison message that Islamist students received from the imprisoned leader was *Risalat Nashr al-Dawa* (the message for the spread of *dawa*). That unsigned message, according al-Maḥboob 'Abdelsalam was not more than 20 pages in length. In that message, al-Turabi assured his Islamist readers that the time of freedom was coming soon, and they had to stay prepared; as he foresaw, the elements that supported the call for an Islamic constitution before the 1969 coup would come to life anew and be energized when freedom comes.[4]

Furthermore, during that period and due to that intractable and troublesome situations of prison and exile, members of the older Islamist leadership, who

4 Al-Maḥboob 'Abdel Salaam, *al-Haraka al-Islamiyya al-Sudanyya*, 16 (see Chapter 1, n. 6).

were suspended or even frozen within their pre-Nimeiri political traditions and experiences, were turned on their heads, if not on their side by a new and younger generation of Islamists. Thus, there is not only a situation that describes opportunities, but one that creates them as well. In this particular period, the continuous activation and even reinvention of the Islamist group, within the younger generation of ʻAlī ʻUthmān's class as a growing geography of centrality within al-Turabi Islamism, shifted from the leader to the foster father'ʻAlī ʻUthmān and his group. After those seven years, the era that ushered on both age groups of the Islamists in the Sudan, and Islamism in general, was anything but simple. Perhaps, that was the most unnoticed development, especially among many of the older generation of the Islamists and among most observers. It is in this period, however, and the unpredicted changes unfolded and set the way for the gradual process of dwarfing the senior leadership. It was the time when the kittens ate their father. That time, every aspect of inter and intra-politics—during the interregnum between the execution of the coup and now—had been charged and defined by violence, while Islamism itself became perverted from disintegration on its way to oblivion. Some people overlooked such developments of absence, the critical transformations, and the consequences, opportunities, and misfortunes that came out of these developments even though they remained manifest throughout the last four decades of the history of Islamism in the Sudan. Here, in tandem with these developments, some of the old Islamist traditions that perceived and approached life and politics "as a game of chance" surfaced and became the norm, as some Sudanese world political traditions and practices dissolved, and their edifying tenets collapsed. Whereas most previous Islamist personalities' ascension to power marked a clear path by stage managing their images through a history of detention by ruling authorities, self or forced exile, interparty power struggles, push and pull of specific interest groups, and/or ratification, election, and promotion through party congresses or conferences, none of these were the most rewarding for ʻAlī ʻUthmān . His accession to power had none of these.

Most clearly, a few of these traditions or roles of political upward mobility were relevant in the case of ʻAlī ʻUthmān. ʻAlī ʻUthmān and some of his generation of Islamists' peculiar and a non-progressive way of getting to the top had its singular and different path that had been masked by some ambiguous, if not mysterious, internal and external developments in the Islamist field of action. This peculiar method for getting to the top worked hand-in-hand with unorthodox "two item sets" of dictatorial changes in the state, the country's political spheres, and the manner in which these developments supplanted a production of "lifestyles," including polygamy as rites of passage, into the urban middle-class changes of status.[5] ʻAlī's

5 Some of the Islamists public statements that show change of status or introduction to urban middle-class milieu is the phenomenon of a semi-collective tradition of marrying multiple wives from urban middle-class families. ʻUmar al-Bashir himself, who took a second wife, encouraged the Sudanese male population, in a public statement, to take more than one wife.

mode of ascension to power is fundamentally different from the norm in previous Sudanese social and political life, and the latter political generations as it sets all other ways of power assumption as dissimilar if not old-fashioned. He has never been to prison like some of the most famous Islamists and non-Islamist Sudanese politicians and activists in the recent history of the country. He was never forced or had to choose to live in exile or study abroad like others. And he never wore a military uniform.

Strangely, while curious questions and possible answers to the phenomenon could be attempted and partially or wholly answered, this most stubborn question here—the enigma of absence as an opportunity—needs more attention and investigation. It is striking to see when one examines the entire history of Islamism in the Sudan that 'Alī 'Uthmān is undoubtedly the most successful Islamist to reach and maintain the highest position in the state of any, including Ḥasan al-Turabi.[6] Paradoxically enough, with his success, he has by no means developed his own personality cult or even a cult of precocity similar to al-Turabi's. Nor has he been endowed with the prestige and recognition from fellow Islamists that normally comes with the position of vice president. Even if 'Alī 'Uthmān had achieved a position that al-Turabi and other Islamists failed to reach, he has still been perceived as a representation of a "little man's syndrome" of sorts by his Islamists colleagues and countrymen.

Many things about 'Alī 'Uthmān and al-Turabi are similar: they both were well-known for being the at top of their classes throughout their school days; they both graduated from the University of Khartoum School of Law; and they both have been described by those who knew them better that they complement each other in being scheming. Nevertheless, nothing could bring out the contrast between the two men more than the ideas behind the Peter Pan and little man's syndromes and the stereotypical impulses that come with them. These conceptions lie in contrast to the family relation-based modes of acquisition, the cult of the master (teacher), and the articulate ideologue that al-Turabi maintained. Taken as a whole, 'Alī 'Uthmān's political experience and success reflects an era in Sudanese political life. It also reflects rationality and irrationality in dealing with the problems, the challenges, the complexity, and the oppressive nature of that polity and its policies as they have been fashioned according to that era's own capacities. In effect, 'Alī 'Uthmān shaped and was shaped by the possibilities, the misfortunes, and the opportunities endowed by a peculiar and an empty-hearted world of repeated periods of military rule in the country. Additionally, however, the most significant factor accounting for the Islamist experience in the Sudan and the course of events it has taken since its very early days in the 1940s (particularly

---

6 I excluded 'Umar al-Bashir who, most stories attribute the role of his relationship to 'Alī ' Osman in recruiting him before the coup. At the same time, there are serious doubts about his relationship to Islamism. It was only after *al-Mufāṣala* in 2000 that al-Bashir claimed that not only himself but his father too was a member of the Muslim Brotherhood. Ḥasan al-Turabi publicly contested al-Bashir's story.

during the leadership and time of Ḥasan al-Turabi and after) is that Islamism has no essence, but it has an accidental character. This accidental character became the gripping ordeal of these experiences and from which new if peculiar traditions were and continue to be invented.

'Alī 'Uthmān appeared in the national scene during the absence of democracy after the 1977 national reconciliation between some of the political parties—including the Islamists—and the Nimeiri regime. It was Nimeiri's regime that appointed him as part of the national reconciliation deal to the position of *Raid Majlis al-Shaab* (the majority leader in the parliament).[7] The case is clear enough, and it is supported with evidence that even the absence of democracy could turn into an opportunity. However, in that particular case, many were caught by surprise that such a young and obscure figure who was hardly known within the Sudanese political circle would be appointed to such a high position. It was something that was unheard of in the history of Sudanese politics before. Moreover, that particular case represented a real paradox as somebody who had no inside knowledge of the regime and its government, which his Islamist group raised arms against two times and had opposed for about seven years to become, over a night, its legislative senior parliamentarian. There might have been some objections or silent anger among the old generation of al-Turabi's Islamists for placing young 'Alī 'Uthmān at the top of the state structure. An important point here for al-Turabi's Islamism is how far the effect of that particular single event went, what it meant, and where it led as a master signifier attached—to a certain extent to all fields of Islamism—to its new and younger group. What was clear, one might say, from this uncompromising start that the message 'Alī 'Uthmān sent to his emerging Islamist new class, especially those who were disillusioned by the National Reconciliation with Nimeiri's regime, was that his appointment marked a break in the cage that set the lion free—but not completely as he still remained within the same zoo's courtyard. At issue here is how that process had made sense for many as it opened a new door for those who were deprived of power before. Hence, the silent message that young Islamists read was that there were opportunities waiting for them, and that what happened to 'Alī 'Uthmān was the start of a pie-in-the-sky of opportunities awaiting for them. It did not take long for 'Alī 'Uthmān to give the "good tidings" to different generations of Islamists. In 1979, 'Alī 'Uthmān expressed good news to a group of Islamist students from the University of Khartoum when he told them that the "Islamist movement

7 According to the Nimeiri regime, this position is equivalent to the position of the prime minister. The other Islamist who was appointed to the position of *Raqieb Majles al-Shaab* (equivalent to an opposition leader) was Yasin 'Omer al-Imām. Yasin, who was considered by many at that time as the second person in rank within the movement after al-Turabi, was offered a position lower in status and rank in comparison to 'Alī 'Uthmān's.

has been moving diligently to see *Lailat al-Qadr*[8] [the Night of Power]."[9] In considering the ambiguous characteristics of 'Alī 'Uthmān's appointment as an event that worked to lighten the heart of his rise to power, that particular event could be interpreted as *Lailat al-Qadr* and the most important event in the history and fortunes of 'Alī 'Uthmān . It was the long "occultation" of the leader and the absence of other leading, old-generation Islamists that became the source and the giver of an authority that was legitimized by the second coming of the leader himself from prison. It was the outcome of the absence and the coming back of the leader that institutionalized his Islamism not as an ideology that could be codified, learned, and advocated, but as a practice that could be emulated and utilized to bring together and promote the political operational coordinates of that particular political community of the community of the state. That marks two important developments in al-Turabi Islamism.

First, although the occultation of the leader shifted the unified principle of al-Turabi's Islamism from an ideological to an operational movement, the functional necessity for his presence after his release in the position of *al-Amin al-'Aam* (the uncontested supreme leader) at that critical time involved the recognition of his Islamism and its harmony as a master signifier of the movement. Since the day he was released from Nimeiri's prison, al-Turabi became a prisoner of his own circumstances. He remained inside a virtual prison controlled by this emerging new class of his "disciples," who kept him by limiting his movement within the objective necessity of the signifier field all the time. He also put himself in Nimeiri's virtual prison by associating himself with a regime and a state that concentrated all powers into the hands of Nimeiri himself. Nimeiri's callousness to assign him a senior position in the state's one party system, the Sudanese Socialist Union (SSU), succeeded only by keeping him in a state of suspended misery by moving him from one position to another. It was one of the requirements for survival in such a situation to praise the "genius" and superior qualities of *al-Rais al-Qaid* (the president leader).[10] But with regard to al-Turabi, the Islamist leader and his experience and relationship with Nimeiri and his regime, he became emasculated as he was changed from *al-Rais al-Quid* to one of those whom Nimeiri could

8 *Lailat al Qadr* (the Night of Power), according to most Muslims exegesis marks the night in which God first revealed the Qur'an to Prophet Moḥamed. Muslims regard this as the most important event in history, and the Qur'an says that this night is better than a thousand months (97:3). According to this Sura, on that night the angels descended to earth. The Sudanese believe those who would be blessed to see that night could have all their wishes fulfilled.

9 Al-Maḥboob Abdel Salaam, *al-Haraka al-Islamiyya al-Sudanyya*, p. 4 (see Chapter 1, n. 6).

10 Nimeiri became the focus of songs, poetry, and words of praise, especially during his presence that exhibited some sort of hypocritical devotion. One of these words of praise was *al-Rais al-Qaid* that represented a personality cult built around Nimeiri. For more about that personality cult, see: 'Abdullahi Gallab, *The First Islamist Republic*, 70–72 (see Chapter 1, n. 1).

humiliate—the same way he used to do with others—in front of other members of the SSU. Not only that, but it was clear from the start that Nimeiri could fire him or change his position at any time without consulting with him. So done, Nimeiri continued moving his former high school class mate Ḥasan al-Turabi from one position to another until finally he appointed him as "foreign affairs advisor where, as he said at the time, he received more advice than he was allowed to give, and where he received no official reports from relevant government agencies."[11] The tragedy here is that, *ṭiech hantoub* (the one at the bottom of his high school class [Nimeiri], outwitted the top student of that class [al-Turabi]).

But a more fundamental transformation was that Nimeiri in fact abolished al-Turabi's Islamism and replaced it with his own Islamism of *al-Nahj al-Islami kiaf.*[12] What will concern us here is to show how al-Turabi Islamism in its approaches to life and politics "as a game of chance" in one sense turned al-Turabi's own experience, to borrow Nandy's words, into "bastions of violence and irrationality"[13] directed by and against him. Needless to say, the violent historical role of al-Turabi's Islamists toward their leader, when they were outside the fields of state power and particularly after the coup when they turned their state into a violent totalitarian regime of domination, has no equal in Sudanese history. But even before the end of the Nimeiri regime, al-Turabi's Islamists turned their leader into a program of Islamism conforming to the logic of the operational political system and the growing corporation that developed during his absence. At the same time, they perfected it and turn it into hypocrisy and greed during Nimeiri's regime and ferocious wilding in the period after that. By default, not by design, his role within the myth was shrouded and transformed to adapt to these fast-moving metamorphoses in the country, the Nimeiri regime, and the fate of Islamism in the country and the region. Whenever he tried to move outside that field or attempt to revise his method, he found himself moved to the actual prison. This form and its system of violence grew and stayed alive to become the source of state authority that hung together in its different fashions and styles after the 1989 coup. One can easily say that nobody before or after that time suffered such an inferno from his own disciples and their absolutist state as al-Turabi has. Within the violence his disciples displayed toward him, he

11 'Abdel wahāb El-Affendi, *Turabi's Revolution*, 126 (see Chapter 3, n. 14).

12 Nimeiri appointed two lawyers, al-Nayal Abdel Gadir Abu Qurun, a son of a religious leader of a minor *Qadri ṭariqa*, 'Awad el Jeed Mohmed Aḥmed, a relatively young lawyer but a friend to al-Bayal, who both graduated from the University of Khartoum Law School in 1970, to write to him what was later known as *Qwanien September* (the September Laws). Nimeiri was reported to have told the two young lawyers in 1983 that they had to observe strict secrecy of their assignment and not to discuss the new laws with anybody, especially the "the man next door" who was Ḥasan al-Turabi and al-Nimeiri's advisor then whose office at the presidential palace was next door to the two lawyers.

13 Ashis Nandy, *The Savage Freud and Other Essays on Possible and Retrievable Selves* (Princeton, NJ: Princeton University Press, 1995), viii.

has been given actual detention, house arrest, and high-security virtual prisons. Actually the state, its institutions, and the Islamists who created them were all inseparable from the rise of, so to speak, the Islamists' violence that contrived to be the representation and the scene of the Islamist strategies and mode of conduct and system of governance.

Second, once again, what emerged out of the absence or occultation of al-Turabi, whether in his real or virtual imprisonment or other forms of absence, became the ultimate or the exclusive reason behind all the effects or the opportunities of 'Alī 'Uthmān's regime that carried significant implications and bred identifiable strides toward his rise to higher political positions. Only one time, such an "absence" as an opportunity for change acted against him. When his competitors took advantage of his six-month absence from the presidential palace while he was negotiating a peace agreement with John Garang, and hence al-Nafie Ali al-Nafie,[14] gained the opportunity *liyakoon lahou 'adowan*

14 Dr. al-Nafie 'Alī al-Nafie (1948–), the Sudanese presidential assistant and deputy chairman of the ruling NCP rose to his current power position within the Sudanese state apparatus and the ruling via a route similar to that of 'Alī 'Uthmān . During the absence of the latter, he took advantage of that situation to introduce himself as a critic of the CPA and as a person who could serve him better than 'Alī 'Uthmān . What made him closer to al-Bashir is that he came from a modest family background living in a small village in the rural hinterland of Shendi, a town in the riverain region to the north of Khartoum. Al-Nafie acquired his political promotion as one of 'Alī 'Uthmān emerging younger class of civilian Islamists and protégé of Ḥasan al-Turabi. He earned a PhD in Genetics from University of California Davis in 1980. When Nafie entered the University of Khartoum as a joint faculty in agricultural studies that year, the time 'Alī 'Uthmān gained prominence in the movement, he was still regarded as a relatively low-profile member of the movement. He undertook a career turn after a period at the Islamists Information Bureau (the NIF intelligence Bureau). Many claim that he took security and intelligence training in Tehran in 1981 under the cover of conducting further studies in the field of agriculture. There are claims also that he traveled to some Muslim and Arab countries making contacts with various militant organizations in Afghanistan and the Beka'a valley of Lebanon. He was one of the main founders of the Islamists' own security apparatus of Islamist regime and its notorious *Biyuot al-Ashbah*, which gave him an unappalled hatred among the Sudanese public. He was dismissed from this post, for his involvement in the 1995 assassination attempt on Husni Mubārak in Ethiopia. Nafie broke decisively with al-Turabi in 1998 when he, alongside a number of other senior Islamists, signed the Memorandum of the Ten, which signaled widespread discontent within the Islamic movement toward the policies pursued by al-Turabi during the 1990s. In the aftermath of al-Bashir's split with al-Turabi in 1999, Nafie grew close to al-Bashir, and took on a number of senior positions, acting as a presidential advisor during the peace talks with South Sudan and then as federal affairs minister. His rise to power and his influence has infuriated his arch-rivals in the NCP, especially 'Alī 'Uthmān and Salah Gosh. Their rivalry recently reached a peak during a series of confrontations that were heavily publicized by the media, as Gosh attacked Nafie for his hawkish stance and opposition to reconciliation with other parties. It has also been reported that in recent NCP party meetings Nafie has accused 'Alī 'Uthmān, who helped negotiate the 2005 Peace

wa hazanan (he became an enemy unto him and grief).[15] As we have seen, the "occultation" of the leader and the appearance of Ḥasan al-Turabi's Islamism in place was an important development in the history of the movement. Al-Turabi Islamism functioned as a master signifier in the political arena and the movement's internal organizational fields.

In connection with this practice and the fulfillment of duties, two of those who were outside prison at that time and who were endeavoring to influence rose to the position of the leader without occupying it or replacing the leader. A young physician from Darfur, 'Alī al-Ḥaj, who was assigned by Ḥasan al-Turabi to act as the party's executive authority,[16] and a young lawyer from Khartoum, 'Alī 'Uthmān, rose to their positions as the overseers of the students bureau and became the two men who temporarily inherited the position of the Secretary General, but not that of the leader. Certainly, their assumption of that position was to regulate and housekeep the affairs of al-Turabi Islamism as a master signifier. But there were other facets to that development.

There was the sense and the seismic effects of the modes of development that emerged after and as a consequence of the National Reconciliation that established new changes and conventions in the field of al-Turabi Islamism. The exuberances of that were not the same for all members and groups of the Islamist movement. An aggregate of serious effects followed as a result of the above-mentioned moves that came after 'Alī 'Uthmān's quick accession in the movement and state power. One of the consequences of this development was the creation of senior Islamist leadership, such as Moḥamed Yusuf Moḥamed, Yasin 'Umar al-Imam, Aḥmed 'Abdel Rahman, 'Uthmān Khalid, and 'Abdel Rahim Ḥamdi. It also included those whom al-Turabi described as the traditionalists: Ṣaldiq 'Abdullah 'Abdel Magid and his Egyptian school of Muslim Brotherhood. Yet, all were either completely or partly dwarfed.

Simultaneously, a younger group came to the fore as a consequence of 'Alī 'Uthmān's rise to power. However, the ripple effect of that single act was far wider than what affected the old group of Islamists. Furthermore, that event put more distance between 'Alī 'Uthmān—in particular—and 'Alī al-Ḥaj—to a certain extent—and other, slightly older, functionaries of the Islamists, such as el-Tayib Zean al-'Abdin, Rabi'i Ḥasan Aḥmed, Ḥafiz al-Shiekh al-Zaki, Aḥmed

---

Agreement, of being behind the secession of South Sudan. It is an over simplification to follow some analysts' argument that these rivalries reflect an ethnic character of Jaaliyyin of al-Bashir in opposition to 'Alī 'Uthmān as Shayqiyya.

15 The Qur'an says that the Pharaoh picked child Moses from the Nile to become an enemy unto them and a source of grief. 'Alī 'Uthmān threw Nafie away from a position of significance when the assassination attempt of Husni Mubārak went wrong to be picked by al-Bashir during the absence of 'Alī 'Uthmān. That day, Nafie became the sworn enemy and source of 'Alī 'Uthmān's grief.

16 'Alī al-Haj Moḥamed, interview by author, audio recording, Bonn, Germany, July 24, 2012.

Ibrāhim al-Turabi, to name a few. At the same time, the rise of 'Alī 'Uthmān could be seen as a phase in the rise of the totalitarian impulse and practice and the third generation of the Islamists' group who came into the field of power after the 1989 coup. After the coup, the new young generation of the Sudanese found themselves in fierce competition, sometimes cut throat competition, and other times sharp conflict with each other. 'Alī 'Uthmān and al-Haj, for example, represented the main competing actors if not rivals for the second position in the state and the party before and after the death of al-Zubair Moḥamed Saliḥ, the first vice president who died in a plane crash in 1998. The power struggle between the two 'Alī s continued throughout the lifetime of the first Islamists Republic only to take a different shape after the downfall of al-Turabi in 2000. 'Alī al-Ḥaj lives now in exile in Germany. Mysterious circumstances put an end to another hidden form of individual competitors, rivals, or ambitious personalities who came from outside the civilian Islamists' third generation. These included Al-Zubair Moḥamed Salih, Ibrāhim Shams el-Din, and those from inside that class who presented a challenge to 'Alī 'Uthmān, such as Majzoub al-Khalifa.[17] All lost their lives in peculiar circumstances without serious investigation to the causes. On the one hand, another power base, which the Sudanese describe as the Shaigiyya tribe gang from 'Alī 'Uthmān's same generation. And this new class, who formed a core group around 'Alī 'Uthmān and included 'Awad al-jazz and 'Alī Kurti, constituted the foundation of a core group that held power through their control of the money, the security apparatus and army, and the militia. On the other hand, there are those the Sudanese satire describe as *al-Ḥijar al-Karima* (precious stones) who include al-Bashir, his family, and his relatives—whose original home was around villages called Ḥajar al-'Asal and Ḥajar al-Ṭair—and their axillary team that included Nafie 'Alī Nafie, Qutbi al-Mahdi, Amin Ḥasan 'Umer and other members of the existing "Deep State." That of course did not exclude those of 'Alī 'Uthmān's competitors who stayed alive, if ineffective, such as Ghazi Salah al-Din, those who resented and disagreed with the whole Inqaz arrangements from first day, such as Dr. el-Ṭayib Zean al-'Abden, those who expressed their dissension later, such as Ḥasan Mekki, 'Abdel Rahim 'Umar Muhi el-Din, El-Tigani 'Abdel Gadir, and 'Abdel wahāb al-Affendi, Khalid al-

17 Al-Khalifa, a dermatologist that Ḥasan al-Turabi sarcastically described "even his speciality is superficial" He was a serious competitor to 'Alī 'Utman. He was well-known for aggressive and bully behavior. Alex de Waal described how Khalifa operated in negotiations as "retail politics". The Sudanese satire described his ambitious derive as *wazir bi makanat raies jamhouria* [a minister with a president engine]. He served as a minister of agriculture and information. He headed the negotiating team in Abuja talks that led to DPA signing of peace deal with some of Darfur rebels. His last position in government was an advisor to the president. He died in a mysterious car crash in June 2007 on the road from his hometown Shendi to Khartoum.

Tigani al-Nur, and others who had not identified themselves with the state and who opposed its regime at different times of its life.[18]

Yet, the depth of the Sudanese dissension in general, of course, goes beyond that small groups of Islamists and should not be glossed over. At issue here is also the question of the mysterious death of some the leading personalities of the Islamists like Magzuob al-Khalifa, Ibrahim Shams eldin, al-Zubair Moḥamed Ṣaliḥ, who perished in atypical circumstances when airplanes and SUVs turned into fast-moving coffins.

The elimination and riddance of those and other local competitors and rivals to ‘Alī ‘Uthmān poses a serious question that goes beyond *al-qadaa wa al-qadar*[19] (fate and divine decree).[20] What is striking is that no official investigation report of any of these death incidents was ever published, even though the ghosts of each one of those victims still looms around seeking straightforward answers to complicated questions. The last three decades have seen many other Islamist personalities dropped through the cracks. What all that is in relation to ‘Alī ‘Uthmān and his rise and stay in power might be an important feature of al-Turabi's Islamism, which approached life and politics as a game of chance. Accordingly, al-Turabi Islamism addressed all aspects of life as something to be dealt with through violence, intrigue, and greed.

Hence, the interconversational conflicts and the battles that arose out of it cannot be defined by the inclusion or exclusion of Islam as a religion or Islamism as an ideology. By the same token, neither Islam nor Islamism can be a product of any forms of its discourses as in their place violence and toxic talk sought to substitute for both. That is why none of those within the Islamist divide ever attributed their internal wars to the actions of the Supreme Being, nor did any group attempt to issue *fatwa* or *takfir* of the other side. That might help explain ‘Alī ‘Uthmān's journey through the corridors of power in sociopolitical terms rather than religious terms.

But at one point, we need to look at how and why these Islamist individuals and groups together with al-Turabi Islamism transformed, developed, and modified the emergence and falling-off of some or all of those individuals and groups within the overground period of its life. This was during the democratic period from 1985 to 1989 and during the nondemocratic first and second Islamist republics from 1989 to the present. The fact remains whether implicitly or explicitly, these developments were productions on net of what, as said before,

---

18 Totalitarianism here is inherent in al-Turabi's Islamism as explained in previous chapters, coercing the melding of society and the state.

19 Most of the time, within Sudanese culture, people attribute instances of death that they do not know to an apparent cause or what they call fate and divine decree.

20 In his book, *al-Haraka al-Islamiyya al-Sudaniyya*, p. 372, al-Maḥboob ‘Abdel Salaam (see Chapter 1, n. 6), hinted to the increased frequency of airplane death accidents that lead to the death of many politicians of the regime that there might have been conspiracies behind them as the Sudanese opposition circles claimed.

was their web of significance. It is interesting that whenever those individuals and groups faced new developments or when they perceived their momentous possibilities, they addressed them with violence and with an open eye instead of taking refuge in the dispositions of the past or with an ideological textbook or reference. It is clear now that remembering or talking about the reality and the way these events and conflicts took place and materialized into serious hostilities among the Islamists brings no comfort to most of those who lived these experiences. Such an attitude could be attributed to what I call "an Islamist moral panic," which is part of the opposing voice of some of the Islamists over what they consider un-Islamist governmentality. This is conduct that they call *fitnat al-sulta* (the arrogant behavior) of other Islamists in power. Different forms of it are somewhat dated, but the discourse remained exceedingly bitter. The bitterness reflected itself within each one of these groups' proximity to the Islamist state, which overtly or covertly rejected one person, group, or another. That "Islamist moral panic" impulse also reflects itself in a feeling of inferiority or shame that manifests in a constant need for an institutional reassurance that would be approved by being employed by the state; otherwise they would live in a state of suspended isolation blaming their fellow Islamists. Aḥmed al-Tigani Ṣaliḥ, one of those who found himself in a similar situation wrote expressing his bitterness, that "the topmost of the *Mashāish* singular *Shaikh* [the older leadership] who have been sidelined from positions of leadership in the movement and the party ... continue to meet together in breakfasts, lunches and sweet dinners and reminiscence [in bitterness] the good days and conclude by saying: *nsamaa j'aj'atn wa la nara ṭaḥnan* [hear bluster but we see no crushes]."[21] Other individuals and groups who suffered from being sidelined continued to claim that they had been betrayed by being ejected out of the state and the privileges that came with it. Those groups, and especially the ones who joined Ḥasan al-Turabi's *al-Motamar al-Shabi* (the Popular Congress), have an attitude of moral panic that was exhibited in feelings of anger and search for revenge as in the case of al-Turabi himself. It is interesting that al-Tuarbi set the tone for this trend of moral panic by presenting the split among the ranks of his Islamists as something that happened to him as an event in history that strands alone initiated by *naqd al-'ihoud* (betrayal to promises).[22] In looking at the internal structure of the regime, especially for those who succumb to this civic siege, it can be painful to be an Islamist and show identification or empathy

21 Aḥmed el-Tigani Salih Abu Bakr, *al-Siyasa wa-l-Hukm: al-Nuxum al-Sultaniyya Bayna al-Usul wa Sunan al-Waqi* ([The Sudanese Islamic Movement After Fifty Years; Where it is: An analytical Critical Assessment] Khartoum, Sharikt Matab'i al-Sudan lil 'Umla, 2008), 8.

22 Al-Turabi here evokes a fundamental Islamic tenet, which *al-wafaa bi al 'ahd* as the Qur'an says, *wa awfu bil-'ahdi in al-'hada kana musula* (and be true to every promise—for, verily, [on the day of judgment, you will be called to account to every promise which you have made]).

to a manifestation of a credence that gets all things—almost—horribly wrong. The Shakespearian Hamlet of the regime, Ghazi Salah al-Din al-'Atabāni for example, whose loyalty to Islamism made him angry at Claudius who killed Islamism and got married to its state. So, his ongoing moral panic took on a more ideological form as expressed in conscious soliloquies that brought out his complex mental state by claiming that he "feels ashamed to say that the Islamists did not rule."[23]

Beyond this, there is another further development that is principally related to absence as an opportunity that 'Alī 'Uthmān met at the midpoint between the front and the back stages of both the Nimeiri regime and the Islamist. Both collaborated with him and the developments in each one's field of action. The first quarter of 1985 was a time when both parties were entangled in a serious struggle for life and death. The state of affairs worried about both parties. It was not only the view inside the regime that made it disproportionally disturbing for both parties that their state of dependency on each other had provided an insight into the terrible fact that each one's survival seemed dependent on the other one's destruction. The extent of the institutionalized and semi-institutionalized relationship that members from each party exercised regardless of the position they held, or were perceived to have held, seriously worsened their reputational problems and overshadowed the national and international debate about the regime and the Islamists. The opposition to the imposition of Shari'a and the criticism of the use and abuse of its implementation for both parties came from all national and international political fields and sectors.

For example, the outbreak of the war in the southern part of the country in mid 1983 was perceived as an outcome of the Shari'a that reflected both Nimeiri and the Islamist parties' opportunism. For the Islamist, it was clear by that time that Nimeiri was on his way to recycling them the same way he did with other political groups before. However, the Islamists who did not read Nimeiri correctly thought they should "maintain business-as-usual attitude[s]. In their analysis, Nimeiri was saying these things [against the Islamists] in order to pacify the West. Nimeiri was apparently not thinking of a crackdown on Ikwan [Islamists] at first, but rather to isolate them and remove them from the centre of power."[24] For Nimeiri and his regime, *Al-Nahj al-Islami kayfa?* (The Islamic Path How?)[25] al-

23 He reiterated this in an interview with the author, recording, Khartoum, Sudan January 4, 2006.

24 'Abdel wahāb El-Affendi, *Turabi's Revolution*, 128 (see Chapter 3, n. 14).

25 Nimeiri's Islamic political approaches and policies were explained in three books, two of which were ascribed to his authorship but were actually written by his ghost and speechwriter, Moḥamed Mahjoub Suliaman. The first one is titled, *Al-Nahj al-Islami limadha?* (Why the Islamic Path?), which was published in Cairo in 1980. The book described in an autobiographical style why and how he found his true self since the early years of his rule in growing observance of Islam. He ascribed to the abortive Communist coup of July 1971, the beginning of born-again Islam. The second book was titled *Al-*

Turabi and his group had exhausted their function, and he began to pull the strings out of the whole costly experience with the Islamists and its memories. It is true that "Nimeiri's new-founded position as imam, religious leader, and head of an Islamic state was particularly distasteful in a country as religiously diverse as Sudan."[26] But the Islamists who cut themselves loose in the savage world of Ja'afar Nimeiri "had lost greatly in popularity and support within the vital modern sector, especially among vocal educated elite, because of their opposition to trade union demands for higher pay. In 1984, they lost control of the key students unions at Khartoum and Omdurman Islamic universities."[27] In January 1985, the execution of Republican Brothers Leader Mahmoud Muhammad Ṭaha "for expressing opposition to Nimeiri's Islamization program brought strong condemnation from many quarters, and the fallout rebounded on Ikhwan, although Ikhwan's role in the bizarre events that led to the man's death was not at all central." It did not take Nimeiri long to turn against the Islamists. In February of the same year, "the involvement of Ikhwan in clashes at Khartoum University campus gave Nimeiri that pretext to lash at them and probably influenced his later decision to act against them."[28] The more Nimeiri could find a group to blame, the more he could find a safe way out to a new field of a coming game. His long experience in playing the similar game with other political groups taught him that once the designation of blame is assumed, it is equivalent to treason. The violent ways of the state would justify its act against that group and need not be cast in doubt. By March 1985, Nimeiri launched his campaign against the Islamists and rounded up most of their leaders. 'Alī 'Uthmān was among the few who escaped that witch hunt and went underground. This situation of 'Alī 'Uthmān being outside prison had served him very well. As soon as the demonstrations began in Khartoum, many saw his shadowy figure in various places. But most importantly, he was there to meet with a new opportunity during the absence of Ḥasan al-Turabi who was in El-Obeid prison.

Through a successful move of civil disobedience after the collapse of Nimeiri's regime on April 6, General Swar al-Dahab and some of high-ranking generals seized power. As 'Abdel wahāb El-Affendi explained, what the Islamists

Nahj al-Islami kayfa? (The Islamic Path How?), which was scheduled to be published in August 1983, but appeared only in April 1985, the month Nimeiri's downfall from power through civil disobedience. It was the intention of Nimeiri and his power group, antagonistic to Islamists, to explain and illustrate how the Islamic path was to be implemented. The third book contains the proceedings of an international Islamic conference, held in Khartoum in September 1984, to celebrate the first anniversary of the implementation of the Shari'a and to eulogize the "great imam," Ja'afar al-Nimeiri. It was published by the Sudanese parliament under the title *'Am 'ala tatbiq al-sharia al-Islamiyya fi al-Sudan* (One Year since the Implementation of the Islamic Shari'a in the Sudan).

26 Mansour Khaled, *The Government They Deserve: The Role of Elite in Sudan's Political Evolution* (London: Kegan Paul International, 1990), 327.

27 'Abdel wahāb El-Affendi, *Turabi's Revolution*, 128.

28 Ibid.

immediately confronted "was the extent of political isolation of the movement internally and internationally as a result of the policies pursued during the preceding years."[29] Moreover, the professionals, trade unions, and political parties who led the civil obedience movement against Nimeiri's regime were bitterly hostile to the Islamists and their leader Ḥasan al-Turabi for his collaboration with the regime. John Garang described the new *Intifada* government as *Mayo 2* (the second phase of J'affar Nimeiri May regime) and refused to stop the war in the South of the Sudan or to meet with the new government to negotiate a peaceful negotiation to the problem. The one serious attempt by the entire political body of the Sudan was that the Islamists "must be excluded completely from the new order and must be punished severely for supporting Nimeiri's excesses."[30]

But despite the problems surrounding them, the Islamists organized a rally, which they called *Aman el-Sudan* (the security of Sudan), in support of the Sudanese armed forces which were demoralized by the poor performance of its troops in the South. The army, the generals who assumed power, and the Islamists needed each other. It was an opportunity, with the previous Islamist leadership in prisons, for 'Alī 'Uthmān to seize power. A hardly established group that included some of the three entities and called *Aman el-Sudan* (the security of the Sudan) was put together. 'Alī 'Abdalla Yagoub and el-Fatih 'Abdon,[31] an ex-army general and a personal friend of Nimeiri, played an important role in mobilizing a big crowd that went to the headquarters of Sudan Armed Forces where 'Alī 'Uthmān talked to the crowd and told the army that they came to give them their unconditional support. The most important aspect of that was that 'Alī 'Uthmān became a central figure among the Islamist officers in the army.

In the broader scheme of things, however, while the dictatorial role of Nimeiri paved the way for 'Alī 'Uthmān to assume one of the highest positions, *Raid Mujlis al-Shaab,* the coming of democratic rule in the country in the first elections after the downfall of Nimeiri, which was held in 1986, gave 'Alī 'Uthmān the opportunity to assume an even a higher position in the state as the opposition leader in the absence of Ḥasan al-Turabi, who was defeated in that election.

29 Ibid.

30 Ibid.

31 'Alī 'Abdalla Yaqoub and al-Fatih 'Abdon organized a big rally that celebrated the first anniversary of the implementation of Shari'a in the Sudan, which they called a One Million March Rally. A very successful international conference that brought more than 200 international Islamists was convened in Khartoum. Suspicious Nimeiri was alarmed by the ability of the Islamists to mobilize such a gathering while his own party *al-Ithad Ishtraky al-Sudani* (Sudanese Socialist Union) with all the facilities provided to it by the state could not mobilize 10 percent of that number.

The Crumple of the Invisible Divide

T. Abdou Maliqlim Simone noted that 'Alī 'Uthmān Ṭaha, "NIF deputy general secretary and head of the party's military 'radical' youth wing, was the most powerful man in the country."[32] Certainly, one might concede that was an outcome of a long and careful attempt at taking advantage of opportunities that availed themselves over more than 20 years of the Islamist movement. 'Alī 'Uthmān was able to take special advantage when al-Turabi Islamism turned its political authority over to 'Alī al-Ḥaj as a caretaker during the absence of the supreme leader who was the only ideology giver. But as the caretaker and the other "artisans" who followed him and institutionalized the idea, not the ideology, that political class continued to grow and develop a life of its own. During the interregnum days of the 1989 coup when al-Turabi was in prison and the *mufāṣala* was stripped from all power, the hidden and apparent conflict between al-Turabi and that new class and its leader, 'Alī 'Uthmān, grew and surmounted in one form only to provoke itself and surface in another more intensified if not aggravated form. For a considerable time, this conflict was kept silent and to a certain extent secret, but it began to become an open secret after the coup; and the state was used to embody the agenda, strategies, and violence of a certain group who directed its power against the other group—*Shaikh* Ḥasan in particular. In that sense, the state became the signifier of Islamism while Islamism itself mutated from disintegration to oblivion. However, it took Ḥasan al-Turabi a very long time to hint at that. When a foreign journalist asked him after *al-mufāṣala* if his deputy 'Alī 'Uthmān stood behind 'Umar al-Bashir in what he did, Al-Turabi with his familiar sarcasm answered "but he stands in front of him." That might be true; however, how does this long-term concern for Ḥasan al-Turabi tie up the development of the two Islamist republics? What was happening, in fact, was that the greatest opportunity that 'Alī 'Uthmān had in his entire life was the one that emerged in the absence of Ḥasan al-Turabi and other senior member Islamists who went to prison on the first day of the 1989 coup. He carried out the integration of every field of power. 'Alī al-Haj explained that all the lists of nominees for ministerial and senior state employee who would be appointed to replace the purged state bureaucracy were even given to him. By controlling the Islamist new middle class, the military and the civil service, the Islamist coup produced a monster from its first day. That monster was called 'Alī 'Uthmān. Hence, when considering the efforts being made to confront any potential dangers that might threaten the new regime and its state from outside, he made additional efforts to erect his state structure and prepare his plan for how to handle the challenges and threats that laid at its heart. As for the first expected danger or potential threat, the regime put in practice *'aqidat al-'onf* (ideology of violence)[33] as its mode of operation. As for the threats that lie at its heart, 'Alī and his team created a very

32 T. Abdou Maliqalim Simone, *In Whose Image?*, 66 (see Chapter 5, n. 35).

33 The term was coined by al-Maḥboob 'Abdelsalaam in his book *al-Haraka al-*

efficient system by keeping Ḥasan al-Turabi confined in his real prison at Kober for six months instead of one month according to the agreement between him and his deputy. After that, he was transferred to house arrest for a longer time. After that and until 1995, the time of the assassination attempt on the Egyptian President Husni Mubārak, both Ḥasan al-Turabi and 'Umar al-Bashir were at different locations on maximum-security virtual arrest. During this time, the two men never met face-to-face without the attendance of 'Alī 'Uthmān and other members of his team: 'Alī Kurti and 'Awad al-Jazz in particular. 'Alī 'Uthmān administered and filtered all the reports each of the two men—al-Turabi and Bashir received. Later in 1992, Hashim Badereddin, a Sudanese exile who was a black belt in karate, knocked al-Turabi unconscious upon his arrival to the Ottawa airport in Canada. Al-Turabi, who was left nearly dead after the attack, suffered severe head injuries and spent about a month in a Canadian hospital in a coma undergoing observations for his injuries. Al-Turabi "himself later called it a Western-inspired assassination. The Security Intelligence Review of the Canadian government prepared a report on the assault that has never been public."[34] According to al-Maḥboob 'Abdelsalaam, a conspiracy was hatching at home as 'Alī 'Uthmān started to prepare for al-Turabi to be moved to a European capital on the pretext that he needed more time away from the country to recover. However, al-Turabi surprised 'Alī 'Uthmān and his government by planning secretly for his return to Khartoum after he recovered.[35]

It is worth looking more seriously into certain characteristics of 'Alī 'Uthmān's class of young Islamists. After the coup, they perpetuated themselves and considered capturing the state as *kasb* (opportunity) and had self-serving motives. Their new relationships carried the message that the new class belonged to the state and its republics rather than to al-Turabi Islamism. Hence, they utilized *kasb* and the state organs that facilitated and transformed *al-tamkeen* into some sort of wilding, regulated, and distributed new and old forms of violence as the mode of governance. Thus, they did not emerge as a dominant class by virtue of being a professional, religious, or even an ideological group endowed by private power; they emerged as members of their own class and within its own personal and collective attributes that followed its own unequivocal system that developed their own technologies of power and violence from the invention of its membership. All too often, some Sudanese and non-Sudanese observers attributed this development to a tribal or *shiqqiyya* or/and *jaliyeen* '*asabiyya* or solidarities. This is by all means an over simplistic characterization of a deeply dithering phenomenon.

It was clear from the early days of the coup and the emergence of its state that there was a strong temptation to get rid of al-Turabi and his Islamism. It is true

---

Islamia al-Sudaniyya (p. 118) describing how the regime unleashed its violence from its early days.

34 J. Millard Burr and Robert O. Collins, *Revolutionary Sudan: Ḥasan al-Turabi and the Islamist State 1989–2000* (Leiden: Brill, 2003), 99.

35 Al-Maḥboob 'Abdelsalaam, *al-Ḥaraka al-Islamiyya fi al-Sudan*, 127 (see Chapter 1, n. 5).

that 'Alī 'Uthmān and his group in power grew into a class within the Islamist community; however, they differentiated their actions by the way they acquired their ambivalent status and their positions as a world apart from al-Turabi and his Islamism, as well as the Sudanese religious, civic, or even ethnic nationalism. That would be the source of so many calamities inflicted on Sudanese citizens, such as ghost houses, the Janjaweed violence, and the separation of the south to name a few. Likewise, that explains why and how they treated their leader and mentor Ḥasan al-Turabi in such inhuman way. It was clear from the very start that they did not intend to release him from prison only to keep him under house arrest in a similar way as Jamal 'Abdul Nasser did with Moḥammed Naguib.[36] Although that attempt to keep al-Turabi under house arrest did not succeed the same way Naguib's did, other plots against al-Turabi continued to hatch in different forms.

And yet, the more 'Alī 'Uthmān and his group continued to establish themselves as the state, the more a representation of themselves as a nation and as the heart of the Sudanese social life, the end became even clearer. In this sense, we can see how getting rid of Ḥasan al-Turabi materialized. A year before the events of December 1999, when al-Turabi was stripped of power, 10 of the regime's emerging, young, leading Islamists surprised the meeting of the *Majlis a-shura* (the Shura Council) by distributing a memorandum that was not scheduled in the meeting's agenda. The memorandum criticized the experience of the Islamic movement in power since 1989 and suggested conferring a number of al-Turabi's powers as Secretary General of the "Congress Party" to al-Bashir. The memorandum was called the Memorandum of Ten because it had 10 signatories, including seven of the young Islamists, one from the old guard, one from the military, and another from the second generation of the Islamist movement. They were Sayyid al-Khatieb, Ghazi Salah al-Din al-'Atabāni, Aḥmed 'Alī al-Imam, Aḥmed Torien, Bakri Ḥasan Salih, Ibrahim Aḥmed 'Umar, Bahaa al-Din Hanafie, Mutrif Sidiq, Nafie 'Alī Nafie, and 'Uthmān Khalid Modawi. The memo was a critical assessment of the 10 years of the Islamist experience in power and offered suggestions for reforming the governing structures of the ruling Congress Party. The proposed reforms stripped al-Turabi of his powers as Secretary General and concentrated them in the hands of al-Bashir. According to 'Abd al-Rahim 'Umar Mohi el-Din, the memo was written by an obscure Islamist by the name of Bahaa' al-Din Hanafi who used to describe himself as antisocial. Dr. Hanafi, who was a graduate of an American university, was known among the Islamists for being openly critical of al-Turabi. Ghazi Salah al-Din al-'Atabāni, one of the 10 and the Information Minister at the time, told *Voice of America* that he "was not

36 Major General Mohammed Naguib (1901–1984) was the primary leader of the 1952 coup that ended the rule of Egypt's royal family or Mohammed Ali Dynasty in Egypt. He was the first President of Egypt, who served from the declaration of the Republic on June 18, 1953 to November 14, 1954. Naguib's power struggle and disagreements with Jamal 'Abdul Nasser led to his forced removal from office, and subsequent 18 years of house arrest that continued until President Anwar Sadat released him in 1972.

viewed as part of a plot against Professor Turabi, but he says it started a process that culminated in the December 12 emergency measures." In actual fact, what transpired then was the extension of the influence of one faction of the Islamists at the highest level of institutional power.

The conflict that split the Islamist National Congress Party into two antagonistic groups was embedded in the revitalization and the deconstruction of race and ethnicity questions within the Islamist groups and the country at large. The group of Western Islamists who stood behind al-Turabi and constituted a substantial number in his party leadership represented more than an ordinary political association. They represented a project of a community with specific cultural and ethnic characteristics and "tactical necessity and common interest."[37] On the other hand, because al-Turabi himself was not a *gharabi*, his leadership might have helped break the closure practices enforced by the northern dominant groups. In this respect, it seems that the regional and race issues brought two things within the ranks of the Islamists: cultural prejudice and ethnocentrism on one hand, and the creation of different techniques of breaking the barriers and closure to get these groups in the Sudanese mainstream on the other. When these two processes came together, an interesting phenomenon emerged, which is worthy of exploration. It seems that the conflict between the two groups was rife even before surfacing in 1999, and I think the *Black Book*, which was printed and widely distributed after the split, was one of the delayed bombs of the propaganda war between the two groups.

Of course, the demise of the first Islamist republic was more complicated than a mere changing of the guard. It was a transformation that marked the end of the first republic; and it was a direct result of serious corrosion from within augmented by external forces. The conflict between al-Turabi and al-Bashir and their supporters that came out in the open in 1999, after years of power struggle between the two men, was only the tip of the iceberg. Because al-Bashir wanted to keep his military attire and his supporters their ideological garb while maintaining the continuity of the Islamist project without al-Turabi's leadership, the history of these developments, al-Turabi's character, the state model, and the ideas that governed the entire experience deliberately distorted, and al-Turabi himself was also openly attacked and even thrown into prison on more than one occasion. Further, al-Turabi continued to express in different forms and forums similar negative and distorted claims about his opponents and the entire experience. In his newly published a book, *al-Siyasawa al-Hukm: al-Nusum al-Sultniyabayna al-usulwa Sunnan al-Waq'ai* (Politics and Governance: Ruling Orders between the Fundamentals and the Conventions of Reality), which he wrote while he was in prison, al-Turabi writes that he "intended to establish a complete extrication from the history of al-Ingadh while condemning it without a forthright confrontation

---

37 C. Geertz, *Old Societies and New States: The Quest for Modernity in Asia and Africa* (Glencoe, the Free Press: 1965), 56.

with that past." So, although the conflict reflected a serious crisis within the regime, the state, and the Islamist movement at large, many observers and even some of the Islamists themselves did not yet comprehend the depth and breadth of the end of the first Islamist republic. The fault line here could have been seen more clearly within the latent and manifest intervening factors that augmented the end of the first Islamist republic. The effects of these intervening factors had been operating through a mediating process in which conflict among the Islamist power groups had become, in turn, the medium that affected the outcomes.

In examining these factors it is important to stress the formal and informal activities and strategies of political and religious actors, as well as the debates and critical activities of intellectuals, journalists, and politicians, as part of the mechanism of generating a new political culture that could mediate new spheres to curb the regime's political and totalitarian designs. All these sets of factors and events worked to accelerate the regime's uneasy transfer of power and to usher in the end of the first Islamist republic. This might be seen as what Gramsci calls "one of these cases in which these groups have the function of 'domination' without that of 'leadership:' dictatorship without hegemony." In the second Islamist republic, the focus of the system was a Nimeiri-like military state where, this time, a "narrow clique" of the Islamist elite were managed, ruled, and "protected by the armor of coercion" represented by 'Umar al-Bashir. It seems that in analyzing the regime, factors of political conflict have been overemphasized at the expense of other factors, such as religion and societal change. This chapter focuses on these underlying developments and accentuates their role in the disintegration of the first republic.

The state, which they hastily created, has concentrated power in the hands of 'Umar al-Bashir, who now has all the power to manage that narrow clique. At the same time, the NCP, which was once described as the ruling party, has also been turned into the party of the state.

In December 2013, 'Alī 'Uthmān stepped down as a first vice president. He was purged by the person he recruited one day to lead the coups of 1989 and 1999. After years of holding the state, the party and all the Islamist men hostage in a web of significance he carefully and furtively spun, it was surprisingly clear he was easily removed. Yet one would search in vain for an understanding of what was the function of 'Alī 'Uthmān in terms of Islamism? When he ascended power and nobody celebrated that, and when he descended that nobody missed him. Should we say that was the destroyer of Islamism? It might be more than that. It was the fate of Islamism itself.

Chapter 9

The Great Exodus: Walking Out of the Islamist Regime and its State and the Liberation and Citizenship Debate

The Sudanese pride themselves in the fact that Sudan was the first African country to gain independence from British colonialism. Ismā'il al-Azhari,[1] whom many Sudanese revere as the father of independence, claims that the vocation and the main objective of independence is *tahrir wa liysa t'amir* (liberation but not development). Nevertheless, the Sudanese people have not been liberated yet. To move such a claim from its observed and experienced premises to the specific, normative social and political positions, many debatable steps may be needed. Liberation comes in many different forms, which must be taken seriously to qualify for *liberation as a process* that is separate from not only all forms of colonial and totalitarian rule at the hands of local systems, including the existing Islamist regime, but also—as we have already indicated—from two distinctive practices. These practices must be well defined if they are to become cherished. But if they become cherished, must these distinctive practices simultaneously work together and separately to somehow successfully establish an order on one side and keep a promise on the other? Would such practices materialize as innovative endeavors that are genuinely liberating the state concurrently with human life in their content and consequences in a way that could endow meaning to human beings as citizens and give value to their acts, rights, duties, and existence?

1 Ismā'īl al-Azharī (1900–1969) was considered and revered by most Sudanese as the father of independence. He played an instrumental role in achieving the Sudan's independence in 1956, and he served as the first prime minister from 1954 to 1956. Ismā'il al-Azharī was born in Omdurman, the son of a religious notable, grandson of Ismail al-Azhari the Grand Mufti of Sudan (1924–1932), and a descendent of the nineteenth-century Asyyid Ismā'il al-Walī. He was educated at Gordon Memorial College at Khartoum and graduated in mathematics at the American University of Beirut in Lebanon, 1930. He was a leading figure with other Sudanese-educated elite in forming the Graduates' General Congress in 1938 and al-Ashiqqa Party, and he was the president of the National Unionist Party (NUP) when it was formed in 1952. His party won an overwhelming victory in the elections of 1953. After the October 1964 Revolution, al-Azharī reemerged as the head of the NUP, and in 1965 he was elected as the permanent president of the Supreme Council (i.e., head of state). He remained head of state until the military coup on May 1969 ended his political life. He died in August the same year.

These two practices include, first, the liberation from a myriad series of contrivances, practices, and mentalities of "totalist" politics, ideologies, and systems that have plagued the Sudanese experience of governance since the early colonial days of Wingate and his state, in particular, and have taken different turns and forms up to now. To state the matter even more explicitly, the Sudanese need to liberate the state that represents the inherent and inherited system and structures of power and coercion developed as part of the colonial experience. This state experience, that needs to be liberated, has sat from the first day in an entirely awkward and fractious situation and has harmed the Sudanese life, individuals, and communities. From the colonial time onward, systems of governance primarily have been founded on the principles of sovereignty of violence rather than sovereignty of citizenship. Hence, neither the Sudanese state nor the civil society and their social bonds have been advanced nor has a moral law been attempted that normally creates and maintains "a well-ordered society" in which all citizens act or be regarded.

The second practice is the liberation from the devices the state created and upgraded to maintain and to give effect to the above-mentioned systems of rule that have always denigrated innate human dignity and abused people's intrinsic moral worth. David Harvey stated that regimes also "come and go, shift locations, merge, or go out of business, but states are long-lived entities, cannot migrate, and are, except under exceptional circumstances of geographical conquest, confined within fixed territorial boundaries."[2] Hence, the Islamist model captures the state and fuses the regime and the state, while in actual fact it introduced a savage separation of religion from the state. Accordingly, and because the regime's only mode of governance has been based on violence, different groups of Sudanese citizens have resorted to various actions—civil or military—to resist, challenge, or confront the regime and its state. At the same time, it is not difficult to see the disintegration of the regime and the runaway world of Islamism toward oblivion and the rise of what the Sudanese describe as the "tribalization" of the state and what I describe as separation of religion and state where the state is designated the function of violence. Many Sudanese would argue that, the internal power struggle among the Islamists themselves emerged out of that so-called tribalization together with the climate that overshadowed all fields of action in the country involving incalculable consequences of such an approach to the political process.

The *al-t'amir* that Ismā'il al-Azharī referred to does not occur by accident. The theory and goals of the colonial "state-centered" system of development facilitate for extraction and resource flow from the periphery to the core. The wealthy colonizing state is thus different from a new system and mode of governance, of an independent state, that enhances national growth and maintains a well-being of a "citizens-centered" approach to liberation. Through such a system the main objective of development is to "attack the 'five giants of Want, Disease, Idleness, Ignorance and Squalor'" through a vision and plans that realize and "meet the

2 David Harvey, *The New Imperialism* (Oxford, Oxford University Press, 2005), 27.

aspirations of authorities with the lives of individuals."[3] Within this respect, both *al-Tahrir* and *al-t'amir* propositions, the Sudanese human well-being, dignity, and rights should and could be advanced as one. However, time and again there have arisen loud voices, violent actions, and recalls to those Sudanese who have been seeking ways to undertake a necessary reconstruction through liberation. In this scheme of events, the Islamist regime represents the latest and highest stage of suffering the Sudanese citizens have ever experienced.

It is true that the Sudan in its 1821 geographical borders was born out of human sufferings. Nevertheless, the Sudan, within its hundreds of years of historical experience and human life has faced and survived trying times; its different groups of historical people have undergone time and again periods of severe hardships. This is because neither Mohammad 'Alī nor the British invented the Sudan. It existed, as Thornton said about India, "for hundreds of years in its civilization."[4] But the most important aspect of the recurrent developments of the Sudanese experience is that the runaway Islamist world and the simultaneous southern walk-away from the Islamist regime and its state represent a multiplicity of important events of Sudanese modern times. They both indicate that the winds of liberation from Islamism are blowing as strongly as possible in the Sudan. This chapter focuses on three aspects of a single phenomenon. Though they are not identical, they constantly intervene with one another to add to the complexity of the idea of the Sudan within its particularities, its deep reaffirmations of its moral and human universe, and its multilayered realities of unity and difference.

One Foot in a Different Field Liberation

July 9, 2011, will go down in history not only as a momentous day for the new state of South Sudan, but also as a significant signpost in the lives of millions of people in that state, in the greater Sudan, in Africa, and in the world at large. The Southern Sudanese people decided to liberate themselves from an oppressive regime and a state that has a long track record of uneven distribution of power, material resources, and violence toward its citizens. This is a factor that contributed to the already long-existing marginalization and inequalities that the tyrannical and totalitarian regime produced. It is a state that only brought dictators, violence, and misery to all the Sudanese people. That action of the Southern Sudanese represents in its true meaning "a one foot in a different field" of liberation. It so happens that, out of what we have witnessed in the Sudan, the debate over the after-effects of peril facing the Sudan as a country stretches

3 Nicolas Rose and Peter Miller, "Political Power beyond the State: Problematics of Government" *The British Journal of Sociology*, 61 (2010): 271–303.

4 Quoted in D.N. Panigrahi, *India's Partition: the Story of Imperialism in Retreat* (London: Routledge, 2004), 2.

and sidesteps forward by the minute. Still one might say, although the Southern Sudanese walked away from the regime and its state, they did not walk away from the Sudan and the Sudanese fields of action. Here, we need to introduce variants that might be revealing within this scope. It is still the case, even after the separation, that the majority of the Southern Sudanese citizens feel they have numerous other human attachments, political associations, religious affiliations, and different collective identities within the Sudanese greater human society that are very important. Sometimes described as the embodiment of the former southern rebel movement, then political party, and the current government of South Sudan,[5] Pagan Amum, Secretary General of the Sudanese Peoples Liberation Movement (SPLM), told the crowd at the independence ceremony "when he lowered the old Sudanese flag for the last time—in preparation for raising of South Sudan flag—that he would not be handing it over to Khartoum in gesture of good riddance." Rather they would hold on to it "for the soon-to-be-formed national archive in memory of their shared history, their shared struggle, and indeed their shared future that northerners and southerners have and would continue to experience together." However, one goes beyond what Pagan has said as we need to recognize the effectiveness and maybe the fortitude of the idea of the greater Sudan. The idea is not a political or an applied label but an existential lived history, a human experience, and a sustained passion that stayed alive and independent of the tribulations and sufferings that are reflected in the heralding signs of incidental and material circumstances and events.[6]

Asif Faiz, captured the symbolic connections between that event and the historic moment in his home country more than a half century before when he listened to President Salva Kiir Mayardit's eloquent oration on July 9, 2011. Faiz remembers that some three score and four years ago, Jawaharlal Nehru delivered his landmark oration, "Tryst with Destiny," which was considered to be one of the greatest speeches of all time. Faiz elucidates that both Nehru and Kiir "delivered their speeches in English, an alien tongue incomprehensive to more than 99 percent of their fellow citizens; in both instances, the assembled masses across their new nations listened to the orations with reverence and attention." He adds that, "neither Nehru's Indian audience nor Kiir's million or more Southern Sudanese left in the North and along an undefined north–south border must be wondering about their fate after listening to their leader in South Sudan."[7] What Faiz forgot to mention was that spirits, memories, and legacy of these two different, great personalities who faced tragic deaths each at a different time were hovering over those who attended each of these historic events. Those were the spirits of Gandhi of India

---

5 Noah Salomon, "The Politics of Religious Freedom: Freeing Religion at the Birth of South Sudan" (Washington, DC, the Immanent Frame, SSRC, 2012), blogs.ssrc.org./tif/2012/04/12/freeing-religion-at-the-birth-of-south-sudan/.

6 Asif Faiz, "South Sudan's Tryst with Destiny" (Washington, DC, Africa Arguments, SSRC, 2011), africanarguments.org/2011/07/19/south-sudan's-tryst-with-destiny/.

7 Ibid.

and John Garang of the Sudan. What made such presence stronger was that the South Sudan independence ceremony was held at the mausoleum of late rebel leader John Garang, who died just months after he signed the peace agreement in January 2005. The spirit of a third personality, Moḥammad ʻAlī Jinnah and his two-nation theory, the story of India's partition, and the creation of Pakistan came alive too.

Nevertheless, it was not "Midnight's Children," however, that constituted the allegory for events that dealt with the South's transition into a new state. It was rather the actual presence of ʻUmar al-Bashir to the ceremony which was considered by local and international attendees problematic. Khartoum's daily newspaper *Al-Ahdāth* quoted unnamed sources that said "some countries particularly in Europe have yet to name their representatives at the ceremony. Western officials have avoided meeting with Bashir since an arrest warrant was issued for him by the International Criminal Court on charges that he masterminded war crimes against humanity and genocide in Darfur." However intertwined with similar issues that immediately emerged, was al-Bashir's hope, which he impatiently mumbled in his address that day, that the South's independence would lead the United States to lift sanctions against the Sudan. That request by itself was a reminder of the United Nations Security Council Resolution 1556 (2004) that imposed sanctions in the Sudan in response to the ongoing humanitarian crisis and widespread human rights violations, including continued attacks on civilians. But what was more important, however, for the entire Sudanese citizenship, the Sudanese consciousness, and their understanding of their political, moral, and human considerations was that the Islamist type of rule in particular has been more responsible than many precolonial and postcolonial regimes in giving insignificant opportunities and reasons not only for its Islamist ideology to disintegrate but also for forcing different Sudanese communities to walk away from their regime and its state.

The presence of ʻUmar al-Bashir in Juba that day was a reminder of another bizarre celebration for the same event in Khartoum. Al-Ṭayib Muṣṭafa, owner of the radically Islamist Just Peace Forum, the notorious daily newspaper *al-Intibaha*, and al-Bashir's uncle—who the journalists' satire describe as the presidential uncle—celebrated the South's secession by slaughtering a black bull and lifting placards expressing their jubilation. Muṣṭafa and his forum members toured different parts of Khartoum during which they distributed sweets and claimed that secession of the South marked Sudan's true independence. Muṣṭafa, his paper, and his forum zealously advocated for the separation of the South on blatant racist and religious grounds. They agitated that the north and the south constituted two irreconcilable entities in terms of race, religion, culture, and political affiliations and orientations. But this is not all. Muṣṭafa and his forum were not alone in harboring such racist attitudes toward Sudanese citizens. Al-Bashir was famous for using racist slurs, epithets, and unacceptable terms to describe other Sudanese from the South and Darfur. Yet, to take the problem of negative impulses seriously, the key issue is that Islamism by itself has been a chief source of the deeply embedded counter-revolutionary attitude and an iron cage in which it and its members have been imprisoned for ages. This attitude has been permeated by other "isms" including colonial and postcolonial totalitarian traditions and experiences, which became remarkably similar but paradoxically enough complementary to the Islamist one. Yet no matter how people evaluate these turn-of-past events, that particular story was in many respects a reminder of one of many missed opportunities.

The presence of former US Secretary of State Colin Powel and the former US representative to the UN, Susan Rice, among the dignitaries who attended the ceremony in Juba along with the commanding presence of President Barack Obama at the upper echelon of United States seat of moral and official power was a reminder of a new age of citizenship that had already moved beyond race, religion, sects, and ideologies. This development marks in essence a transformation of consciousness that could announce the threshold of an epoch of hope and rebirth. Within such new consciousness there could have been a potential for social change and nation and state building for a new Sudan as a new world is unfolding in front of Sudanese citizenship with open-ended dynamics. But it seems as Robert Bellah once said, "there are many ways in which apparently open doors may turn out to be closed."[8] Nevertheless, it behooves us to envisage how such missed opportunity came to exist. Yes, history has vacillated from such a lateral of opportunity to the other. This is not said lightly.

Like all events of scale, a historic moment made itself available for the Sudanese people to grasp and to use to rebuild a new country, a nation, and a state. It was an opportunity for the world—and for especially concerned entities such as the United States—to help facilitate the emergence of the new Sudan as they played a major role in securing the 2005 Comprehensive Peace Agreement (CPA). Whatever some may think of the merit of the CPA, it corresponded with the three main influences on President George W. Bush's policy toward Sudan: the American evangelicals, the war on terror, and oil interests. It was a missed opportunity for President Obama, a global politician whose choice as the new American president was empowered by and empowering to a vibrant global civil society. His election reenergized a citizenry impulse eager to actively and effectively transform the world in that direction, and he was widely expected to offer "hope" and "change."

Instead, the Sudan has recently been singled out as an example of internal strife, especially as stereotyped by Western journalists. Others categorize the Sudan as an example of a failed state. However, many Sudanese and non-Sudanese rue such impositions because they do not produce "objective, positive knowledge" upon which a program of action can be built. It is true that the Sudanese state is a product of a unique and complicated encounter between imperial designs of exploitation, hegemony, ideology, and control, which was as an anathema to civil society that inhibited its discourses and repressed its liberating forces. But it is also true that the Sudanese struggle for a possible new Sudan is noteworthy for the

8 Robert N. Bellah, *The Broken Covenant: American Civil Religion in Time of Trail* (Chicago, IL: University of Chicago Press, 1975), 91.

range and depth of this program of action. The multifaceted chain of events—the collective grievances and the hierarchies of discontent that have been reflected for a half century—is in its essence a quest for change. An opportunity availed itself for a negotiated comprehensive peace agreement that would incorporate the collective demands of the Sudanese for rebuilding their nation, their state, and their sociopolitical order.

But, as the Indian epic poem Shri Ramcharitmanas says "the chariot that leads to [such] victory is of another kind." Had Naivasha been the starting point for a sovereign citizen system—one that would endorse a vision of a new social contract—it would have refashioned into a nation-state that promotes, protects, and maintains communal harmony and welfare. This is the new Sudan, where collective propensities, all-embracing responsibility and long-awaited democracy, freedom, equality, and dignity can be observed. It could have been negotiated and supported by the Sudanese experience of past and ongoing struggle for a comprehensive peace agreement; it could have shaped the Sudanese future. The citizens themselves could have set a model—through all the Sudanese parties and the civil entities roundtable conference—for a stable, free, and equitable future to be shared by all the Sudanese people. If the CPA of 2005 (which has been criticized by many Sudanese as a non-comprehensive arrangement) is considered a seminal peace-building attainment of the United States, an abundant opportunity has availed a significant shift of direction with profound social and political change that could have provided for a new model for nation building. For President Obama and the United States to steward such a process would have provided a model for others to follow to peacefully resolve similar situations. That was the missed opportunity within the grasp of a historical moment.

John Young, who describes the peace process between the SPLM and NCP as flawed, explains in his book, *The Fate of Sudan,* that the "failure to widen the peace process contributed to many of the problems that emerged in post CPA period."[9] The larger promise remained moot, in actual fact, for reasons over and above what Young has characterized. The predicament of the Sudan goes beyond the war, which was wrongly described as a "civil war" between the Muslim north and Christian, animist south, which paradoxically lost in the geographical description as the problem of the south. That is untrue because the first characterization was totally misleading because the war was against the state, and it had never been perceived in religious terms until the advent of the Islamist regime in 1989. At the same time, the geographical description is a very partial one. These wrong characterizations led to wrong approaches for solving it including state violence, violence against the state, and unsustainable agreements. The preliminary issue here is what the Sudanese themselves describe as *al-Qadiyya al-watanyyia* or the national issue. At the center of this national issue is how to develop the collective demands of the Sudanese citizens for both *al-taharir wa al-t'amir* and a new social

---

9 John Young, *The Fate of Sudan: The Origins and Consequences of a Flawed Peace Process* (London: Zed Books: 2012), 109.

contract as an effective foundation of a modern state that could come to terms with the Sudanese dream of a well-ordered society where equality, human rights, dignity, and welfare could be preserved.

These desires hark back to 1964 when the Sudanese public sphere lead a successful civil disobedience act against the ‘Abboud military regime and brought it down. The ‘Abboud regime then executed oppressive measures in the southern part of the country in an attempt to put an end to the rebel movement. The Sudanese public sphere within its civil organization put an end to the regime and put the issue of the southern grievances at the center stage of the national discourse of the national project where people could perceive and would shape their reality. The October Revolution generated the value that the citizens are the source of the state's legitimacy. It postulated equality, affirmed citizenship, and recognized human and civil rights at the heart of the idea that the democratic nation and the good society. All that led the Sudanese to develop a working model, which is the roundtable conference as a platform that could help transform society and move their consciousness and experience forward on the roads of practical application of and a new model of liberation.

John Garang's visit to Khartoum on July 2005, revealed another world, which was long in the making. Garang was given an electrified and electrifying welcome in Khartoum on his first visit to the capital since the war began in 1983 and after signing the Naivasha accords. The event and the passionate reception Garang received, which was the first of its kind in the history of the Sudan, had a very significant message for the regime. It was the north—not the Islamist regime, and other southern constituencies in the country that made that day historic and meaningful even though the Sudanese people and their representatives were denied participation in the negotiations in Naivasha. From the very beginning of the peace negotiations at Machakos in 2002 to the final signing of the CPA "none of the two [parties SPLM and NCP] were willing to include the other [Sudanese] political parties [or Southern military or civil groups] in the process."[10] As Peter Woodward noted that "throughout it had been negotiated by only two parties, the NCP and SPLM/A, both of which had numerous critics and probably represented only a minority of the population in northern and southern Sudan respectively."[11] Moreover, "the international community saw other claimants to participation either as comparatively weak, and/or likely to complicate the negotiating process. A multi-party negotiations of the kind that took place in South Africa with the end of apartheid had been ruled out with the sidelining of Libyan–Egyptian initiative. This was a blow for the Umma Party and the Democratic Unionist Party in particular, which had been the two dominant parties in Sudan's three previous

10 Lovise A. Alen, "Making Unity Unattractive: The Conflicting Aims of Sudan Comprehensive Peace Agreement," *Civil Wars* 15 no. 2 (2013): 173–91.

11 Peter Woodard, "From CPA to DPA: 'Ripe for Resolution,' or Ripe for Dissolution?" In *After the Comprehensive Peace Agreement in Sudan*, ed., Elke Grawert (Suffolk, James Currey, 2010), 235.

periods of democratic governments."[12] In light of all this, it seems that the millions of Sudanese who received John Garang in Khartoum and those who followed the event via TV and radio were endorsing the idea and vision of a new Sudan rather than that of the CPA. They were there to mark a new beginning and a true birth of the New Sudan. The New Sudan, which was a vision of Sudan affording equality and rights to all citizens, has always been part of the Sudanese discourse. But John Garang gave it new vitality when he presented his vision "to abolish the Old Sudan and establish a New Sudan; a new political dispensation; a Sudanese sociopolitical entity; a transformed Sudan in which all Sudanese are equal stack-holders regardless of their race, tribe religion, or gender; a democratic Sudan where religion is constitutionally separated from the state; a Sudan which governance is based on popular will, the rule of law and respect for human rights."[13]

The Sudanese public endorsement of John Garang and his New Sudan vision meant as Garang himself told "his closest advisers: 'after this, Sudan will never be the same again.'"[14] Yasir Arman says that after this experience "Dr. John was born again."[15]

But it did not take long to see that the CPA—in its development into a political project after Garang's historic visit to Khartoum—and the popular support of the New Sudan vision were not able to overcome inherent Islamist and counter-revolutionary efforts against them. Many Sudanese from the North, in particular, strongly internalized and reflected the behavior of those who were unhappy about such an endorsement of Garang and the New Sudan vision. Hilde Johnson perceived that political project and its endorsement "had frightened some of the National Congress Party (NCP) core leaders. They had seen nothing similar for themselves, and they had certainly not expected such massive expressions of support. They understood that they now had a national political leader in their midst."[16] In actual fact, this new political project stood in opposition to the Islamist project of the civilization mission and its state, which was born from an Islamist project. Additionally, 'Alī 'Uthmān and his Naivasha team were to face his Islamist colleagues with their long knifes to slaughter the individual and group leadership ambitions of that team and its leader. Ṭaha's Islamist enemies and competitors used his long-time preferred strategy of absence as opportunity to prepare the scene for that day by getting closer to al-Bashir. As 'Abdel Gahni Aḥmed Idris explains, when the first vice president came back from his 16-month long stay in Naivasha and absence from Khartoum, he found a different situation similar to what had happened during al-Turabi's absence in prison after the 1989 coup. New

12 Ibid.

13 In Paanuel Wel: South Sudanese Bloggers: John Garang, Dr. John Garang, Khartoum Press Conference by Phone (April 13, 20012), paanluel2011.worldpress.com.

14 Ibid.

15 Hilde F. Johnson, *Waging Peace in Sudan: The Inside Story of the Negotiations that Ended Africa's Longest War* (Brighton: Sussex Academic Press, 2011), 195.

16 Ibid.

teams of Islamists, including Ṣalah Gosh, Usama ʻAbdallah, and Kamal ʻAbdelatif became closer to the president, who began to appreciate their views. This time, the Islamists were not interested in repeating their mistake when they put down al-Turabi in 1999. They feared that ʻUthmān might join hands with al-Turabi who "did not go quietly in the night, and instead continued to be both an irritant and a threat to the NCP government."[17] This time they kept ʻUthmān in the palace in a political cardiac arrest situation.

At the same time, Garang faced "opposition within the movement he had given birth to, and on the eve of independence and less than a year before he died, he was almost overthrown by his compatriots."[18] However, and regardless of the persistent suspicion among Sudanese in general and many Ugandans on the truth of a Ugandan helicopter crash that killed Garang and his team, "even his enemies in the SPLM/A elevated Garang to the status of an 'African hero' and loudly proclaimed that his vision would never die. But in practice, Garang's call for democracy had already been fatally tarnished before he died, and his appeal for a united Sudan would die with the January 2011, referendum. It was only his legacy of militarism, authoritarianism, and government that would continue."[19]

Hence, the aftermath of the signing of the CPA was "a race to the bottom" as the orphans of the late John Garang's vision compromised with the Islamists of the regime—Ḥasan al-Turabi's children of divorce—and hence underbid and parted company with the grand ideals of the New Sudan. In this sense, it takes no extraordinary acumen to identify how such a development materialized. The death of Garang, as Young rightly argues, left a major gap in the peace process. Waithaka Waihenya noticed that "the man who spent 21 years fighting in order to achieve peace had spent only 21 days in office." Soon, many expected that Kiir would be the natural successor to the deceased leader. However, "many doubted that he had the stature of the fallen leader. He was a good soldier, many said, but would he be a good politician?"[20] For the Sudanese who hoped for a new beginning and for a New Sudan, it quickly became "apparent [for them] that Salva Kiir and his supporters had a different approach."[21] Questions regarding why the CPA failed to mention anything about the New Sudan began to surface. Andrew Natsios, US Special Envoy to the Sudan from October 2006 to December 2007, argues that "Garang's greatest legacies are a transformed south, however incomplete, with oil revenues that led to independence; and a large army capable of acting as a deterrent to northern aggression."[22] Natsios adds that "ironically, Garang's death removed

---

17 John Young, *The Fate of Sudan*, 75.

18 Ibid.

19 Ibid.

20 Waithaka Waihenya, *The Mediator: Gen. Lazaro Sumbeiywo and the Southern Sudan Peace Process* (Nairobi: Kenway Publications, 2006), 147.

21 Ibid.

22 Andrew S. Natsios, *Sudan, South Sudan, & Darfur: What Everyone Needs to Know* (Oxford: Oxford University Press, 2012), 176.

the one major impediment to the South's independence. Had Khartoum's security services orchestrated that accident, they would have also have been ensuring the secession of the South."[23] According to Natsios, only *awlad John Garang* (Garang Boys), chief among them are Yasir Arman, Malik Agar, Mansour Khalid and Luka Biong, were perceived by some Southerner as Communists. It was "feared they would be isolated and attacked by Khartoum if the South seceded (which indeed they later were)."[24] Meanwhile, as explained before, 'Alī 'Uthmān, "was, as one SPLM respondent put it, 'a victim of the CPA.' With the death of Garang he lost considerable authority, and his policy of making concessions in the peace process to normalize relations between Khartoum and Washington did not bear fruit. ... As a result 'Alī 'Uthmān was increasingly attacked by NCP hardliners led by Nafie 'Alī Nafie, who held that he gave away too much at Naivasha and was naïve to believe American promises."[25] When Hilde Johnson visited 'Alī 'Usman at his home in Khartoum in October 2005, she noticed that he "was a different man ... subdued. The internal political dynamics in Khartoum were now a major concern and, for 'Alī 'Usman, clearly a matter of political survival."[26] Not only that, but many rumors continued to surround 'Alī 'Uthmān and to cast suspicions about his ambitions behind Naivasha, the thing that poisoned his relationship with al-Bashir. The talks ended up in the hands of Garang and 'Alī 'Uthmān which "left the fate on the peace process in their hands and assumed (wrongly as it turned out) they would continue to be in positions of authority to implement the agreement they reached, risked a complete breakdown of the negotiations if their talks failed, and played to the institutional weakness of Sudan by making the process dependent upon two personalities."[27] Moreover, that opened the door for endless rumors that these two personalities "were making private deals, which even some of Garang's closest colleagues thought was possible." Young adds, "we cannot know if there were any secret deals or if the talks represented the inauguration of 'Alī 'Uthmān's proposal for a 'political partnership' between the NCP and the SPLM/A, but some of the decisions that came out of the talks suggest it. Thus while the strong resistance of the NCP to proposals for international guarantees of the peace agreement were predictable, Garang's opposition to them was harder to understand."[28] But the most common rumor was the one that alleged that al-Bashir knew 'Alī 'Uthmān's treacherous nature and that he worked in a subtle way to ride it to the seat of the presidency on the back of the SPLM/A and the international community.

For many Sudanese from different generations, political affiliations and intellectual orientations, the 'New Sudan' is an idea and a dream for which too much blood and mental and physical resources have been devoted. The idea of the

23 Ibid.

24 Ibid.

25 John Young, *The Fate of Sudan*, 107.

26 Hilde F. Johnson, *Waging Peace in Sudan*, 205.

27 John Young, *The Fate of Sudan*, 107.

28 Ibid.

Sudan is mainly concerned with the surface issues and the underlying realities of the Sudanese life. Such thoughtfulness reveals the honest concerns of millions of Sudanese individuals and communities who have been engaged in all aspects of Sudanese life from the social, to the intellectual, religious, and political. It includes freedom of religion, separation of religion and state, democracy, human rights and—over and above the formation of a democratic and legitimate order—a new social contract and a state where citizens can attain and exercise their human rights.

Had the CPA or the Naivasha agreement been taken as the starting point for reconstructing a new Sudan—of which John Garang was one champion—in which civil society could be revitalized and the state rebuilt by changing the environment of public discourse to accommodate and adopt the inner resources, the historical resentments, and the self-definition of a new Sudan, these and other conditions could have produced a new social contract out of the collective aspiration of the Sudanese people for a good society. This could have also provided for the much-needed subversion of the vicious cycles of totalitarian rule and could have paved the way for the reconstruction of a new state built on citizenry, justice, inclusive social and political life, and a solid foundation for the repair of the social sphere. The Sudan could have provided and presented to itself and the world a new model for creating a nationality, a state, and a country. For these entities are neither simply there nor God sent; they are creations and processes of action that people build according to their fortitude and imagination. It is this fact that those who believe and work for a new Sudan regard as their dream that motivates their past, present, and future involvement.

Yet things took a different turn. Lovise A. Alen argues that two developments emerged during the period of the implementation of the CPA through the establishment of the government of national unity between the SPLM and the NCP after 2005. The first development was that "through the establishment of National Unity Government (GoNU), the former foes' positions were fortified in the post-war era. The power-sharing efficiently secured their power and resources until elections were held. This made it impossible for other political parties to challenge their positions, ultimately enabling the incumbents to consolidate their positions at 2010 national elections."[29] The second development was emerged out of "the fundamental lack of trust between the parties of the GoNU, the power-sharing arrangements did little to contribute to a national reconciliation after war, which was one key aim of the CPA. Instead, the disappointment and the disillusionment at the lack of cooperation within the GoNU, particularly from the SPLM's perspective, fueled the demand and desire for a partition Sudan."[30] Even so, and the most important development that the environment created by the processes of constructing making unity attractive had created a situation that reduced that goal not only to the minimum but consolidated that mistrust to the maximum. The

29 Lovise A. Alen, "Making Unity Unattractive: The Conflicting Aims of Sudan Comprehensive Peace Agreement," *Civil Wars* 15 no. 2 (2013): 173–91.

30 Ibid.

way the regime continued to control the state even worse than before and to deny their new partner actual trustful and sincere partnership that could construct a different system of power that could convince the southern partner that unity could be attractive was the main reason that brought old bitter experiences alive. Hence, the Southern Sudanese decided to liberate themselves from the oppressive regime and its totalitarian state. Especially as that would continue on resulting continued oppressive politics and inequalities and evoking in the open new language of racism. Moreover, the Southern Sudanese had their unequal share of suffering with other Sudanese from an ugly face of a state that brought to the Sudanese people dictators and misery, starting with its grand manufacturer, General Sir Francis Reginald Wingate Governor of the Anglo-Egyptian Sudan between 1899 and 1916, and continuing to its existing one, 'Umar al-Bashir, who came to power through a military coup in 1989. There are, on the other side, clear indications that there has been progressive deterioration after the walkout process of the SPLM as a partner to the ruling NCP to the speedy pace of runaway world of the Islamists and their regime towards oblivion.

Many have argued, and would argue still, that the Islamists' hostile attitude toward the South is a complex reality that defies simple explanation. Each wave of change accepting this attitude, in the end, has reconstituted the South in the eyes of the Islamists as the categorical enemy of their ideological pursuit and political designs. Even before assuming power through a military coup in 1989, the Islamists perceived the South as an idea that was born out of opposition and antagonism to Islam and Arabism in the country. Against such a background, the Islamists' hostility toward the South ignited one of the most vicious cultural and real military wars in the history of the Sudan. Meanwhile, their call was "let the South go if it is going to be the obstacle against the implementation of Shari'a in the Sudan."

During the Nimeiri Era, their other involvements were clearly in support of separation, and during the early days of the Islamist state, they launched jihād against what they described as an unholy alliance of crusaders and Communists under the leadership of John Garang in the South. Through the long negotiations in Kenya at Machakos in 2002 and Naivasha where the CPA was produced in 2005, the Islamists were forced to seek negotiations after their regime was weakened by internal and external factors. Chief among these factors was the inability to achieve a decisive victory against John Garang and the SPLA (Sudan People Liberation Army) in the South through Jihād, encroachment, and the progression of the regime's incessant unpopularity and the split (the uneasy divorce) within the Islamists ranks that led to the downfall of Ḥasan al-Turabi in 2000.

At a more profound level, however, the National Unity Government (2005–2011) between the SPLM and the NCP after the signing of the (CPA) was a sort of control of the SPLM from without by the NCP. Aggressive rhetoric, suspension of participation in the government, and even military posturing were the main characteristics of that agonizing relationship between the two partners. Given this pattern of conduct, it was not surprising at all to see how the cultural divide went far beyond disagreement among them. Al-Ṭayib Muṣtafa ('Umar al-Bashir's uncle)—the man of the moment—completely devoted himself, his forum and his paper, *al-Intibaha*, to the ugliest form of hate speech against everything that related to South Sudan and southerners before, during, and after the official separation of the two partners on July 9.

The Genealogy and the Residue of Unfinished Liberation

The Sudanese human experience—before the founding of the Sudan as a geographical and human space—has transformed into a series of complex developments and different forms of interrelationships. These developments, similar to other human situations elsewhere "wrought fundamental transformations in existing forms of political memberships, status, and identity, and they also set in train further sweeping changes."[31] The different modes and systems of development, and their environments, have created the Sudanese as a people "defined by two dimensions: the historical community and cultural specify."[32] Significant human experiences have molded and shaped the Sudanese mutual encounter with time and place, have acted together and separately to internally and externally provoke violence, and have allowed for systems of domination of nature over each other and the means of production and modes of regulation. Such an address to the idea of the Sudan does not keep the point at issue not only in respect to "the *value* of the situation of the national community but also its *signification*."[33] But the question that has never received significant attention and importance is the impact and the cost of looking at the Sudan from a disparaging or belittling angle. The problem, however, is that the past three centuries, most particularly since the first (1821–1875) and the second (1898–1956) colonial periods, have not been favorable for the idea of the Sudan. The high cost or the consequences of this experience and its outcome have made it difficult to understand the Sudanese predicament or what is sometimes described as the Sudanese dilemma. Nevertheless, there is more to the idea of the Sudan and the Sudanese experience in its complexity than meets the eye.

Since the creation of the Sudan in 1821, the Sudanese saw their lifeworld colonized, civil experience constrained, and "the topography of cruelty"[34] advanced by oppressive regimes who continue to be produced and rule over them,

---

31 Roger M. Smith, *Stories of Peoplehood: The Politics and Morals of Political Membership* (Cambridge: Cambridge University Press, 2003), 10.

32 Dominique Schnapper, *Community of Citizens: On the Modern Idea of Nationality* (New Brunswick: Transaction Publishers, 1998), 16.

33 Etienne Balibar, *We, The People of Europe: Reelections on Transnational Citizenship* (Princeton, NJ: Princeton University Press, 2004), 12.

34 Ibid.

while the evolution of their civil society is deferred.[35] The referendum that took place in Southern Sudan during January 9–15, 2011, on whether the region should remain a part of a united Sudan or become independent, was a walk-away from the Islamist regime and its state but not from the Sudan as stated before. The new state of South Sudan maintained the name of Sudan for its new republic. At the same time, the declaration issued on July 9, 2011, that split North and South Sudan occurred because the Islamist regime withdrew from the Sudan to *Amarat al-Sudan*[36] in an attempt to exercise a tighter grip over the Sudanese lifeworld. The Islamists attempted effect tighter control through different forms of coercive measures and combinations of violence and neglect for progressive marginalization by remapping of their project which is called Ḥamdi Triangle; as will be explained later in this chapter.

The Islamists have split Sudan into two states. The first has been open for hot war while they turned the rest of the country into a closed district for a cold battlegrounds between the regime and other Sudanese groups. That Cold War started by inventing the ghost houses as champers for torturing true or potential opponents. The ghost houses represent the Islamist gulag that continued since the early days of the regime in the capital and other northern parts of the country. Again, it now largely depends on how the form and the intensity of each one of these hot or cold wars could work to find a critique of the other or how they both become concrete as they emerge and develop to arouse citizens' feelings with or against the essence of Islamism and its regime. Both, however, represent a situation in which Islamism in practice in a non-Islamist setting (Muslim, Christian, and other African religions), and its relationship to the entire Sudanese community or the majority of it. Through its oppressive framing devices of war, violence, and torture that deal with each one of these situations based on where Sudanese person resides regardless of his or her relationship to humanity is considered by the ruling Islamists as an enemy to the regime, the country, and to God. Hence, for the colonized Islamist mind, which has been caught in the prison house of its Islamism, it has always been entrapped in its callus and unchanging discourse of reason and conduct of oppression. Their prison is further defined by cruelty as a system of governance, which has been based on the savage separation of religion and state and its zealously guarded condemnation of the other. All that

35 See Abdullahi Gallab, *A Civil Society Deferred: the Tertiary Grip of Violence in the Sudan* (Gainesville, FL: University Press of Florida, 2013).

36 The Islamists changed the tribal chiefs' title to *Amir* and their locality is recognized as *Amāra* an emirate. That system, which is similar to the colonial *idarra ahliya* (native administration) served to increase the power of local despotic chiefs, reduce the cost of administration to the minimum, increase marginalization of rural Sudan, and perpetuate and deepen what the British administration designed or recreated as tribes. After the downfall of the Egyptian president Muḥammad Morsi, an Egyptian paper published a letter claiming that it was sent from Omar al-Bashir to Morsi describing their two countries as Islamic emirates. Neither 'Umar al-Bashir nor Morsi denied the authenticity of the letter.

continues to be an unchanging storehouse of Islamist violence from which its apparatus of physical and toxic verbal violence finds its self-aggrandizing subject of governance asserting an inseparable totalist system.

Nothing, it would seem, was left in the legacy of Sudanese Islamism. The cruel and protracted trail of other violent Islamist groups was all that remained to make the Sudanese people feel good to find an emancipatory aspect of Islamism. However, in the scheme of things proposed here, there can be no doubting that ripping the country into two republics is an outcome of the Islamists' experiences as they tried to reproduce and add to their own history within the colonial and postcolonial contexts of the totalitarian state in the Sudan and their pursuit to create their state within its own domain of governance. Whether it does or does not depends largely on what the Sudan has been undergoing before and for a considerable period of time. There is reason not to see that the Islamist enterprise has been promoting a continual segmentation of the Sudanese realm into separate and stratified racial zones. Again, it is almost equally clear that there might be several other implications and indications that come out bearing the essential characteristics of that crisis, and it might be serious enough to threaten the country with more fragmentation in the future. But, similar to other serious situations, the diagnosis of the Sudanese condition and its consequences are at the heart of Sudanese and non-Sudanese academicians' inquiries and of intellectuals' and knowledge workers' *ijtihād*.

In our search for an explanation, we have to consider the accumulative and singular role that the central state has played in the Sudanese life since 1821. From the time of the Ottoman Walī Muḥammad 'Alī's invasion of the Sudan and the creation of a centralized state in 1821, to the current totalitarian rule of the Islamists (1989 to the present). The state in its different formations has focused on several main tenets: (1) the charters of the conventions of hidden and manifest structures of violence; (2) the all-embracing and monopolizing power over all means of a brand authority by which the conduct of the population is governed, disciplined, and coerced; and (3) the Islamist state, as the highest stage of violence in the history of the Sudan, represents a savage separation of religion from state in which the state offers privileges to some but denies them to others while designating the field of violence as a coercive force to control and exploit the Other.

Central to such experiences, the state continued to act as a vessel for extraction, a major manufacturer of inequalities, racial engineering, and social stratification on a grandiose scale. Its public and heavy hand has always been a silhouette in the shadows and a hound in the light of these developments. The state continued to be utilized as "a locale form 'power containers'—circumscribed arenas for the generation of administrative power" as Anthony Giddens once said.[37] The Islamists, however, tended to increase and maintain that power by expanding the violence, greed, and *tamkeen* size of this container to the extent that they turned the state

37 Anthony Giddens, *The Nation-state and Violence: Volume Two of A Contemporary Critique of Historical Materialism* (Cambridge: Polity Press, 1985), 13.

into a" coercive-intensive" if not a coercive-only entity. Stated more precisely, the Islamist state within its different formations and designations through time became a secular Tertullian theology. "I believe it because it is absurd and I know it because it is impossible." Going against that state or persuasion of any act of resistance to its tyrannical grip would most likely be considered as *kufr* (heresy) that should be dealt with in the most violent manner. The surge of peaceful or violent resistance to state designs must always not only be criminalized but also be destroyed as an enemy force.

The state during the Turkiyya period (1821–1875), the Mahdiyya period (1875–1898), under British colonial rule (1898–1956) and under every form of military rule (1958–1964 and 1969–1985) continued to be the central focus of all these forms of conduct that ferments from the center only to be nurtured and intensified through time. Within its rhizome-like nature, the state is based upon a system originally established by colonizing powers and military rule in both colonial and postcolonial periods. This is what, paradoxically has never been studied in comparison among the colonial state, the military rule, and the current Islamist system. However, the Islamist regime, like all other totalitarian systems and more than most of Sudanese regimes, constituted a continuum of historical events that shared guiding differentialist ideologies based on violence. It is true that each operated within its own historical and material circumstances; yet, they together contributed to the construction of the conditions that deeply affected the creation of the country's center and its margins and what we witness today of cold and hot wars and their consequences and ramifications. In this sense, we can see how the Islamist regime is still fermenting from the Wingate, to 'Abboud, and on to Nimarie totalist and coercive experiences.

By 1998, the Islamists began their systematic withdrawal from the Sudan by developing an imagined Islamist character as an important part of the country. This character materialized later and shrank into Ḥamdi's Triangle. The Islamists let one part of the country walk out of the regime and its state. They turned that part into a political unit, but when they adopted Ḥamdi's Triangle, they withdrew from the Sudanese human society at large. The different and complicated dynamics of these historical processes have been completely missed if not entirely overlooked by local and foreign scholars of Sudanese social sciences and historians within their recorded history.

From Auto to Homo-referential Racism

The residue of that abuse and oppression, exercised by the two colonial states, piled up in the collective memory and the popular consciousness that shaped individual and group worldviews. All versions of violence experienced by that state against the Sudanese continued to have their distant historical resonance. Yet the nature and intensity of each form of violence, together with the territorial differentiation that emerged out of that experience, planted and maintained something that has reached beyond generalities and generations. Most importantly, that experience—which entailed certain racist postures as auto-referential impulses that lead to the construction of different, real and imagined communities and districts that could be colonized and opened up to different systems of subjugation—was also subjected or "closed" to another form of subjugation as during the British colonial period. That situation produced what I would call a form of homo-referential impulse.

A homo-referential impulse and its different forms of prejudice emerges when the practice of auto-referential racism leads some of those who were subjected to prejudice and colonization to begin to see themselves as different from other groups within their same human milieu. Colorism is typically characterized in the Sudanese case by how dark one's skin color is. But what makes colorism a moral predicament is that it defines social distance between and among groups of the same human milieu. Moreover, the psychological fixation surrounding colorism, as a way of thinking and acting for the creation of social distance, has made of that homo-deferential impulse the "last taboo" among the Sudanese, who have discriminated against one another for decades. Because it has long been considered unmentionable, it has always been denied and never mentioned within the national discourse.

The focus of such a differentiation, which ranks groups and individuals in terms of specific and sometimes imagined phenotypic characteristics and attributes, reflects a subtle way of social positioning of those particular and comparable groups and individuals: riverians or shamaliyyin (from Northern Sudan); garaba (Western Sudanese); Nuba (from the Nuba mountains region); Ghanobiyyin (from South Sudan); and halab (from Turkish, Egyptian, or Levant origin). Like other types of prejudice, homo-referential impulses, and its consequential production of the social zoning of the Other, which can be traced back to the time and auto-differential racism of the Turkiyya colonial experience, are historically and culturally rooted, socially learned, and self-regulating in response to different or new conditions, confrontations, or structural situations. A tremendous progressive trend in this respect was clear during the Mahdiyya period toward al-Khalifa ʻAbdullahi and those who were called *alwalad al-Gharib* of Western Sudan. Remnants of that period's expressive culture are still alive. It has been even clearer in the attitudes of some of the ruling groups of the Islamists toward the Darfurian members of the party and South Sudanese citizens who were not members of the party.

The attitudes related to colorism reflect three aggregates of identity management. The first reflects itself in the social status, aptitude, ethnic relations, and attitudes that qualify or disqualify individuals and groups from (or for) certain rewards. These groups within their distinctive regional and ethnic characteristics and backgrounds came to be housed in a collective imagined stratum within the changing Islamist structure as a less worthy class. The enormity of the feelings of that group and the consequences of such actions added to the grievances of the Darfurians toward the state and their fellow Islamists and served only to further their call to arms against the regime. The status inconsistency between those

Darfurians' achieved and ascribed status located them in "a place of involuntary exile" within the Islamist community. When Daud Bolad broke away from his Islamist colleagues and joined John Garang to start his military insurgency in Darfour, Garang asked Bolad the young ex-Islamist leader what brought him to the SPLM? Bolad's answer was that he discovered that blood is thicker than Islam. Bolad's ill-fated dissention and Khalil Ibrahim's bitter fight against the regime stand as prime examples of the effects of this development.

The second, the homo-referential attitude toward the South as a peoplehood—and the Nuba of the southern region of Kurdofan, who are all Sudanese citizens in the first place and who include Muslims—nevertheless instigated jihād by the Islamist state and was propagated by its media. The third is the Islamists' homo-referential impulse's expressed in hidden language highlighting certain tribes' superiority—organized and fashioned within the daily conversations and jokes but which became the end result of notions and actions that rank these tribes according to position of power. This conduct supports very specific forms of what is described by the Sudanese as tribal domination and tribal damnation—as the Islamist state continued to be the prime distributor of rewards and inequalities. The promotion of the tribe among the Islamists represents a phenomenon that is psychological rather than physical, exclusionary rather than inclusionary, and to some extent an absurd tribal supremacist agenda in which the association of the individuals to a group accentuates belonging to a communality that binds together some of those competing groups within the ranks of the Islamists.

The current regime, which is a strange mix between Islamist totalitarianism and militarism, added to the state colonization of religion. This has been explained before along with new and additional factors that declare jihād against what the regime labeled as the alliance of pagans and their supporting crusaders and communists in the south of the country. Those who were tormented with such aggressions were, in the first place, Sudanese citizens. The Islamist state upgraded the capacity of the state apparatus of torture—which was sponsored as a mode of "divine" conduct and practice—to deal with its opponents in the northern part of the country as well.

However, the Islamists' withdrawal from the Sudan was underway even before July 2011. By putting into effect the "Ḥamdi Triangle" plan, which the former Ingaz Finance Minister 'Abdulrahim Ḥamdi proposed in 2006, and the NCP Conference accepted, became the cornerstone for withdrawal through deferential treatment and exemptions of all marginalized regions of the country from all public livelihood duties. In his paper, which was titled "Strategy for the Elections," Ḥamdi proposed the Islamists and their regime focus future development and investment in what he described as the Dongla, Sennar, Kordofan axis. This imaginary triangle would exclude the already marginalized regions of the country, which includes Darfur, the old and new South, and the eastern parts of the country. Some observers believe the Ḥamdi Triangle outlines the locations where the "core regime supporters"[38] are concentrated. However, according to Tim Niblock's early characterization of this triangle, it represents the basis of inequality in the Sudan where "the condominium's development efforts were concentrated."[39] Ḥamdi's plan and the NCP who adopted it, might have considered that Southern Sudan was already out of the "Civilization Oriented Project" equation; hence, they did their best to make "unity seem like an unattractive option." Whether the Islamist regime had lost hope in Darfur and other marginalized areas or they consciously saw Ḥamdi's plan as a way to mimic colonial rule, the Islamist party and its regime certainly considered Ḥamdi's plan as a way to direct the development of Sudanese oil revenues and external financial resources within the Dongola-Sinnar-Kordofan axis. The exclusion of these parts of the Sudan by limiting economic investment to one specific region, the "Ḥamdi Triangle," would by the end of the day drive the rest of the country out of the Sudan through epistemic violence of an unending marginalization of economic scarcity and poverty. 'Abdullahi el-Tom concluded that this triangle represents the hard core of historic and future Arab-Islamic Sudan. Following segregation of the south, as given by Ḥamdi, this triangle guarantees power for the NCP of 'Umar al-Bashir in future democratic Sudan. The Arabs of Darfur have a lot to contemplate about in their alliance with the riverians people of Sudan.[40] Not only the Arabs of Darfur but the entire marginalized areas of the Sudan including the South should consider their relationship with the regime and its state. As such an act will produce a huge gap between the state and the human content of citizenship and belonging. On this, Benaih Yongo-Bure argues that "the consolidation of power by a minority to the exclusion of most Sudanese, especially those from outside 'Hamdi's Privileged Triangle,' and the consequent concentration of economic development in that Triangle to the neglect of the rest of the country are the underlying causes of virtually all the wars in the Sudan, whether it be war in the south, Nuba Mountains, Blue Nile, the East and now Darfur."[41]

One would agree with many that when an understanding of the Sudanese consciousness is able to influence a walk-away from the current regime and its oppressive state, a new and a trustworthy debate might become a starting point to initiate and evoke the virtue of a new Sudan. This debate would have a

38 Richard Downie and Brain Kennedy, *Sudan Assessing Risks to Stability: A Report of the CSIS Africa Program* (Washington, DC: Center for Strategic and International Studies, 2011), 14.

39 Tim Niblock, *Class and Power in Sudan: The Dynamics of Sudanese Politics 1898–1985* (New York: State University of New York Press, 1987), 143.

40 'Abdullahi El-Tom, commenting on 'Abdel Rahim Ḥamdi, "Future of Foreign Investment in Sudan: A working paper for the National Congress Party." *Sudan Studies Association Newsletter*, 24 no. 1 (2005): 11–14. October, Internet Publication (Translated from Arabic by Abdullahi El-Tom).

41 Beniah Yongo-Bure, "Marginalization and War: From the South to Darfur," in *Darfur and the Crisis of Governance in Sudan: A Critical Reader*, eds Salah M. Hassan and Carina E. Ray (Ithaca, NY: Cornell University Press, 2009), 68.

profound meaning, extremely rich in its human and existential means of growth to posit a political possibility of a bigger geographical field than what the colonial borders mapped out in their day. In this sense, past attempts and the ever-growing accumulation of human capital of what we know as the Sudan in its broader meaning, historical potent identity, and sociopolitical consciousness, are not marginal to the constitution of "a reasonable comprehensive doctrine" to move the public sphere within its human diversity from the margin to the center. In this sense, liberation could turn and materialize into an advanced step reflecting the powerful myths of belonging and long-lived and enduring disposition of historical events. Was there a missed opportunity to come to terms with an "open-ended" transformation into such a development within the Naivasha or CPA, which many would agree with John Young was a "flawed peace process? ... Even the efforts to achieve negative peace were never fully realized, and the CPA 'was closer to a suspended war during which local conflicts erupted frequently.'"[42]

Yes; it was a missed opportunity for bringing all the Sudanese together within their political and intellectual actors to negotiate a more comprehensive peace agreement that would have led to people-making and state building. It would have also represented the essence of a New Sudan or the liberation from a state that is "an apparatus distinguished by the fact that it involves a monopoly of coercion"[43] and an Islamist ruling political community that does not accord to "equal respect to the moral claims of each citizen."[44] An effort of this kind alone can give meaning to a project of a new Sudanese citizenship. It alone can disengage people from what I described before as practices and mentalities of "totalist" politics, ideologies, and systems that plagued the Sudanese experience of governance since the early colonial days of Wingate that took different turns and forms, such as the Islamist ruling regime. Thus, in the absence of an effort of that kind, the failure of the CPA became an entry point to a new cycle of internal (within the regime) and external (against the regime and its state) violent acts. The internal one was represented by the emergence of the Hawkish group within the Islamists ruling community. It was led by Dr. Nafie 'Alī Nafie who seized the 16-month absence of 'Alī 'Uthmān outside the country in Naivasha as an opportunity to have a direct communication and a close relationship with the president of the republic 'Umar al-Bashir. This began 'Uthmān's demise as gatekeeper to the president. It is ironic that 'Uthmān orchestrated this same practice to manipulate the enigma of absence as an opportunity or a route to power. Moreover, hardliners spread rumors in covert and over manners in order to exploit the weaknesses, fears, and jealously of al-Bashir and to forge true or false evidence that 'Uthmān was trying to exploit

42 John Young, *The Fate of Sudan*, 7.

43 Murray Forsyth, "State" in *The Blackwell Encyclopedia of Political Thought*, ed. David Miller (Oxford: Basil Blackwell, 1987), 505.

44 Quentin Skinner, *The Foundation of Modern Political Thought, Vol. 2* (Cambridge: Cambridge University Press, 1978), 353.

the international, regional, and local recognition of his role as a peace maker to become president of the Sudan.

The Sudanese, who are experienced in leading successful uprisings and civil disobedience movements against dictatorial rule (which they did in 1964 and again in 1985), are certainly able to do it for a third time to finally liberate themselves from the tyranny and totalitarianism of the inherited state and its current and similar regimes. Then, perhaps, there would be a new opportunity for building a new Sudan out of the Sudanese collective order and its emerging good society. By that time, surely, the Sudanese "habits of the heart" that ameliorated and molded the Sudanese character and its deeper sense of civility (not the state or its regimes) would help them examine themselves, create new political communities, produce a new social contract and thus ultimately support and maintain conditions of democracy, freedom, equality, and human dignity. Then, the gentler side of the Sudanese life, and the people's propensity for it, would, should, and maybe will, as Alexis de Tocqueville describes, "spontaneously [help create] the bonds of friendship, trust and cooperation that lie at the heart of civil society." The dominant impulse by that time, I would say, will be that a change for the State of South Sudan will also be a change for the new Sudanese Sudan.

Hence, this multifaceted chain of events—the collective grievances, the hierarchies of discontent that have been reflecting themselves for centuries—is in its essence a quest for change. An opportunity availed itself for a negotiated comprehensive peace agreement that would incorporate the collective demands of the Sudanese for rebuilding their Sudanese nation, state and a new sociopolitical order. Yet, "the chariot that leads to [such] victory is of another kind."

Chapter 10
Conclusion

Three important events took place in Sudan between November 2012 and January 2014; separately and together, these events have shaken the Islamist regime from both inside and outside. To tie these three events together might help define the Sudanese model of Islamism as a social phenomenon and help to come to a conclusion regarding what transformed within its describable and indescribable essence. It is true that events, actions, and reactions toward the society the Islamists ruled unfolded with different impacts and pace of successions from the very early days of the regime in 1989, and they have been faced by repression ever since. So the Sudanese experience represents a showcase of "a retrograde consummation of the essence" of Islamism and its model of the savage separation of religion and the state. Civil collective actions, military insurgencies, coup attempts, and non-movements within the urban centers, the marginalized areas, and in the diaspora have played and continued to play an important role in the Sudanese political climate and the regime's violent counter actions for the last quarter century. The Islamist state has been facing serious challenges from its first day not because of its relation to Islam, but because of its totalitarian and violent nature. As a coercion-intensive state, the Islamists have created a garrison state in which they cannot believe or imagine it could exist in peace with itself or with its citizens. Most if not all of these movements against the Islamist regime, regardless of their forms and efficiency of their organization and organizations, represent self-conscious and relatively sustained mobilizations with identifiable and unidentifiable leadership but through one specific goal, which is *isgat al-Nizam* (the overthrow of the regime). Different Sudanese groups found themselves at the head of opposition against the regime. However, for anyone who would attempt to interpret the fields of power and the political climate in the Sudan for the last quarter century, they cannot miss: (1) how that violent experience has shaped and galvanized the Sudanese political discourse and social actions; (2) the development and fortification of an autonomous and transformed coercion-intensive state where violence has prevented the Sudanese urge for a good society to develop to its full potential; (3) how such a violent experience has changed the Sudanese internal and external geography and might continue to do so in an open-ended manner; and (4) Islamism within its very nature and pursuit is a counter-revolutionary force and by being so, the Islamists, their state, and political experience, therefore and above all, have produced their own gravediggers. Hence, it is proceeding along the line of other "isms."

The First Episode

The 8th[1] general conference of the Sudanese Islamic Movement[2] was held in Khartoum November 16–17, 2012, and whatever significance is attributed to it, it was an open book for and a reminder of the route that Islamism in the Sudan is headed for oblivion. The Conference was preceded by a vigorous debate and hot-tempered exchange among former and existing Islamists and followed by a military coup attempt. For a month before the conference was convened, former Islamists debated vigorously with Islamist state officials on the issue of whether there is anything remaining of what they once called an "Islamist movement." Most of the Sudanese and outside observers would agree with Mona 'Abdel Fatah in her assertion that the Inqaz government relied mainly in holding that conference to assemble "the remaining some of the dispersed population of the Islamist movement whom it neglected for more than two decades."[3] 'Abdel Fatah continued to ask the pertinent question, "after sixty years to the founding of the Sudanese Islamist movement, and after its transformation from an ideological movement into a state of influence and authority, who would be more deserving of the inheritance of the Sudanese Islamic Movement? Are they the ones who were excluded or their brothers who have been enjoying the luxury of power?"[4]

So what is new or significant about this particular conference? Angry self-centered Ḥasan Al-Turabi, the father of Sudanese Islamism who was eaten by his kittens, addressed some of the unavoidable conclusions in a letter addressed to foreign Islamist movement leaders attending the event. First, he described the conference as a charade planned by those hypocritical politicians who sought their own personal gain to monopolize Islamism and exclude him. No

1 According to the official history of the Islamist historians, the first conference was convened on August 21, 1954, at the Omdurman Cultural Club. It was called the Eid Congress. At that conference, there was a serious conflict between the Egyptian Ikwan-oriented group and the Bābikir Karār Sudanese-oriented group. The al-Ikhwan group won the day. They removed Ali Talib Allah, Moḥamed Khair Abdel Gadir (Egyptian educated) and replaced him; and the name al-Ikhwan al-Muslimoon was adopted. Bābikir Karār and his follower seceded, and they established their own organization which they called it *al-Jam'aa al-Islamiyya* (the Islamic Group). It was difficult for the Islamists to hold a conference during military dictatorial rules in the country, which was why they convened the second one 1969 in al-Aylafoon, south of Khartoum. After the Islamists assumed power in 1989, they started holding it once every four years.

2 It was al-Turabi who came with the name after the end of 1970s to distance himself from the Muslim Brotherhood and to operate under a different name during the Ja'afar Nimerei regime.

3 Mona 'Abdel Fatah, al-Hukuma al-Sudaniyya al-Taluq bi astar al-haraka al-Islamiyya (the Sudanese Government covering [itself] with the clothing of the Islamist Movement, al-Dawha, al-Marifa: aljazeera Net, 2012), http://www.aljazeera.net/opinions/pages/ae33f9976-e0e-4bd3-a1ed-e00ba62c6b41.

4 Ibid.

doubt al-Turabi knew that he had not only been excluded by those "hypocritical politicians" whom he once considered his own disciples, but he knew they had sent him to prison for a long time as well. Second, al-Turabi contended in his letter to foreign Islamists that the "genuine Islamists are excluded and languishing in prisons as political detainees."[5] Third, the former leader and the sole ideologue of Sudanese Islamism, who has left no space for an intellectual, an ideologue, or a political thinker other than himself to emerge within his movement, complained that "he knows of no intellectual, political or ethical connections [between the conference] and what can be truly ascribed to Islam."[6] In an interview with the *Sudan Tribune*, al-Turabi described the Islamic Movement, which he disbanded after the coup, as "nothing but an NCP-affiliated organization … whose members are united only by power and tribal links." He also revealed that "his party intends to meet Islamist figures from outside the country to explain the PCP position on the conference and why they decided to boycott because they want to disassociate themselves from the 'faces that tarnished the image of Islam.'"[7]

The Islamist Shakespearian Hamlet of the regime, Dr. Ghazi Salah al-Din al-Atabāni, whose loyalty to Islamism made him angry at Claudius who killed Islamism and got married to its state as described before, spent more than a year writing articles, and maybe a book,[8] while giving lectures at home and abroad by himself and trying to pave the way for reform as a new strategy for challenging his long-time rival 'Alī 'Uthmān. Dr. Ghazi, who was the main challenger to 'Ali 'Uthmān in the 2008 General Conference, and the one some Islamists described as the heir potential ideologue of Ḥasan al-Turabi, and who presented himself this time as the "hope for reform" candidate. He and other Islamists outside the establishment debated before the conference about what they described as the merger of *al-Ḥaat al-Thalatha* (the three Ḥs) *al-Ḥaraka* (the movement), *al-Ḥizb* (the party) and *al-Ḥkouma* (the government) as one. That was the very late recognition of the fact that 'Ali 'Uthmān's class of Islamists, which included within their leadership Ghazi Ṣalāḥ al-Din and his reform group, were the ones who perpetuated the crime within a new development that emerged out of the coup as *kasb* (opportunity). Accordingly, self-serving motives and the wilding that emerged as the new

5 Sudan's Turabi repudiates the "Islamic Movement" Conference: *Sudan Tribune*: Plural News and Views on Sudan, November 16, 2012: http://www.sudantribune.com/spip.php?article44552.

6 *Sudan Tribune* obtained a copy of the letter and gave a brief summary of its contents in the above cited story.

7 Ibid.

8 It is rumored that he and not his son-in-law 'Abdel Ghani Aḥmed Idriss was the real author of the book: *al-Da'wa lil Dimogratiyya al-alIslah al-Siysi fi al-Sudan: al-Islamiyoun azmat al-Roya wa alQiyyada* (The Call for Democracy and Political Reforms in the Sudan: The Islamists and the Crisis in Vision and Leadership). Abdel Ghani has been living in London as the owner and director of Sinnar Publishing House.

relationship that brought them together within this new class who merged these three Ḥs to the state and its republics and by delinking themselves from al-Turabi Islamism. Hence, they utilized *al-kasb*, and they interwove it into everyday life. They hooked their actions on every level to the state organs that facilitated and transformed *al-tamkeen* into some sort of wilding, governed their personal and official performance, and regulated and distributed new and old forms of violence as the mode of governance, which I describe as savage separation of religion and the state. Ghazi and his supporters advocated in locally published articles, in a few public lectures, and in communications with like minds at home and abroad for a modest reform in the separation of the movement from both the party and the government. After the end of the conference, Ghazi wrote a long article in which he reflected on the conflict that "crystallized around two clauses in the draft constitution presented to the the 8th Conference, one dictating the election of the Secretary General from the *Shura* Council instead of the General Conference, and a second clause that provides for the establishment of a 'Supreme Leadership' for the SIM composed of its committed members in the leadership of the government, the ruling party and the 'special branches,' i.e. the security services."[9] The outcome of that is that 'Alī 'Uthmān and his group out maneuvered Ghazi Salah al-Din and his supporters by down grading the functions, role, and authority of the Secretary General, and stripping his office of all authority. According to that, "President Bashir and his deputies in the government and the party, i.e. 'Alī 'Uthmān Moḥamed Ṭaha and Nafie Ali Nafie, as well as the Speaker of the National Assembly, Ahmed Ibrahim al-Tahir, and security and military chiefs, will continue to watch over the shoulders of the Secretary General lest Turabi's ghost settle into his jellabiya."[10] Hence, the call for reform and liberating the movement from the government and the party ended in despair.

The new Secretary General of the Sudanese Islamic Movement appeared the next day on the Blue Nile TV in what al-Turabi scornfully described as his renegade Islamists who learned from him "*libs al-Shal wa Istimal al-Joual*" (wearing neck shawl the and using cell phone). The Sudanese blogger and fellow of the Rift Valley Institute Magdi al-Jizouli described the do-nothing al-Zubair 'Ahamed al-Hassan, as he stroked a generous white-grey beard and responded to the calibrated questions of a prudent host, "until a day before only an Ustaz, the title of the Sudanese effendi, al-Zubier was now the 'Shaikh', a veneration that ranks him equal to the grand heads of Sūfi tareeqas (brotherhoods)." Al-Zubeir in that interview "defended the worth of his office against Ghazi's critique, and went further. In rejecting the benign notion of coordination between the SIM, its ruling party and its government in the form of a coordinative Supreme Leadership the opponents of the new constitution were attempting to lift the Secretary General of

9 Magdi al-Gizouli, *The Sudanese Islamic Movement: a parastatal tareeqa, Sudan Tribune*, 2012: http://www.sudantribune.com/spip.php?article44594.

10 Ibid.

the SIM above the President."[11] Hence, rather than "liberate" the Islamic Movement from the state, the 8th General Conference consummated its "nationalization" as it were.

A few months before the conference, news of a memo circulated that had been signed by 1,000 members of middle-rank leadership of the Islamist movement criticizing the ruling leadership and asking for reform. For a while, the government and the party denied receiving such a memo. It is for precisely this reason that some of the ruling party leaders argued that the news of the memo was mere fabrication. Later, and when the memo circulated via email to a number of key Islamists and to Sudanese websites, some circles within the ruling party attributed that to hostility between Ḥasan al-Turabi and his former deputy 'Ali 'Uthmān. They rumored that the memo was written and circulated by supporters of Ḥasan al-Turabi in response to a memo against him prepared by al-Bashir's vice president. The director of the National Intelligence and Security Service Moḥamed 'Atta made those rumors a reality by accusing al-Turabi's party of conspiring with the other rebel groups against the regime. Khartoum based daily newspaper *Al-Tayyar*, owned and edited by former Islamist 'Uthmān Merghani, quoted sources who said that the idea of the memo might have emerged from the members of the ruling NCP's parliamentary caucus whose leader is Ghazi Salah el-Din. The NCP caucus was outraged by refusal of the party's leadership to consider a reform memo they had previously raised. Ghazi Salah al-Din al-Atabāni, however, said he did not know anything about the memo.

But the defeat of Ghazi at the conference and the withdrawal of his candidacy for the position of the Secretary General of the movement has brought to the forefront other tangible factors and new emerging groups involved in the complication of the Islamist conflict. *The New York Times* correspondent, Ismail Kushkush reported that the Islamist reformers who later disclosed their identity on their Facebook site and were behind that memo "were eager to push their agenda of fighting corruption and expanding dialogue with the opposition. But when the movement elected a conservative, conciliatory figure as a new leader, frustration soared among the camp supporting change."[12]

It would be inconsequential to imagine that such frustration and anger emerged spontaneously out of the conference events and an outcome of power struggle that it reflected itself only that day. Reading the group's Facebook and watching the number of videos they posted on YouTube, one could see how the recent developments and the growth of that group came to be in relationship to and out of the roots and practices of Islamist violence: but who was that group?

The Islamist regime created what they called the Popular Defense Force (PDF) as an alternative to the national army. They found its recruits from four sources that included tribal militias, volunteers and recruits from the ranks of Islamists, compulsorily conscripted students and civil servants, and forcibly

11 Ibid.

12 *The New York Times*, December 8, 2012.

drafted males between the age of 18 and 30 according to the *Popular Defense Forces Act of 1989*. Under the *National Service Law of 1992*, all men between 18 and 33 years of age are liable for military service. Military service is for up to 24 months, with 18 months for high school graduates and 12 months for university and college graduates. To obtain a secondary school certificate, a requirement to enter university, boys aged between 17 and 19 were obliged to do 12 to 18 months of compulsory military service under a 1997 decree. The PDF recruits received military training by instructors from the army and indoctrination from a group of Islamist ideologues headed by Ibrāhim al-Sanoussi, a senior Islamist and a very close ally of al-Turabi. TV programs such as *fi sahat al-Fidaa* (in the fields of sacrifice) devoted hours every day propagating the PDF and their jihād in the South of Sudan. After weeks of training in the camps, they would be dispatched to the military zone. As Burr and Collins explain, it was clear that the Sudanese PDF would "become neither a revolutionary guard nor efficient paramilitary organization. It was a rabble in arms, volunteers, used by the Sudan army in its southern civil war as cannon fodder whose depleted ranks had to be filled by forced and unpopular conscription."[13] Out of those indoctrinated young recruits, emerged groups of *mujahdeen* (jihādists) and *dababeen* (tank pumpers). Many of those young groups died in the field; others were neglected after *al-mufāṣala*. Some of these "disheartened *mujahedeen* met 2012 to follow up on one another, check on the families of fallen soldiers, and reminisce. Reminiscence, however, turned into a desire to put things straight. Out of those meetings came an informal group whose members remain connected mostly by Facebook. They chose a name, *Al Sa'ihun*, or the Wanderers, from a special operations unit active in the civil war." The group began to gain momentum with the former *mujahedeen*, holding meetings in houses, on soccer fields, and under bridges. They took their concerns to Sudan's top leadership late last year through a memorandum, "The Memorandum of One Thousand," which was a call for reform signed by members of the group. The new memo brought back to memory famous memos including the "memo of the ten" in 1999, which led to the ousting of Al-Turabi, and the *Black Book* whose group of writers according to Khalil Ibrahim "wanted to provide scientific evidence that a minority of northern elite controlled the whole Sudan. More importantly, it wanted to instigate and lead the change, by force, if necessary."[14]

One event during the conference marked and reminded the conference's captive audience and other audiences at home and abroad of the decisive moments of the life and death of the Sudanese Islamist movement and in particular the actors or personalities spun within the web of significance of these moments. The conference brought together the actual figures of those main actors together with the ghosts of others. This actual and virtual presence of these personalities created

13 J. Millard Burr and Robert O. Collins, *Revolutionary Sudan: Ḥasan al-Turabi and the Islamist State, 1989–2000* (Leiden and Boston: Brill, 2003), 18.

14 'Abdullahi Osman El-Tom, *Darfur, JEM and the Khalil Ibrahim Story* (Trenton: the Red Sea Press, 2011), 202.

hierarchies of unease that opened new vistas for many to foresee and feel "*wa tilk al-Ayyam ndawiliha baynan-nasi wa liya lamal-ladhina amanu wa yatatakhida mikum shuhadaa wal-lahu la yuhibbuz-zallimin*" (we apportion unto men such days of fortune and misfortune]: and [this] to the end that God might mark out those who have attained faith, and choose among you such as [with their lives] bear witness to the truth—since God does not love evildoers).[15] Most of those inside the conference room and many of those outside that place bore witness to an era, some Sudanese pondered within their social groups and the peace of their homes, which reflected its deeper effects on their health conditions of the ruling Islamists. To them, this era with all its evil doing has reflected itself into the face of 'Alī 'Uthmān, which turned so dark and wondered if it was true that this was happening to him because of some sort of cancer. All those who were in and outside that conference room listened to the four-minute address of 'Umar al-Bashir and reflected on the condition plaguing the man that silenced him to such a degree. Before that, he was "known for his bellicose and inflammatory speeches, often followed by a round of dance and stick waving in the grand styles of Sudanese riverian patriarchy, theatricalised of course to serve the purposes of state power."[16] For a considerable period of time, Sudanese audiences, although used to his toxic speech, never stomached the vulgarity that he brought to the field of sense and sensibility of the presidency. People ponder on all these issues and wonder if that is God's wrath. Some Islamists who witnessed all that still remember what they said one day about *as-Samiri* (the Samaritan) who led the Israelites astray during the absence of Moses and persuaded them to worship the golden calf. That day, the most indignant person was Ḥasan al-Turabi, the Moses of the Islamists, who led their exodus to the desolate Sinai Desert of the first Islamists republic through the coup of 1989. But they wandered as they witnessed the whole drama to the end and wondered if that happy magician is a false prophet, if that golden calf is hollow, and what kind of sound it produces when the wind passes through it.

Although al-Turabi was absent from the conference hall, and his ghost was looming within the closed and open meetings of the Islamists. Some observers and media reports saw in the gathering of Islamist leaders, within the region and beyond, a reminder or a resurrection of what Ḥasan al-Turabi organized in1991 under the PAIC in Khartoum without Turabi. The delegates who congregated for the PAIC meeting in Khartoum from different parts of the world hoped to promote the Sudanese capital as a major center in the Islamic world and to claim the leadership of the world's Islamic movement. This time, it did not take some neighboring Arab countries long to express their concern when Dubai Police Chief Dhahi Khalfan Tameem suggested that the Muslim Brothers were in Khartoum to conspire against the shaikhdoms of the Gulf. Promptly, the Sudanese chair of the conference, al-Tayeb Ibrāhim Moḥamed Khair, issued a statement declaring

15 The Qur'an, Surah 3, The House of 'Imran: verse 140.

16 Magdi al-Jizouli, "The Sudanese Islamic Movement: A Parastatal Tareeqa," *Sudan Tribune*, 2012: http://www.sudantribune.com/spip.php?article44594.

that the Sudanese Islamist Movement had full respect for the sovereignty of individual Muslim countries. That statement was not enough to quiet rumors that the conference itself was a cover for the secret meeting "al-anzim Al Dawli lil Ikhwan [International Organization of the Brotherhood], the best guarded secret of the Brotherhood." It is worth mentioning that Ḥasan al-Turabi refused in 1971 when he was asked to give Bay'ah (oath of allegiance) to the Egyptian Murshid al-'Aam of what some consider as the mother organization in accordance of 1948 bylaws of *Jam'iyaat Al-Ikhwan al-Muslimeen* (the Muslim Brotherhood). Al-Turabi also refused in a meeting held in 1973 in Saudi Arabia between himself and the Egyptian *Murshid Ḥasan al-Hudiabi* to be part of *al-Tanzim al-Dawli*. He explained in that meeting and another meeting in Khartoum in 1980s that their disagreement was with the al-Bay'ah model of incorporation in the mother organization. He proposed instead a formula of cooperation that has never materialized. Ever since, the Sudanese Islamists have retained their autonomy, and the Egyptians have resented that. Relations between the two have remained sore and sensitive. But what makes this issue more complicated is that al-Turabi once complained that the Egyptian Muslim Brotherhood was behind the vicious campaign against him to which the top Saudi Salafi establishment, including late 'Abdel- Aziz Bin Baz contributed. Today the famous war of words, which erupted between al-Turabi and the Sudanese Salafi group who have been accusing him with *kufr* (apostasy), is a continuation of that saga.

The 8th Conference could be considered as the official death sentence of what the Islamists call the Islamic movement. The competition, conflict, and antagonism between the different personalities, which local media coverage tended to portray as conflict between "hardliners" and the "reformers," was further complicated by three subsequent developments. The first complication was that 'Alī 'Uthmān, the outgoing Secretary General of the movement out maneuvered his competitor and long-time challenger Ghazi Salah al-Din by changing and passing amendments before the 8th Conference that established a supreme council consisting of and chaired by President 'Umar al-Bashir and his deputies. Bitter, Ṣalaḥ al-Din described that development later in an article widely speculated in Sudanese electronic media: "it is true that we recognize their credit as individuals; they were not elected by the bases of the Movement, but by other colleges which are not part of the Movement. For instance, those will include the President of the Republic, his deputies and the Speaker of the National Assembly. It is clear that in this order, the organs and leaderships of the State have become part of SIM [Sudanese Islamic Movement] leadership without having been elected by SIM bodies and under SIM rules. In this way, the Movement has become more linked to the government than any previous time. Under this situation in which SIM Secretary General become surrounded by a clique of men who are more superior and influential than him and, under those circumstances, he would not be able to make any initiative without permission from the higher leadership and be barred from reaching his Shura Council. The main problem of this proposal lies in mixing the positions of the independent Movement and the State. The erroneous belief of the inevitability of a conflict between the Movement and the State if they were not amalgamated is unfounded and unjustifiable."

The second development came out as an outcome of what has been considered by some observers as an attempt to pave the way for the post-'Umar al-Bashir era, as most reports and speculations focus around a power struggle for succession caused by the president's ailing health. On November 22, 2012 the Sudan's National Intelligence and Security Service (NISS) announced that it had successfully foiled a coup and arrested several high-ranking army officers who were accused of plotting the takeover. Former NISS head Salah Gosh was also arrested. Among those detained individuals were some of the most prominent Islamist Army officers who included Brigadier General Moḥamed Ibrahim 'Abd al-Jalil, a popular officer among the young Islamists who call him "emir al-mujahideen," better known to some admirers as "Wad Ibrāhim," and the very person who once commanded the president's guard. Other senior army officers detained included the former commander of the Sudanese–Chadian Border Force Fath al-Raḥeem 'Abdalla Suleiman, and the senior military intelligence officer 'Adil al-Tayeb. Ghazi Ṣalaḥ al-Din was rumored to be not only a suspect but also one of or the key coup planner. What is very peculiar about that development is that it was the first time in the history of the Sudanese army that suspected high-ranking officers were detained by the security force, as the army has its own intelligence unit principally responsible for carrying out such operations.

Third, some of the younger Islamists within the PDF, expressed their frustration in different ways—including social media—after they were denied representation at the 8th Conference by the government who organized the event.

The fourth issue is the public appearance of what the Sudanese describe as the Sudanese Taliban who call themselves al-Saihoon in reference to the Qur'anic verse that praises the God-seeking wanderers (jihādists). This group, which emerged as both militant and frustrated with the corrupt, long-time leading Islamists in power and the deficient performance of 'Abdel Rahim Moḥamed Ḥussian, issued a statement under the name of the "NCP–Reform Platform" pleading President el-Bashir to release detained suspects of the foiled coup. Al-Saihoon's statement holds the minister of defense responsible for the poor performance of the Sudan Armed Forces and the paramilitary PDF in the Sudanese war zones and directly to blame for the failure of the army to respond to repeated Israeli attacks on the country. Two other statements came from London-based Islamists who made some observers look at the reform Platform group within a wider scope. The first statement was signed 'Abdel Ghani Aḥmed Idriss who claimed the position of the direct of the NCP—Reform Platform. Abdel Ghani is the son-in-law of Gahzi Salah al-deen who has been living in London as the Director of Sinnar Publishing House. In July 2013, he published a book titled *al-Da'wa lil Dimogratiyya al-alIslah al-Siysi fi al-Sudan: al-Islamiyoun azmat al-Roya wa alQiyyada* (The Call for Democracy and Political Reforms in the Sudan: The Islamists and the Crisis in Vision and Leadership). Many saw Gahzi's ideas and style of writing in the book. The other was an article written by 'Abd al-Wahab El-Affendi, a Sudanese former

Islamist journalist, the first Information Counselor at the Sudanese Embassy in London to be appointed by the Islamists regime, who currently works as a reader in politics at the Centre for the Study of Democracy at Westminster University. Dr. El-affendi praised 'Wad Ibrahim' the man who has not been stained by corruption. But more importantly, El-Affendi made two important points. The first was that he claimed Salah Gosh (the devil) who was arrested together with 'Wad Ibrahim' (the noble officer) was an evil attempt to smear the "good reputation" of the latter. The second point he made was a call for a "move by the army," which he described as the least costly route to achieving democratic change in the country. He concluded that whether an initiative of the army supported by the people or a popular movement of the people supported by the army, the countdown of the regime has started.

Perhaps this brief overview of the developments within the Sudanese field of action does not only point to the corrosion of Islamism in the Sudan, but also to its progression, like other "isms," to oblivion. The contemporary in-fighting between the Islamists themselves, the fragmentation, and the lack of meaningful narrative or discourse are structural consequences of how this phenomenon evolved in time and place.

The conference organizers boasted that the conference was attended by 150 foreign Islamists. Those who attended the conference included: Moḥamed Badie al-Murshid al-aam of the Egyptian Islamists *Jamiyyat al-Ikhwan al-Muslimoun*: Khalid Meshaal, the leader of the Palestinian Islamist organization Hamas; Rashid Ghannushi, the leader of Tunisia's Islamist Movement Ennahda; Bashir 'Abd al-Salam al-Kebti al-Murshid al-aam of the Libyan Moslem Brotherhood; 'Ali Sadr al-Din al-Bayanouni, the Deputy al-Murshid al-aam of the Syrian Moslem Brotherhood; and Syed Munawar Hassan, the Emir of the Pakistani Jamaat e-Islami. Among the international attendees at the conference were representatives of Islamist movements from African countries such as Chad, Senegal, and Nigeria, and leaders of Islamist organizations, such as the Pakistani women's league leader of the Jamaat-e-Islami Begum Aisha Munawar.[17] It should be no surprise that the conference and the environment that encompassed Islamism in the Sudanese field of action has overwhelmed the scene with serious issues that culminated in Islamist political activism in the Sudan since the Islamists assumed power in the country in 1989 through a military coup.

17 The presence of this big number of high-level Islamists from Egypt Ikhwan and other Islamists from different parts of the Muslim world led to the speculation that the conference was designed that way to camouflage to the secret meeting of '*al-anzim Al Dawli lil Ikhwan* (International Organization of the Brotherhood). The London-based *al-Aarb* newspaper described—in an unconfirmed story—that the principle issue at the meeting was to discuss the proposal from Qatar to create a new political entity headed by Khalid Mish'al to be located in Cairo.

Second Episode

The very way the Sudanese people expressed their attitude toward the Islamist regime during the 10 days following September 23, 2013, constitutes a whole experience whose dissimilar characteristics of defiance and state violence, by both the Sudanese population and the regime, enabled the local and world population to see the events unfold through modern systems of communication. Citizens in most of the Sudanese cities and cosmopolitan centers of the world witnessed the largest anti-government protests. In the Sudanese cities, many of the protesters upgraded the scale and extent of their unprecedented movement. The protesters clearly defined their goals behind the protest and turned anger against government's new economic policy or cut in fuel subsidies into outright rejection to the regime.

After a quarter century in power, 'Umar al-Bashir, the Islamists sorcerer's apprentice, has nothing more to give to the Sudanese people except for asking them to be grateful to him because during his time in power he brought them the hot dog. His Finance minister, 'Ali Maḥmoud 'Abdel Rasoul, boasted that the Sudanese during the Ingaz's long rule have been introduced for the first time to pizza and luxury housing. Qutbi al-Mahdi argued that the larger sector of the Sudanese population is will not be affected by the new economic measures because they use donkeys for their transportation. However, at the very moment when unarmed civilians took to the streets protesting the government policies, the regime, as usual, deployed the police and security services in civilian clothes to respond with lethal force. According to Amnesty International, Human Rights Watch, media reports, and other sources who gave authoritative reports of the "brutal crackdown" and as US State Department Spokeswoman Jen Psaki described, they took the lives of 210 unarmed protesters, more than 2,000 men and women were rounded up and detained in unidentified places, and a similar number was injured.

The protests and the protesters evoked the memory of previous successful uprisings of the April 1985, popular uprising that brought down Ja'afar Nimeiri's regime and in particular the October 1964, Ibrahim 'Abboud military rule. They brought together the leadership of the October 1964 Revolution—chief among them Farouq Abu Eisa—and the April leadership—in particular Amin Mekki Medani—together with the younger digital generation of Griffna, Sharara, and the Sudanese diaspora. The central fact about this development is that a Sudanese revolution that consists primarily of a global composition and dimension of protest against the Islamist regime is in the making, and it may herald episodes that step toward liberation from not only the Islamist regime but also the state and a myriad series of contrivances, practices, and mentalities of "totalist" politics, ideologies, and systems that have plagued the Sudanese experience of governance since the early colonial days of Wingate and his state and took different turns and forms up to now.

The emergence of what could be described as the twilight of a new era is summarized by the street slogan: *huriah, salaam was 'adalah, al-thawrah khiar al-shaab* (freedom, peace and justice, revolution is the people's option). The slogan reflects the accumulation of the Sudanese collective memory and collective urge to be liberated through an open-ended revolution.

In January 2014, Ḥasan al-Turabi was the center of the Sudanese public gaze at home and abroad when he attended the first time in 14 years an NCP event. 'Ali 'Uthmān caught their attention too when he for the first time in 24 years took a back seat among those present at the Friendship Hall attending the same event. 'Umar al-Bashir disappointed the Sudanese population who expected his speech that day to carry an initiative of significant magnitude: to resign or delegate his powers to his comrade in arms he recently appointed as First Vice President Baki Ḥasan Salih. However, his speech, which went on for an hour, was a clear *wathpa* [leap] in the dark over the corpus of a long dead Islamism.

The scene of al-Ṣadiq al-Mahdi, Ḥasan al-Turabi, Ghazi al-'Atabāni seated in the front row next to each other listening to 'Umar al-Bashir delivering what was called by the media "his surprise speech" on January 27, 2014. All that can be linked to the historical conditions underlying the long journey of Islamism from its infancy to disintegration and finally to oblivion. What Sudan has become after this long journey is a military state even different than what everybody has experienced and seen since of the June 30, 1989 coup. It took too long for the military coup to materialize and appear in its true colors. The most disheartening of all, may be to most of those who were at the front row, as well as 'Ali 'Uthmān and of those he joined at the back seat, together with all those who were behind the coup that brought the Islamists to power is that they are all now waiting to offer their service to the general as the military returned to capture the state.

Many Sudanese observers were not surprised by al-Turabi's move toward unconditional dialogue with al-Bashir and his National Congress Party (NCP) after the removal out of power of 'Ali 'Uthmān the First and Nafie 'Ali Nafie in December 2013. And yet, one cannot speak of this without drawing the attention to the nature and long-term consequence of al-Turabi's Islamism where acute internal conflicts of attitudes, violence towards each other, including long-term periods of prison to *Shaikh* Ḥasan and some of the close loyalists, can easily be turned into privilege guided by the material interest of one or the other of the Islamists warring parties. Al-Turabi's Islamism, the "child of opportunism" that has died, wrought its ghost upon the air. A few days, after 'Umar al-Bashir's address that "brought nothing new and lacked a diagnosis of the country's problems and offered no fundamental solutions," according to al-Turabi Kamal 'Umer, al-Turabi party's political secretary who was until the last minute acted as the spokesman of the opposition alliance, the National Consensus Forces (NCF), "slipped as if on a banana peel from the antics of 'overthrowing the regime' to slick 'dialogese'."[18] Kamal went even a step further to accuse "the allies of yesterday, primarily the Communist Party and fractured remnants of the Nasserite and Baathist parties, of

18 Magdi al-Gizouli, "New Sudan: Back to the future," *Sudan Tribune*, February 15, 2014.

unwarranted recalcitrance and wished for a reunion of the parties of the historic Islamic Movement, the NCP and the PCP, in a heavenly gush of Islamic accord." Moreover, al-Turabi's deputy, Abdalla Ḥasan Aḥmed, "went further stressing that the PCP holds no grudges against the fellow ikhwan ([Muslim] brothers) of the NCP, not even against Ṭaha and Nafie."[19] At the same time, "reporters close to the PCP 'leaked' stories of reconciliation bids between the eighty two years old Turabi and his most capable disciple, the seventy years old 'Alī 'Uthmān Moḥamed Ṭaha, the latest victim of the dyslexic officer, followed by reports that preparations for a meeting between Turabi and President Bashir were diligently pursued by keen mediators."[20] The multiple consequences of this transformation and the events that followed not only capture a moment unfolding in al-Turabi's Islamism but also explains clearly that al-Turabi himself can be understood only against al-Turabi's Islamism.

But it is possible to ask the question even without reiterating any skepticism with respect to the idea of the end of "isms": under what order or disorder or stipulations might al-Turabi's Islamism become possible again? The answer is an emphatic no way.

19 Ibid.
20 Ibid.

Bibliography

'Abdel Gadir Ḥamid, Al-Tigani. "Islam, Sectarianism and the Muslim Brotherhood in Modern Sudan, 1956–1985," PhD diss. Department of Economics and Political Studies, the School of Oriental and African Studies, University of London, 1989.

———. "al-Ra'simaliyoon al-Islāmiyoon fi sl-Harka al-Islamiyya," *al-Ṣaḥafa Daily* Khartoum, 2006.

'Abdelsalaam, Al-Mahboob *al-Haraka al-Islamiyya al-Soudaniyya: Dierat al-Daw wa Khiout Dhalam.* Cairo: Maktabat Jazīrat al-Ward, 2009,

Abu-Rabi', Ibrāhim M., ed. *The Blackwell Companion to Contemporary Islamic Thought*. Malden: Blackwell Publishing, 2008.

el-Affendi, 'Abdel Wahāb. *Turabi's Revolution: Islam and Power in Sudan.* Grey Seal Islamic Studies. London: Grey Seal, 1991.

———. *Al-Thawrah wa-al-iṣlāḥ al-siyāsī fī al-Sūdān.* Landan: Muntadá ibn Rushd, 1995.

Aḥmed, Akbar S. *Discovering Islam: Making Sense of Muslim History and Society*. rev. ed. London, New York: Routledge, 2002.

Aḥmed, Einas. "The Rise of Militant Salafism in Sudan." Available online at: http://www.cedej-eg.org/IMG/pdf/Einas_Aḥmed_-_The_Rise_of_Militant_Salafism_in_Sudan.pdf

Aḥmed, Zain al-'Abdin Moḥamed. *Mayo Sanuat al-Khusb wa al-jafāf: Muzkirat al-Raid (Rt.) Zaim al-'Abdin Moḥamed Aḥmed.* Khartoum: Markaz Moḥamed 'Umar Bashir lil Dirasat, 2011.

Alen, Lovise A. "Making Unity Unattractive: The Conflicting Aims of Sudan Comprehensive Peace Agreement," *Civil Wars* 15 no. 2 (2013).

Amin, Galal A. *The Modernization of Poverty: A Study in the Political Economy of Growth in Nine Arab Countries 1945–1970, vol. 13*. Leiden: Brill, 1980.

el-Amin, Mohammed Nuri. *The Emergence and Development of the Leftist Movement in Sudan during the 1930s and 1940s*. Khartoum: Khartoum University Press, 1984

An-Na'im, 'Abdullahi. *Islam and Secular State: Negotiating the Future of Shari'a.* Cambridge, MA: Harvard University Press, 2010

Atkins, Stephen E. *Encyclopedia of Modern Worldwide Extremists and Extremist Groups*. Westport, CT: Greenwood Press, 2004.

Ayoob, Moḥammed. "Political Islam: Image and Reality." *World Policy Journal* 21 no. 3 (2004):1–14.

———. *The Many Faces of Political Islam: Religion and Politics in the Muslim World.* Ann Arbor, MI: The University of Michigan Press, 2008.

Azraq, 'Iesa Makki 'Uthmān. *Min Tariekh al-Ikhwan al-Muslimin Fi-l-Sudan, 1953–1980.* Khartoum: Dar al-Balad Publishing, N.D.

Balibar, Etienne. *We, The People of Europe: Reelections on Transnational Citizenship.* Princeton, NJ: Princeton University Press, 2004.

Barker, Raymond William. *Islam Without Fear: Egypt and the New Islamists.* Cambridge, MA: Harvard University Press, 2003.

Bayart, Jean-François. *Global Subjects: A Political Critique of Globalization.* Malden, MA: Polity, 2007.

Bayat, Asef. *Life as Politics: How Ordinary People Change the Middle East.* Stanford, CA: Stanford University Press, 2010.

———. *Post-Islamism: The Changing Faces of Political Islam.* Oxford: Oxford University Press, 2013.

Bechtold, Peter K. *Politics in the Sudan: Parliamentary and Military Rule in an Emerging African Nation.* Praeger Special Studies in International Politics and Government. New York: Praeger, 1976.

Beinin, Joel and Joe Stork. *Political Islam: Essays from Middle East Report.* Berkeley, CA: University of California Press, 1997.

Bell, Daniel. *The Cultural Contradictions of Capitalism.* New York: Basic Books, 1976.

Bellah, Robert N. *The Broken Covenant: American Civil Religion in Time of Trial.* 2nd ed. Chicago, IL: University of Chicago Press, 1992.

Boddy, Janice Patricia. *Civilizing Women: British Crusades in Colonial Sudan.* Princeton, NJ: Princeton University Press, 2007.

Bourdieu, Pierre. *Distinction: A Social Critique of the Judgment of Taste.* Cambridge, MA: Harvard University Press, 1984.

———. *The State Nobility: Elite Schools in the Field of Power.* Stanford, CA: Stanford University Press, 1996.

Burr, Millard and Robert O. Collins. *Revolutionary Sudan: Ḥasan al-Turabi and the Islamist State, 1989–2000.* Leiden, Boston, MA: Brill, 2003.

Chatterjee, Partha. *The Partha Chatterjee Omnibus: The Nationalist Thought and Colonial World, and its Fragments, a Possible India.* Oxford: Oxford University Press, 1999.

Cohn, Bernard S. *Colonialism and its Forms of Knowledge: The British in India.* Princeton Studies in Culture/Power/History. Princeton, NJ: Princeton University Press, 1996.

Colvin, Auckland. *The Making of Modern Egypt*, 3rd ed. London: Seeley, 1906.

Cox, R.W. "Social Forces, States and World Orders: Beyond International Relations Theory." *Millennium—Journal of International Studies* 10 no. 2 (1981): 126–55.

Dabashi, Ḥamid. *The Arab Spring: The End of Postcolnialism.* London: ZED Press, 2012.

Dacey, Austin. *The Secular Conscience: Why Belief Belongs in Public Life*. Amherst: Prometheus Books, 2008.

Daly, M.W. *Empire on the Nile: The Anglo-Egyptian Sudan, 1898–1934*. Cambridge: Cambridge University Press, 1986.

Ḍayf Allah, Muḥammad al-Nur. *Kitab al-Ṭabaqat fi khusus al-awliya'wa 'l-salihin wa 'l-' ulamā' wa 'l-shu'ara' fi 'l-Sudan.* Ed. Yousif Fadl Ḥasan. Khartoum: Khartoum University Press. 1985.

Denoeux, Guilain. "The Forgotten Swamp: Navigating Political Islam," *Middle East Policy* 9 no. 2, 2002.

Downie, Richard and Brian Kennedy. *Sudan Assessing Risks to Stability: A Report of the CSIS Africa Program*. Center for Strategic and International Studies, Washington, DC, 2011.

Duran, Khalid. "The Centrifugal Forces of Religion in Sudanese Politics." *Orient* 26, 1985.

Emmerson, Donald. "Inclusive Islamism: The Utility of Diversity." In *Islamism: Contested Perspectives on Political Islam*, edited by Richard C. Martin and Abbas Barzegar, 17–32, 2010

Faiz, Asif. "South Sudan's Tryst with Destiny." *Africa Arguments*, SSRC, Washington, DC, 2011.

Finer, S.E. *The Man on Horseback: The Role of the Military in Politics*. Boulder, CO: Westview Press, 1988.

Fischer, Michael M.J. "Islam and the Revolt of the Petit Bourgeoisie." *Daedalus* 111 no. 1 (1982): 101–25.

Fluehr-Lobban, Carolyn. *Shari'a and Islamism in Sudan: Conflict, Law and Social Transformation*. London I.B. Tauris, 2012.

Furnivall, J.S. *Colonial Policy and Practice: A Comparative Study of Burma and Netherlands India*. New York: New York University Press, 1956.

Gale, Richard N. "The Impact of Political Factors on Military Judgment." *Royal United Services Institution Journal* 99 no. 593 (1954): 36–46.

Gallab, Abdullahi A. *The First Islamist Republic: Development and Disintegration of Islamism in the Sudan*. Aldershot; Burlington, VT: Ashgate, 2008.

———. *A Civil Society Deferred: The Tertiary Grip of Violence in the Sudan*. Gainesville, FL: University Press of Florida, 2013.

Garawert. Elke. *After the Comprehensive Peace Agreement in Sudan*. London: James Currey, 2010.

Geertz, Clifford. *The Interpretation of Culture: Selected Essays*. New York: Basic Books, 1977.

Giddens, Anthony. *The Nation-State and Violence*. Cambridge: Polity Press, 1985.

Goffman, Erving. *The Presentation of Self in Everyday Life*. Garden City: Doubleday Anchor Books, 1959.

Gramsci, Antonio. *Selections from the Prison Notebooks 1*. New York: International Publishers, 1971.

Gurdon, Charles. *Sudan at the Crossroads*. Cambridgeshire, England: Middle East & North African Studies Press, 1984.

Hallaq, Wael B. *The Impossible State: Islam, Politics, and Modernity's Moral Predicament*. New York: Columbia University Press, 2013.

Hamdan, G. "The Growth and Functional Structure of Khartoum." *Geographical Review* Vol. 50 No. 1 (1960): 21–40

Ḥamidī, Muḥammad al-Hāshimī. *The Making of an Islamic Political Leader: Conversations with Ḥasan al-Turabi*. Boulder, CO: Westview Press, 1998.

Hansen, Thomas Blom. *The Saffron Wave: Democracy and Hindu Nationalism in Modern India*. Princeton, NJ: Princeton University Press, 1999.

Harvey, David. *The New Imperialism*. Oxford: Oxford University Press, 2003.

Ḥasan, Qurashi Moḥamed, *Qasaid min Shiaraa al-Mahadiyya*. Khartoum: al-Majlis al-Qoumi li Ri'āyat al-Adāb wa al-Finoon, 1974.

Hobsbawm, E.J. *The Age of Revolution 1789–1848*. New York: Vintage Books, 1996.

Huntington, Samuel P. *The Soldier and the State: The Theory and Politics of Civil-Military Relations*. Cambridge, MA: Belknap Press of Harvard University Press, 1957.

Ibrāhim, 'Abdullahi 'Ali. "A Theology of Modernity: Ḥasan al-Turabi and Islamic Renewal in Sudan." *Africa Today* 46 no. 3 (2003): 195–222.

____. *Manichaean Delirium: Decolonizing the Judiciary and Islamic Renewal in Sudan, 1898–1985, Islam in Africa*. Leiden, Boston: Brill, 2008.

Ibrahim, Haydar. *Muraj'aāt al-Islamieen: Kasb al-Donya wa kharasat al-Din*. Cairo: al-Hadara Publishing, 2011.

Idris, Abdelgani Aḥmed. *Al-Dawa lil demoqatiyya wa al-Islag fi il Sudan: al-Slamitoun.azmat al-royaa wa al-qiada*. London: Sinar Publishing House, 2012.

Ijaz, Mansoor, "The Clinton Intel Record: Deeper Failures Revealed." *National Review Online*. Available online at: http://www.nationalreview.com/articles/206745/clinton-intel-record/mansoor-ijaz.

Johnson, Hilde F. *Waging Peace in Sudan: The Inside Story of the Negotiations that Ended Africa's Longest Civil War*. Portland: Sussex Academic Press, 2011.

Juergensmeyer, Mark. *The New Cold War? Religious Nationalism Confronts the Secular State, Comparative Studies in Religion and Society*. Berkeley, CA: University of California Press, 1993.

Kandil, Hazem. *The End of Islamism*. London, London Review of Books. 2013.

Khair, Aḥmed. *Kifah jel:tariekh harakat al-khirjeen wa tatoriha fi il Sudan*. Khartoum: al-Dar al-Sudaniyya, 1970.

Khalid, Mansour. *Nimeiri and the Revolution of Dis-May*. London: Kegan Paul International, 1985

____. *The Government They Deserve: The Role of the Elite in Sudan's Political Evolution*. London: Kegan Paul International, 1990.

Lacroix, Stephane. *Awakening Islam: The Politics of Religious Dissent in Contemporary Saudi Arabia*. Cambridge, MA: Harvard University Press, 2011.

Lahoud, Nelly. *The Jihādis' Path to Self-destruction*. New York: Columbia University Press, 2010.

Lowrie, Arthur L. *Islam, Democracy, the State and the West: A Round Table with Dr. Ḥasan Turabi*. Tampa, FL: The World & Islam Studies Enterprise, University of South Florida, 1993.

Maḥmoud, Moḥmed. *Quest for Divinity: a Critical Examination of the Thought of Maḥmoud Muḥamed Ṭaha*. Syracuse, NY: Syracuse University Press, 2007.

Majama' al-Fiqh al-Islami, *Risalat al-Qawl al-Fasl fi al-Radd 'ala man Kharaj 'an al Asl:* Khartoum 2006.

Malik, Ibn (Aḥmed Malik). *al-Ṣārim al-Maslūl fi' al-rad-'Ala al-Turabi Shātim al-Rasūl* (N.I).

Mamdani, Mahmoud. *Define and Rule: Native as Political Identity*. Cambridge, MA: Harvard University Press, 2012.

Martin, Richard, ed. *Islamism: Contested Perspectives on Political Islam*. Stanford, CA: Stanford University Press, 2010.

Marx, Karl. *The Eighteenth Brumaire of Louis Bonaparte*. Rockville, MD: Serenity Publishers, 2008.

Massoud, Mark Fathi. *Law's Fragile State: Colonial, Authoritarian, and Humanitarian Legacies in Sudan*. Cambridge: Cambridge University Press, 2013.

Mekki, Ḥasan. *Al-Haraka al-Islamiyya fi il Sudan 1985–1969: Tariyikhaha wa khitabiha al-siasi*. Kharoum: al-Dar al-Sudaniyya lil Kutob, 1999.

Mendiata, Eduard. *The Power of Religion in the Public Sphere*. New York: Columbia University Press, 2011.

Miniter, Richard. *Losing Bin Laden: How Bill Clinton's Failures Unleashed Global Terror*. Washington, DC: Regnery Publishing, 2003.

Muhi el-Din, 'Abdel Rahim 'Umar. *al-Turabi wa al-Ingaz: Ṣirā'a al-Hawa wa Al-Hawiyya; Fitnat al-Islamiyyien fi al-Ṣulta min muzkirat al-Ashara ila muzkirat al-tafahum m'aa Garang*. Khartoum: Maktabat Marawi Bookshop, 2006

Nandy, Ashis. *The Savage Freud and Other Essays on Possible and Retrievable Selves*. Princeton, NJ: Princeton University Press, 1995.

———. *Exiled at Home: Comprising at the Edge of Psychology, the Intimate Enemy, Creating a Nationality*. Delhi: Oxford University Press, 1998.

Natsios, Andrew S. *Sudan, South Sudan, and Darfur: What Everyone Needs to Know*. Oxford, New York: Oxford University Press, 2012.

Niblock, Tim. *Class and Power in Sudan: The Dynamics of Sudanese Politics, 1898–1985*. Albany, NY: State University of New York Press, 1987.

Nienhaus Volker. *Fundamentals of an Islamic Economic System Compared to Social Market Economy*. Berlin: KAS International Reports, 2010.

Olivier, Roy. *The Failure of Political Islam*. Cambridge, MA: Harvard University Press, 1994.

———. *Holy Ignorance: When Religion and Culture Part Ways*. New York: Columbia University Press, 2010.

Panigrahi, D.N. *India's Partition: The Story of Imperialism in Retreat*. New York: Routledge, 2004.

Piscatori, James P. *Islam in the Political Process.* London: Cambridge University Press, 1983.

Powell, Eve M. Troutt. *A Different Shade of Colonialism: Egypt, Great Britain, and the Mastery of Sudan.* Berkeley, CA: University of California Press, 2003.

Reitter, Paul. *On the Origins of Jewish Self-hatred.* Princeton, NJ: Princeton University Press, 2012.

Rone, Jemera. *Behind the Redline: Political Repression in Sudan.* New York: Human Rights Watch, 1996.

Rosenau, James N. *Distant Proximities: Dynamics beyond Globalization.* Princeton, NJ: Princeton University Press, 2003.

Said, Edward W. *Culture and Imperialism.* New York: Knopf, distributed by Random House, 1993.

Salomon Noah. *The Politics of Religious Freedom: Freeing Religion at the Birth of South Sudan.* Washington, DC: The Immanent Frame, SSRC, 2012.

Sayyid, Bobby S. *A Fundamental Fear Eurocentrism and the Emergence of Islamism.* London, New York: Zed Books, 1997.

Schnapper, Dominique. *Community of Citizens: On the Modern Idea of Nationality.* New Brunswick: Transaction Publishers, 1998.

Shakespeare, William. *Twelfth Night: The Oxford Shakespeare Complete Works.* Oxford: Oxford University Press, 2005.

Sidaḥmed 'Abdel salaam. *Politics and Islam in Contemporary Sudan.* New York: St. Martin's Press, 1996.

Simone, A.M. *In Whose Image? Political Islam and Urban Practices in Sudan.* Chicago, IL: University of Chicago Press, 1994.

Skinner, Quentin. *The Foundation of Modern Political Thought, vol. 2.* Cambridge: Cambridge University Press, 1978.

Smith, Rogers M. *Stories of Peoplehood: The Politics and Morals of Political Membership.* Cambridge, Cambridge University Press, 2003.

Steinberger, Peter J. *The Idea of the State.* Cambridge: Cambridge University Press, 2004.

Tenet, George and Bill Harlow. *At the Center of the Storm: My Years at the CIA.* New York: HarperCollins, 2007.

Tibi, Bassam. "The Worldview of Sunni Arab Fundamentalists: Attitudes Toward Modern Science and Technology." In Martin E. Marty and R. Scott Appleby, *The Fundamentalist Project: Fundamentalisms and Society*, Chicago, IL: University of Chicago Press 1993.

———. *Islamism and Islam.* New Haven, CT: Yale University Press, 2012.

El-Tom Abdullahi Osman. *Darfur, JEM and the Khalil Ibrahim Story with Complete Copy of the Black Book: Imbalance of Power and Wealth in Sudan.* Trenton: The Red Sea Press, 2011.

Trimingham, J. Spencer. *Islam in the Sudan.* London, New York: Oxford University Press, 1949.

Tripp, Charles. *Islam and the Moral Economy: The Challenge of Capitalism.* Cambridge: Cambridge University Press, 2006.

Al-Turabi, Ḥasan. *al-Haraka al-Islamiyya fi el-Sudan: al-tatour, al-kasb al-Manhaj*. Khartoum: Institute of Research and Social Studies, 1992.

———. "Islamic Fundamentalism in the 'Sunna' and 'Shia' Worlds," Part One: Press Conference Given by Dr. Turabi in Madrid August 2, 1994 (Religion File No. 6, The Sudan Foundation. 1998.

———. *Al-Siyasaa wa alhukum: al-Nuzum al-sultaniyya baina al-usool wa sunnan al-wāqī*. London: Dar al-saqi, 2004.

Turner, Bryan S. *Weber and Islam: A Critical Study, International Library of Sociology*. London, Boston: Routledge & Kegan Paul. 1974.

Volpi, Frédéric. *Political Islam Observed: Disciplinary Perspectives*. New York: Columbia University Press, 2010.

de Waal, Alex. "Counter-Insurgency on the Cheap." *Review of African Political Economy* 31 no. 102 (2004): 716–25.

Waihenya, Waithaka. *The Mediator: Gen. Lazaro Sumbeiywo and the Southern Sudan Peace Process*. Nairobi: Kenway Publications, 2006.

Warburg, Gabriel. *The Sudan under Wingate: Administration in the Anglo-Egyptian Sudan, 1899–1916*. London: Cass, 1971.

Wickham, Carrie Rosefsky. *Mobilizing Islam: Religion, Activism, and Political Change*. New York: Columbia University Press, 2002.

Woodward, Peter *Sudan, 1898–1989: The Unstable State*. Boulder, CO: L. Rienner Publishers, 1990.

Wright, Lawrence. *The Looming Tower: Al-Qaeda and the Road to 9/11*. New York: Knopf, 2006.

Young, John. *The Fate of Sudan: The Origins and Consequences of a Flawed Peace Process*. London: ZED Books, 2012.

Yongo-Bure, Beniah. "Marginalization and War: From the South to Darfur." In *Darfur and the Crisis of Governance in Sudan: A Critical Reader*, eds Salah M. Hassan and Carina E. Ray. Ithaca, NY: Cornell University Press, 2009.

Zald, Mayer N. and John D. McCarthy. *The Dynamics of Social Movements: Resource Mobilization, Social Control, and Tactics*. Cambridge, MA: Winthrop Publishers, 1979.

Index